THE
COMPLETE
IDIOT'S
GUIDE® TO

I0642287

Choppers

Russ Austin and Michael Benson

ALPHA

A member of Penguin Group (USA) Inc.

This book is dedicated to my Father. He has always been my role model and inspiration.—R.A.

ALPHA BOOKS

Published by the Penguin Group

Penguin Group (USA) Inc., 375 Hudson Street, New York, New York 10014, U.S.A.

Penguin Group (Canada), 10 Alcorn Avenue, Toronto, Ontario, Canada M4V 3B2 (a division of Pearson Penguin Canada Inc.)

Penguin Books Ltd, 80 Strand, London WC2R 0RL, England

Penguin Ireland, 25 St Stephen's Green, Dublin 2, Ireland (a division of Penguin Books Ltd)

Penguin Group (Australia), 250 Camberwell Road, Camberwell, Victoria 3124, Australia (a division of Pearson Australia Group Pty Ltd)

Penguin Books India Pvt Ltd, 11 Community Centre, Panchsheel Park, New Delhi—110 017, India

Penguin Group (NZ), cnr Airborne and Rosedale Roads, Albany, Auckland 1310, New Zealand (a division of Pearson New Zealand Ltd)

Penguin Books (South Africa) (Pty) Ltd, 24 Sturdee Avenue, Rosebank, Johannesburg 2196, South Africa

Penguin Books Ltd, Registered Offices: 80 Strand, London WC2R 0RL, England

Copyright © 2006 by Michael Benson

International Standard Book Number: 1-59257-452-1
Library of Congress Catalog Card Number: 2005938291

08 07 06   8 7 6 5 4 3 2 1

Interpretation of the printing code: The rightmost number of the first series of numbers is the year of the book's printing; the rightmost number of the second series of numbers is the number of the book's printing. For example, a printing code of 06-1 shows that the first printing occurred in 2006.

Printed in the United States of America

Note: This publication contains the opinions and ideas of its authors. It is intended to provide helpful and informative material on the subject matter covered. It is sold with the understanding that the authors and publisher are not engaged in rendering professional services in the book. If the reader requires personal assistance or advice, a competent professional should be consulted.

The authors and publisher specifically disclaim any responsibility for any liability, loss, or risk, personal or otherwise, which is incurred as a consequence, directly or indirectly, of the use and application of any of the contents of this book.

Most Alpha books are available at special quantity discounts for bulk purchases for sales promotions, premiums, fundraising, or educational use. Special books, or book excerpts, can also be created to fit specific needs.

For details, write: Special Markets, Alpha Books, 375 Hudson Street, New York, NY 10014.

Publisher: *Marie Butler-Knight*
Editorial Director: *Mike Sanders*
Managing Editor: *Billy Fields*
Senior Acquisitions Editor: *Paul Dinas*
Development Editor: *Phil Kitchel*
Senior Production Editor: *Janette Lynn*
Copy Editor: *Keith Cline*

Cartoonist: *Shannon Wheeler*
Book Designer: *Trina Wurst*
Cover Designer: *Bill Thomas*
Indexer: *Brad Herriman*
Layout: *Ayanna Lacey*
Proofreading: *Mary Hunt*

Contents at a Glance

Contents

Appendixes

Foreword

For me it all started in a darkened movie theater when I was 12 years old watching a biker flick called "Hells Angels on Wheels," starring Sonny Barger, the Oakland Hells Angels, and a guy named Jack Nicholson. My favorite scene had Sonny and his brotherhood of Angels riding over the Oakland, San Francisco Bay Area bridge like Jesse James and his endless pack of Outlaws.

I went home and took a lawnmower, bicycle, and my mother's vacuum cleaner pipes and built a chopper mini bike. From that day on, I became a chopper guy. I built all my choppers right in my garage. At the time, the "chopper look" meant the customized, garage-built bike, which consisted of a frame, motor, transmission, front end, "ape hanger" handlebars, and upsweep exhaust pipes. I sure could have used a terrific book such as *The Complete Idiot's Guide to Choppers* to get me started.

Some 26 years later, I became a member of the biggest and baddest motorcycle club in the world, the Hells Angels. We all shared the same common bond, the feeling of being free on the "open road," like a long black carpet in front of you, when you hit that throttle and those horses kick in, you feel the power under your ass and the wind in your face, whether riding solo or with a pack of hundreds, from Sturgis to Daytona or Oakland to New York. I've been there, done that; after 25 years, I am no longer in the club, but the memories and the bike remain.

That's why Benson's book is terrific. Together with co-author and chopper expert Russ Austin, it gives you everything you need to kick-start you into the chopper dream. From the choices you should make about what kind of bike you want, to how to get there either on your own, with a kit, or with the help of some of the most awesome bike builders working today from coast to coast, *The Complete Idiot's Guide to Choppers* has it all. Austin and Benson are the real deal. They offer inside tips and outsider information including detailing, clubs, incredible stories about biker road experiences, and best of all, the feeling of hopping on and taking off.

People who ride know what I am talking about, whether you're a hard core biker or just a weekend warrior. The power you feel on a custom chopper is like no other, and Benson gets you there.

So grab the bull by its handlebars, and ride forever free.

—Chuck Zito, bodyguard to the stars, a former Golden Gloves boxer, martial-arts expert, past president of the New York Nomads chapter of the Hells Angels, and actor on the award-winning drama *Oz*, is the star of the upcoming USA Network series *Chuck Zito's Street Justice*. He lives in New Rochelle, NY.

Introduction

Before I start talking about choppers themselves, let me tell you a little bit about me and how I got to be a chopper enthusiast (that is, nut). I was born in Columbus, Ohio, but when I was little we moved a lot, all throughout the Southeast. We stayed put in North Georgia when I was 9.

I am the youngest of three boys. Each one of us is totally different. The oldest is a laid-back ladies' man. The middle kid is a responsible, fun-loving guy. And then there's me, the runt. I was always—and still am—the workhorse of the family. I don't believe in buying or paying for something if I can build it or do it myself.

I was always the smallest kid around and found the only way for me to get respect was to kick every big guy's ass if he looked cross at me. From early on I was a fighter. I think most of the small guys in the world were at one time.

My parents divorced, and even though it was amicable, it only threw gas on the fire. Of course, I rebelled by being a typical brat to my parents. I needed something to get this "tough-guy/small-man" syndrome out of me.

Over my high school years, you could always find me tearing up the North Georgia mountains on a dirt bike. I had so much fun riding bikes and being with my friends that I sort of, without knowing, alienated myself from the harmful things most teenagers do. I was too busy having fun on my dirt bike to smoke or drink or do drugs. What do you know? I even stopped fighting.

A chopper is a motorcycle with a little bit of dream attached to it.

(Barry C. Altmark Photography)

I also sunk myself into fixing up cars and selling them to make a profit. I wanted to make just enough money to buy a bigger and better car. I now look back and realize I followed the same path as my dad: always trading up to the next bigger and better something.

My dad always had the coolest cars and motorcycles. I wanted to be just like him. My dad was and still is my role model. He is a great father, a successful self-made man, and a good friend. My wish came true: I'm just like him. I'm not sure whether to be thankful or not. We're both as stubborn and headstrong as you can get. However, somewhere down the line he taught me dedication and determination.

At the age of 15, my dad bought a 1986 Honda Rebel 250 for my stepmother. She rode it, I think, 7 feet. She didn't want anything to do with it. As much as I wanted her to learn to ride, I was happy she didn't. I just kind of assumed it would be my little ride now. I begged my dad to let me ride it. One day he let me follow him. He was on his Harley, and I was on my stepmom's bike. I'll never forget when we stopped at a red light and out of nowhere about 25 to 30 bikers, all on Harleys, rode up around us. I was so intimidated, maybe even scared, as this big burly guy looked over at me. I remember him doing a double take when he realized I was just a kid. He smiled and gave a big thumbs up. I thought that was so cool.

Later that year, my dad started really customizing his Harley. There was a project he couldn't quite figure out, and he let me give it a try. We were wiring up a set of custom taillights. My dad hovered over me in a worried, "try not to scratch it" kind of way. What do you know? I got the lights to glow. My dad made such a big deal about it and told everyone, "My son was the one who did that." I felt pride like I never had before—over taillights. From then on, my dad always encouraged me to develop my talents.

My mother, on the other hand, didn't like motorcycles or me riding them—and for good reason. I was 15, with no helmet, no driver's license, and riding a dirt bike illegally on the street. I had my good friend on the back of the bike and I was carrying the carburetor for his bike to my house so I could fix it. On our way home, coming up a hill—*bang!*—we got hit by a nurse backing out of a blind drive in a Ford Taurus. We sailed a good 30 feet and landed on the pavement. Luckily, the car hit the rear swingarm, and we only suffered cuts and some heavy bruising. The nurse knew my mother and wanted to help us, but, of course, we told her we were fine, even though both of us could barely walk. We didn't tell anyone, especially our parents, for fear of getting in trouble. Sure enough, the nurse called my mom to see if we were okay. There went any chance of my dad giving me the Honda Rebel now. My mom called my dad, and my dad sold the Rebel within a week. Thanks, Nurse Lady!

I continued to ride dirt bikes and customize cars throughout high school and into college. I had lost the bug to ride street bikes. I was too busy chasing women. Then I caught one. Or maybe she caught me. Either way, I met a wonderful woman who swept me off my feet. She was the type of girl who wanted to do whatever I did: hiking, camping, backpacking, and rock climbing. She's never stood in my way and has always supported me. I knew she was the woman for me the day she took the keys to my severely lifted and heavily modified four-wheel-drive pickup and drove it off to the stuffy architectural firm where she worked. We got married, I took any job I could find, and we started to make a life for ourselves.

All that time, I knew wanted to be working with cars or bikes. Prior to getting married, I figured I had to get a bike first or I might never get one. I found a 650 Honda and convinced my brother to loan me enough money to get it. I hustled to pay him back in between buying extras to customize them. It wasn't a Harley but it got me riding. I soon found myself in that old familiar pattern of buying and selling. Each exchange would get me a better bike.

Finally, I thought I had enough money to buy a Harley. I was dumbfounded at the prices. Keep in mind, this is when there was a waiting list for Harleys and used ones sold for more than new ones. I was now bikeless, with $15,000 burning a hole in my pocket. I sat down and calculated how I could get a Harley. Remember, I don't believe in buying or paying for something if I can build it or do it myself. So in 1998 I built my first Harley. I wanted a chopper. Everyone said I was crazy and that they would never come back in style. I built my chopper anyway. It had an 80-inch EVO, five-speed tranny, 230 tire, with a 45-degree rake.

I was almost done building it when I found out about a local show and, of course, I wanted to win it. The only problem was that my slack painter gave me my gas tank but wasn't done with my rear fender and wouldn't be for a while. So I fabricated a bracket to hold my seat up and took off for the show.

It looked cool. No rear fender. It was the only chopper there, and it took first prize. Everyone was in awe of how intimidating the then-huge 230 looked without the fender. I was glad I built a chopper. At that point, I knew what I had to do: build bare-bones, fenderless choppers.

As soon as possible, I hustled the fender on the bike and put it up for sale. It sold pretty quickly. And I got a good price. I figured a fella could make a living this way— but would it be too weird? I bounced the idea off on my wife. She was three months pregnant and was not interested in sharing the back of the bike with anyone else (although that would never happen), so she thought it was an excellent idea to build a true "solo" bike. As always she said, "Do it! Who cares what everyone says. If you believe choppers will come back in style, do it!" I took all the money I made from that bike and built a frame jig and my first bike. From that point on, Precious Metal Customs was born.

I took the resulting chopper down to Daytona Bike Week to show it off, as most do, and it caught the eye of a national magazine. They did a photo shoot on the bike, and as soon as it hit the newsstands, my phone started ringing.

My little idea started to grow into a successful company. Sometimes it is hard for me to believe Precious Metal Customs all started from having fun wrenching and riding on stuff as a kid.

I look now at the phone ringing and the orders going out and can't believe it. I recently received a call from an old friend. It was the same guy who was in the bike wreck with me, calling me to help him fix the carburetor on his chopper. Funny how history repeats, isn't it?

Face it, there was a time when mainstream society considered choppers …

- ◆ Outrageous.

- ◆ A counterculture within a counterculture.

- ◆ Just plain wrong.

- ◆ The product of amateur designers messing in a professionals' domain.

But those days are all but gone. What was once considered "outlaw" has now become the norm. Choppers today are considered beautiful, even awesome. It's been awhile since they have angered motorcycle purists. Nobody calls choppers a crime against nature anymore.

Choppers now are like long hair on men. It's still a fashion statement, but it no longer ticks off parents, who, more often than not, wore their hair that way themselves when they were younger.

I've made it my life's goal to put the "outlaw" back into choppers. Have you noticed that many of the custom bikes out there are all starting to look the same? Sure, they may have a couple of different parts, a flashy paint job, and maybe a "theme," but the general look is the same.

I got into chopper building because I wanted to create designs that were truly original. Having a look that separated my bikes from everyone else's was my goal when I founded Precious Metal Customs.

I knew that the only way to be totally different was to attack the heart of the chopper: the frame. Soon Precious Metal Customs' Spoon Style Rigid frame was available to anyone who wanted to ride a truly radical custom chopper.

Beginners should always do their research. If you want to build your own chopper, the first step is not to pick up the phone and start ordering parts. Make sure you understand what you are getting into.

(Barry C. Altmark Photography)

Since then, many amateur and professional bike builders have created spectacular bikes and have had tremendous success using Precious Metal Customs' frames, custom gas tanks, and a full line of radical custom parts.

And now for the legal disclaimer: I intend to show you a little bit about how I build choppers in this book, and there will be tips—do's and don'ts—for first-time builders, but this is *not* a "How to Build a Chopper" book.

If you are a neophyte who plans to build a chopper that will subsequently be ridden on actual streets in actual traffic, do not think you can use this book as your guide. If your front wheel comes off just as you are hitting Dead Man's Curve, do not blame me—and your estate shouldn't blame me either!

How to Use This Book

The Complete Idiot's Guide to Choppers is divided into five parts, each designed to teach a different lesson about choppers. Some parts will be more relevant to some readers than others, but all parts will have some interest for everyone:

Part 1, "What Is a Chopper?" has information regarding what a chopper is and how it differs from other bikes. It also includes a history of choppers.

Part 2, "To Potential Owners (and Builders)" has info for people who are considering whether to become a chopper owner, either through purchasing one or building their own.

All mechanics love to take things apart and put them back together again. **Part 3, "Anatomy of a Chopper,"** is the literary version.

After you've got your chopper, you have to know how to take care of it. **Part 4, "Maintenance with Style,"** is where you look for maintenance and repair info.

It ain't just the bikes, it's the lifestyle. **Part 5, "Chopper Culture,"** has info regarding life in and around choppers—and how to join in on the fun.

Extras

In addition to the main text, there are lots of photos and boxes of information to aid you in your learning experience. The boxes come in these categories:

Road Closed

Cautions. This sidebar warns of and helps to correct common mistakes and misconceptions.

Celebrity Bio

Short biographies of the celebrities of chopper culture and design.

Wheelie World

Insights into chopper culture. This is the "didja know?" box for cool facts. This sidebar provides you with additional information and insight designed to illuminate the messages of the main text.

def•i•ni•tion

Definitions of bikers' unique lingo. This sidebar helps you understand technical or unusual terms and concepts found in the main text.

Flapping Lips

Flappin' as in flappin' in the breeze! Interesting quotes regarding motorcycles in general, choppers in particular.

Acknowledgments

Thanks for all the help to Barry C. Altmark Photography; Jeff Schwen at Aeromach Manufacturing; Tangela Boyd and Janet Kersey at the Daytona Beach Area Convention & Visitors Bureau; Katy Wood at the Motorcycle Hall of Fame Museum; Danny Sutton at Mark Kings Custom Metal Etching; Jay Moody at Jay Moody's HotRodPaint.com; Rick Corgan at Be-Unique Airbrushing; Lisa Weyer, director of the Sturgis Motorcycle Rally; Gilbert Luna at the V-Twin Expo in Cincinnati, Ohio; Jose De Miguel at Caribbean Custom Cycles in San Juan, Puerto Rico; Paul Platts at JIMS Performance Parts and Tools; Andy and Chris Wyzga; Terry McCall; Marc Osmun; and to Dr. Michael Kamalian at Revolution Speed and Custom in Marietta, Georgia.

Part 1

Becoming a Chopper Owner

According to the website hondachoppers.com, choppers are all about boldness, about "that spirit of individuality, that proverbial, 'I am.'" A chopper, the site says, "speaks a language that isn't heard in mass-produced machines."

For starters, we define our terms. In this part of the book, I tell you what a chopper is and how is differs from your run-of-the-mill motorcycle. Together we journey back in time to the pioneers whose lust for customization started the chopper craze several generations ago.

Whether you are a chopper aficionado, a potential chopper owner (or builder), or just someone who is seeking to learn more about choppers, I think you'll find these many factoids and anecdotes entertaining, as we ask the musical question, "What is a chopper?"

What *Is* a Chopper?

In This Chapter

- ◆ Daydream into reality
- ◆ The chop in chopper
- ◆ Hollywood myth from reality
- ◆ What gets chopped
- ◆ Pros and cons

Maybe you rented *Easy Rider* from Blockbuster last Friday night and it lit a fire under your tail. Maybe you watched the Discovery channel on Bike Night and developed an insatiable urge to weld something.

Now you want a chopper. You want to ride one. You want to be seen riding one. You want to look at it when you're not riding it. About 20 times a day you catch yourself in a daydream—a chopper daydream.

The Chopper Daydream

You're cruising down the open road, your butt 17 inches off the pavement, a 100-cubic-inch engine roaring between your legs, the front tire protruding from your bike at a 45-degree angle, a big fat rear tire under you ....

Sonny Knighter's black 2005 Texas Chopper has a 42-degree rake.

(Barry C. Altmark Photography)

Daydreaming while sitting at a desk or staring at the empty space in your garage can often lead to some unwise—perhaps even foolish—decisions. This chapter is the first step toward steering the neophyte (a fancy word meaning you, the guy or gal who's still a little wet behind the ears when it comes to choppers) in the correct direction.

Chopper Defined

Chopper is merely the catchall term for a customized motorcycle. Sometime back in the 1960s, some bikers with some warped imaginations began to buy Harleys (and sometimes other bikes), chop off the parts they didn't like, and add new parts.

Wheelie World _____

The longest bike trip in history was by Emilio Scotto of Buenos Aires, Argentina. It lasted from January 17, 1985 until April 2, 1995. During that time, Emilio rode around the world twice—once clockwise and once counterclockwise—and visited 214 countries. He traveled 457,000 miles and filled eleven 64-page passports.

The results of those first customization experiments were often bizarre mutations, sometimes humorous in their desperate quest to be different. They looked like the creations of a mad scientist, and many of them looked as if they should have stayed in the laboratory.

The Closest Thing to Flying

The folks who started customizing their bikes after World War II, however, did so not because they wanted to make a fashion statement, but because they wanted better performance out of their American-made bikes. The war produced a lot of mechanics and a renewed interest in making motor vehicles go fast. A lot of these guys had been fighter pilots during the war, and riding a motorcycle was the closest thing they could find to flying after they returned to the States. Others went to England, crossed the North Sea on D-Day, and then road-tripped the hard way from Normandy to Berlin.

Here's a 2005 Legend Softail with a belt drive and a progressive suspension.

(Barry C. Altmark Photography)

When these guys got out of the army, those who were into bikes had also developed a love for speed. Quarter-mile drag strips for motorcycles became popular. Where official drag strips were unavailable, a straight and flat stretch of road relatively devoid of traffic, or a dry lake bed, would often suffice.

The Bare Necessities

Back in those days, choppers were almost never built from scratch. Instead, they were created by customizing a pre-existing factory bike, known as the *donor bike*. There were no rules. The donor bike could be almost anything.

def•i•ni•tion

A **donor bike** is the bike you customize to make your chopper. It is the raw material, the blank canvas upon which you paint your masterpiece.

American bikes were the most popular donor bikes then as now, but it was not out of the question to chop a Honda.

The new riders liked Harleys and Indians, but wanted the zoom-zoom-zoom that they could get from the more-powerful bikes being made in the United Kingdom. Part of the problem was that American bikes, just like American passenger cars of the time, were a lot heavier than they needed to be.

Here I am out for a test ride on a chopper I built called 24K. Why 24K? Because it's jewelry you ride, that's why.

(Precious Metal Customs)

There are two ways to make a bike faster. You can either

◆ Give it an engine with more horsepower, or

◆ Chop off all the unnecessary parts so that it's lighter and easier to propel.

The first chopper builders chose the latter. Those were in the old-, old-school days, and choppers weren't called choppers, they were called "bobbers."

The first guys to turn their bikes into choppers were looking for additional speed, just like these guys battling it out for the lead in the Daytona 200 at the Daytona International Speedway.

(Daytona Beach Area Convention and Visitors Bureau)

Only the bare necessities remained. Everything that could be considered a luxury was gone. The turn signals and horn were removed. Who needs a muffler? The front fender—out of here! Front brake? Excuse me? Doesn't that make the bike *slow down* instead of *go faster?* Take it off! That was how it started, but when guys started messing with their bikes, they found that it was so much fun that they couldn't stop.

Here's a bike I built called Elegantly Wicked. You can tell why. As you can see, there aren't any luxuries. There are only the bare necessities. Actually, the bike remained nameless until a young lady came to me and said, "That bike is very elegant—yet wicked!" Women are always right.

(Precious Metal Customs)

The first option—making the engine more powerful—did not go unnoticed either. Getting more horsepower out of the existing engine (without spending money) turned into a science unto itself. Engine heads were ported and polished to manipulate the combustion chamber. Pistons and valves were taken off of hot rods and fitted to their bikes. Flywheels were shaved to increase revolutions per minute (RPMs).

This chopper attempts to show that life really is more than just a bowl of cherries.

(Andy Wyzga)

The World of Aesthetics

Some aspects of the chopper, however, have nothing to do with going faster or riding better. They are there to make the bike look good. Take, for example, the chopper's most famous feature: its protruding front wheel.

Guys who had removed the seat springs were starting to get sore butts, so they lengthened the front end of the bike in an attempt to get more bounce. It didn't work. In fact, if anything, it made it worse. But it looked great. Then someone discovered that if you modified the frame of your bike, you could extend your front tubes even further, and that looked even cooler.

Those long front ends said, "Hey, look at me!" It's the same reason anyone would ride a chopper today. People after the war wanted to be different, to stand out in the pack, and this sure was a way to do that. The guys chopping their bikes discovered aesthetics, and the world of choppers never looked back.

Here's a bike I built called Negative Image. Where are the handlebars, you might ask? Look closely. There they are below the top triple tree.

(Precious Metal Customs)

Fixing Problems

Looks aren't everything, though. Riders and their passengers started having some trouble riding the first choppers. A lighter bike with the same power plant could accelerate wildly, and had a nasty habit of flipping passengers off the back of the bike when getting off the starting line.

To make the passenger more secure back there, riders built the first sissy bars. These looked cool, too. By the time all of the problems caused by the additional performance were sorted out, you had a bike that was recognizably similar to what we know as a chopper.

Wheelie World _____

Today many choppers don't have sissy bars for the simple reason that they don't have room for a passenger.

Choppers are designed to cut through the wind with a minimum of resistance.

(Barry C. Altmark Photography)

David Edwards, editor of *Cycle World* magazine, remembers the old days, and how they differed from the chopper world portrayed on today's Discovery channel TV shows: "It was a different time back then … you got an old second- or third-hand bike and did it yourself."

The Fonda Factor

In 1969, a momentous event altered the history of choppers forever: a Hollywood movie called *Easy Rider*. That movie was good for the chopper movement in that it turned choppers into a craze, a fad. The choppers ridden in *Easy Rider* by the characters Captain America (Peter Fonda) and Billy Bike (Dennis Hopper, who also directed the movie) remain, more than 35 years later, the most famous of all time.

Wheelie World

Two of each chopper were built for the filming of *Easy Rider*, converted from Harleys Peter Fonda bought at a police auction. One blew up during filming, and the other three were stolen, so new versions had to be constructed so that the movie could be finished.

def•i•ni•tion

A **hardtail** is a bike with a rigid frame, essentially suspension free.

Captain America's bike had been thoroughly chopped. It lacked a windshield, turn signals, suspension, seat springs, a front brake, and a front fender. It was also, obviously, a piece of art. The builder, Cliff Vaughn, may not have intentionally set out to design an icon of American freedom and the open road, but he sure as hell did.

The Captain's chopper was a *hardtail* and had lots of chrome—even on the frame. This is a sign that there was just as much Hollywood as reality in the Captain's bike. The frame of a bike gets a lot of abuse even if you're just riding it around your neighborhood on weekends. If you take it cross-country like Captain America (without a front fender!), then any chrome on the frame will quickly get destroyed. In real life, a simple paint job would have sufficed.

Captain America's chopper had lots of chrome on its rear end, too—on the exhaust, and the rear fender. There were also two bullet lights on either side at the rear, which might not have been a chopper staple but, in a nod to reality, would have been a useful safety precaution for a guy who frequently rode backroads at night.

Then there's that American flag–themed gas tank, which is smaller than a stock tank. The builder accomplished this effect by first painting the tank candy-apple red, then adding the field of blue, white stars, and stripes. Peter Fonda's helmet and jacket matched the gas tank, thus the Captain America moniker.

The other distinguishing factor of this chopper was the handlebars, which were very high. Those types of handlebars offer another Hollywood illusion. They look super cool—and they make the rider look super cool, too: relaxed, arms outstretched, shoulders back. Truth is, long trips steering a bike with high handlebars results in pins and needles in the fingers.

Billy's Bike, the one ridden in *Easy Rider* by Dennis Hopper's character, is also a chopper—but not as memorable for the simple fact that it isn't as extreme. For example, it retains its brakes and fenders. The front fender has been chopped short, however. It has the smaller gas tank and the seat is close to the frame, so the bike looks sleek. The paint job is candy-apple red with yellow flames over that.

The chopper ridden by Captain America (Peter Fonda) in the movie Easy Rider *did more than anything to standardize what a chopper was supposed to be—and it remains by far the most famous single chopper of all time.*

(Jim A. Pearson)

Taking advantage of the movie's popularity, the California Motorcycle Company (now a subsidiary of the Indian Motorcycle Company) built replicas of the *Easy Rider* choppers to sell. But they weren't that good. Gray paint replaced chrome. For street legality, turn signals and front brake and fender had to be put on. The basic look is there, but....

Since then, other one-off replicas have been built, and more precisely match the actual choppers used in the film. Maybe one day you'll be lucky enough to see one of these bikes at a show or in a parade.

Much easier to find than a facsimile of the Captain American chopper is a facsimile of Captain America's Old Glory–themed helmet, which is made by Custom Chrome of Morgan Hill, California. The DoT-approved lookalike features:

- Thermoplastic shell
- Three-snap visor
- Plush brush nylon interior
- D-ring retention system
- High-quality paint with a clear-coat finish

> **Flapping Lips**
>
> According to Jacob Roth of NAPStudios: "Some folks say 'Choppers are *not* for beginners.' Bullocks! I had put in less than a year on a 1975 Honda CB500T when I got sick of pumping money into a bike I really didn't like. Then I dumped my money instead into something I had always wanted. I painted it black so I wouldn't worry about accidentally laying down the bike or spend too much time cleaning it. I ran a very dangerous bike with a wickedly wild front end and only a rear brake for a couple of years in a city full of traffic and freakin' idiots. I have broke down on many occasions. Only when I blew the rear tire did I have to have my wife come and pick us up in the truck. Otherwise I always have managed to fix her enough to get her home. Very few people can even start my bike, let alone ride a chopper designed for a 6-foot-4 individual. If you want a chopper, build it."

Fame Equals Standardization

The sudden leap in chopper popularity after *Easy Rider* was also bad because it tended to standardize the chopper. Anyone who had seen the movie knew exactly what a chopper was supposed to look like and wanted theirs to look exactly like it.

Over the years, however, the chopper did evolve. Starting in the late 1980s, it became fashionable for the back wheel on your chopper to be very fat. The fatter the better. It was a look, but those bikes rode very poorly.

> **Wheelie World**
>
> For a time after the movie *Easy Rider*, all choppers had to have a hardtail frame and a big Harley-Davidson twin engine.

def•i•ni•tion

> A chopper's **forks** are the metal tubes connecting the front wheel to the rest of the bike.

In the 1990s, things got better. New technology was developed, and chopper builders learned to apply older technology, too. The result was choppers with stronger *forks*, and fat back wheels that rode and handled well. Even today, however, some chopper builders do not like fat tires.

New technology developed in the past 20 years also allowed chopper builders to use ever-longer frames. The front wheel could angle outward from the frame by as much as 45 degrees. Choppers became longer and longer, and yet they remained rideable.

One of the things you can count on when it comes to a Precious Metal chopper is that the back wheel will be fatter than the front.

(Precious Metal Customs)

Simple with Attitude

Although some chopper builders end up adding more and larger parts than those that they chopped off, the chopper as a rule is a simple machine, often lighter and more powerful than the factory model it was customized from.

Simple, yes—but with attitude. Because choppers are longer and sleeker and sexier than factory models, they convey an aura of rebelliousness. There was a time when all motorcycle riders seemed like rebels, but, let's face it, that is no longer the case.

Celebrity Bio

On August 30, 2004, the chopper world lost one of its greats when Indian Larry died of head injuries sustained when one of his stunts went wrong. Born Larry Desmedt, he was a master mechanic, metal sculptor, and stuntman. He was killed when performing his trademark stunt of riding a bike while standing on the seat. The accident took place during a show at Liquid Steel Classic and Custom Bike Series show at Cabarrus Arena and Events Center in Concord, North Caolina, near Charlotte. He lived in Brooklyn, New York, and was probably best known for his appearances on Discovery Channel's "Great Biker Build-Off" show, and on "The Late Show with David Letterman," where he once rode a bike through a wall of fire. He was born in Cornwall-on-Hudson, New York, and built his first bike as a teenager when he bought a 1939 Harley Knucklehead for $200 and then spent the next nine months putting it back together again. His shop, Gasoline Alley in Brooklyn, opened in 1991. He was a champion of the "old school." His bike Grease Monkey won the Easy Rider award for Chopper of the Year.

Things That Get Chopped

Looking at the vital statistics for a chopper I built recently gives a pretty good checklist of what many motorcycles have that Precious Metal choppers don't. (If you are converting a stock bike into a chopper, you literally chop things off. If you are building a chopper from scratch, as I do, then those parts are never there to begin with.)

Anyway, here's a list of things my chopper named The Pimp does not have:

- Rear shocks (Who needs them? Your butt comes with its own padding, right?)
- Front and rear fenders and fender struts (Fenders are pointless!)
- Turn signals (I can point where I'm going.)
- Oil cooler
- Dash (Speedometer and odometer? I don't care how fast I'm going or how far I've been!)
- Most of the sheet metal (It just covers up what others couldn't make presentable!)
- Mirrors (I still refuse to install a small mirror on the handlebars to make it street legal, a story I'll get into later in Chapter 19.)

The Downside

All right, you're thinking, if what Russ is telling me is true, then why doesn't every motorcycle rider in the world chop his bike? Well, there are several reasons. For one thing, not everyone *is* a rebel. Heck, there are *R-U-B.s* who are content to ride a moped back and forth to their desk job every day.

def•i•ni•tion

An **R-U-B.** is a *Rich Urban Biker*, sort of the biker version of a wannabe. You know who you are.

For another thing, the folks who make the factory bikes aren't idiots. They make bikes that ride well, can carry a load, and need a minimum of maintenance. There's a whole school of bikers who believe that chopping a bike is one way to ruin a damn good bike. That's fine. Some folks like driving SUVs, too.

So hey there, daydreamer. Here's a list of questions you need to answer truthfully for yourself:

- Do you want to buy a motorcycle, or do you want to buy a chopper?

- Are you really brave? Would you like to convert an old bike into a chopper?

- Would you like to take a crack at doing what I do for a living and build a chopper from scratch?

It's up to you. Hopefully the information in this book will help you make up your mind.

The Least You Need to Know

- Folks started customizing their bikes in the 1940s not because they wanted to make a fashion statement, but because they wanted better performance out of their American-made bikes.

- At some point, motorcycles were no longer customized for practical reasons, but just as a way to get attention.

- The choppers ridden in *Easy Rider* remain, more than 35 years later, the most famous of all time.

- The chopper is a simple machine, lighter and more powerful than the factory model it was made from.

- If you are converting a stock bike into a chopper, you literally chop things off.

2

Owning the Right Chopper

In This Chapter

- Knowing what you want
- Knowing your capabilities
- Three necessities
- East vs. West Coast
- Learning to scrounge

This is a book about dreams coming true, so in this chapter we are going to focus on the dream. Your dream. What's the use in purchasing or building a chopper if, when you're done, you can't say, "This is *exactly* what I wanted"? Talk about disappointing!

So, to make sure it doesn't happen to you, let's take a closer look at the dream, the better to transform it into reality.

What's Your Dream?

Close your eyes. What's your dream chopper? Can you envision it? Good. Don't forget that image. There may be reasons why you can't make your dream come true. Maybe you lack the money for such a magnificent creature. But even if you have to make compromises, always keep that dream bike as a master guideline. If you don't have to settle for something less, don't.

That's another way of saying do not make things up as you go along. Plan. Plan. Plan. Plan. Have your bike blueprinted out from the very start. Even if you are just going by a simple sketch, or from a photo you took of that perfect bike you saw in the tavern parking lot, have a vision and, as much as is possible, stick to it.

If your dream is going on long runs on your chopper, don't build one that can barely make it around the block. If your plan is to build a totally wild but impractical chopper, don't plan to take it cross-country.

To Buy or To Build?

The great majority of this book's readers are more interested in purchasing a chopper than building one. Most of you, I'm sure, would just as soon build your next TV set as build your chopper. Some things you just go to the store and buy. That's okay by me. Selling choppers is what I do. If you want me to build it for you, great.

Maybe you don't know which category you're in. Sometimes customers ask me if they should buy or build a chopper, and I always find it a hard question to answer. What should a person consider when determining whether to buy or build? Maybe part of you thinks you've got the right stuff to build your own chopper, and another part feels like riding the new chopper *now!* I guess the first consideration is: Do you want instant or delayed gratification?

To buy a chopper outright offers instant gratification. That may be enough for some people, just hop on a bike and ride. To build a chopper takes time, but the reward is an undying, overwhelming, you-did-it gratification.

Look Deep Inside

I think a person knows deep down inside if he or she is the right person to build a bike. It requires a lot of patience, a fair number of tools, and knowledge about how to use them. Don't think that your profession means anything either.

Sometimes I have doctors call me to order a rolling chassis, and they are able to jump right in and complete a beautiful bike. Other times I have mechanics order a roller, and they can't build a decent bike if their life depends on it. Bottom line: It doesn't matter what your day job is, just what's inside. You know if you have what it takes.

> **Wheelie World** _____
>
> I can't think of anything I can do on a regular bike that I can't on one of my choppers. And if couldn't do it on a chopper, why bother?

Before you decide to build your own chopper, take a long, hard look at yourself in the mirror. It's a big job, and it demands a certain level of mechanical thinking and motor skills. Not everybody is up to the task. If you are the sort of person who dreads Christmas morning out of fear that Santa has delivered a toy that needs "some assembling," building a chopper is probably not for you.

> **def•i•ni•tion** _____
>
> A **gearhead** is a man or woman who is a born mechanic, the sort of person who could take a bike apart and put it together again, the first time he or she tried, without an instruction manual.

On the other hand, maybe you're a major *gearhead*. Maybe you like to take everything you own apart, just so you can put it back together again. If that is true, building a chopper will be more than just a rewarding experience; it will be fun. What are you waiting for?

Shopping

If I didn't already have contacts in the chopper world, and I was looking to purchase my first chopper, my first step would be to buy every bike magazine on the newsstand. Some are just about choppers, and some are about motorcycles in general. The latter often have articles about choppers, too.

Then I would look at the ads. That's the fastest and best way to learn what's out there. Then get on the horn and start making phone calls. Get an idea of how much things cost. Figure out what you can afford and who sells it. If possible, find a shop near you.

Celebrity Bio

Yasoyoshi Chikazawa, better known as Chica, learned his mechanical chops while working for Honda in Japan. While there, he bought a Harley and learned to love tinkering with it. While still in his homeland, he and a group of friends opened up Chica Motorcycle Service, which did mostly maintenance and repair work. Chica came to the United States in 1995, and settled in Huntington Beach, California. He soon began to build his own choppers and opened up his own shop. His bikes earned immediate attention because they were on the cutting edge, yet each paid homage to some aspect of American pop culture. For the first few years, most of Chica's bikes were purchased by Japanese customers, but that is no longer the case. "I'm still looking for my style. I am never satisfied," Chica told reporter Adrian Blake.

Special Insurance Problems?

Here's something you might not have thought of. If you build a chopper and it has a flaw, then you take it out for a ride, crash and die, you only have yourself to blame. If you build a chopper and let your friend ride it, and, because of a flaw in the construction, he crashes and dies, you are gonna get sued big-time.

Wheelie World

If you are going to build a chopper and let someone else ride it, be sure that you have liability insurance up the wazoo.

For this reason, guys who build choppers that others are going to ride have to buy liability insurance to cover themselves just in case something goes wrong. Guys who ordinarily would build a chopper from scratch, including the design and creation of the frame, now outsource the building of the frame to larger places because only a place with some volume can afford the liability insurance for frames.

Road Closed

Do not build a chopper unless you are 100 percent into the project. I think a person knows deep down inside if he or she is the right person to build a bike. It requires a lot of patience, a fair number of tools, and knowledge about how to use them.

The Kit Option

Don't forget that you can combine the two schemes. You can purchase kits that make assembling a chopper easier. In some cases, when you get the package, some of the toughest work has already been done for you.

You can build part of your bike and have part built for you. If you love to work with motors and sheet metal but are afraid of electricity, get a pro to do your wiring for you. If you are great with a set of tools but you aren't exactly an artist, hire out to get that hot custom job applied.

Now a word from our sponsor: at my shop, Precious Metal Customs, we sell products to both the buyers and the builders. You can shop for a finished chopper (photos of which you'll see throughout this book), or you can come to me to buy aftermarket parts.

Things You'll Need to Build

You need six things to build your own chopper, in order of importance as follows:

- Determination
- Tool knowledge
- Space
- Time
- Money
- Two extra people (explained later)

If you are lacking in any of these all-important commodities, you are not ready to start building a chopper. Let's take them one at a time.

Determination

Ask my wife and she'll tell you I am hardheaded. Ask my father and he'll tell you I have a one-track mind. Ask my mother and she'll tell you that I am determined. To those who have no obstacles in their way (plenty of money and time, and so on), determination might not seem so important. But to the majority of us (who have obstacles we must overcome), determination is a commodity that you must rely on.

Pitfalls happen in every bike build, and at every stage. These pitfalls may be something that is totally out of your control. It could be that the paint peeled off the bike because of a poor application. Maybe the product had a manufacturer's defect, or maybe a tire was sent to you out of round. Or maybe it was you who screwed up. Determination will get you through these "I-give-up" moments.

> **Road Closed** _____
>
> Some folks have a single dream, and they cling to it dearly. Then there are people who don't have that kind of attention span. These people have a different dream every week. One week they want to become a downhill skier. They buy expensive skis and hit the mountain. By the end of the second weekend, the urge to ski is gone. But they want to build a chopper, so they buy a bunch of books and a bunch of parts, but by the second weekend, the urge to build the chopper is gone. If you change obsessions once every couple of weeks, skip the whole idea of building a chopper.

Tool Knowledge

You can't build a chopper with a screwdriver and a hammer. If that's all you have lying around the house, you are going to need to do some shopping. Don't worry. A little later on, I give a complete rundown of the tools you need.

When you own a chopper, life becomes a never-ending parade.

(Daytona Beach Area Convention and Visitors Bureau)

Space

If you live in the desert, you can probably get away with building your chopper outdoors. If you live anywhere else, you need some sort of indoor space. A garage without a car in it is the most popular space. Some are lucky enough to have a house with an extra room or two, one of which can be converted into the shop. If this is you, no problem. But if building a chopper means you are going to have to move one of your kids into the backyard, maybe this isn't the right project for you.

Time

Even those who earn their living building choppers, such as me, are keenly aware of how time-consuming it can be. The problem is, building a chopper always takes longer than you think it is going to. Something always goes wrong. Some part you ordered doesn't fit. Some mistake is made. Whatever. Rare is the bike that is finished exactly when you thought it would be finished. Even rarer is the chopper that is finished early.

If that happens to those of us who attempt to crank out bike after bike, who have professional shops fully equipped with all the tools necessary to perform any task and work out any problem, imagine how long it is going to take you to build your first chopper in your garage!

If you want to build a chopper part-time, there is no point in putting yourself on a deadline. Remember, many of you have other obligations—family, home, career, things like that. The worst thing you can do is rush your first build.

Money

Whoever said, "The best things in life are free" never tried to build or buy a chopper. Make sure, before you start, that you have enough money to complete your chopper project. This is easy if you are buying a prebuilt chopper. If you are building your chopper, it can be tricky.

You have to figure out ahead of time how much the whole project is going to cost and then

Road Closed

If you're a first-time builder, don't rush. Take your time and make sure you do it right. Every professional builder has rushed a build and will likely do it several more times—but ask them if they enjoyed the stress, aggravation, and sleepless nights they endured.

Wheelie World

A lot of people think that many choppers lack mufflers as an expression of the rider's attitude. A rude bike should sound rude, is the thinking. That's not necessarily the case. Choppers, when riding in traffic, can be difficult to see in the rearview mirror of a car or truck. As a safety precaution, many riders prefer to keep their choppers loud so that they can be heard, as well as seen.

determine whether you will have the money to pay the bills. Nothing is worse than running out of money in the middle of a chopper project. That half-finished chopper could sit in the back of your garage for the rest of your natural life!

Two Extra People

Everyone needs two extra people on their first build. The first person, probably a good buddy, might be there to give you an extra hand when things get tough. He may set up the motor in the frame, or hold the front end straight while you put on the front wheel, or he might just be the person who gives you the encouragement to get through the build. Everyone needs a "you can do it" and an "atta boy (or girl)" every now and then.

The other person is probably the most important person to the build. All first-time builders must have someone they can call for help. Maybe it's the mechanic at the local shop. Or maybe it's someone at the company you bought your *roller* through.

def•i•ni•tion

Roller is short for rolling chassis, the frame and wheels combo that is the starting piece for most first-time chopper builders.

Or maybe it is just someone who has walked the path that you're on right now. Whoever it is, he or she will be the person at the other end of the line when you pick up the phone and ask for help. Make sure you have made this contact and you know who this person is before you start your first build.

Finding the Perfect Chopper

Before you can decide what the perfect chopper is for you, you need to know who you are. What makes you tick? Take a good long look at yourself in the mirror. Only when you know yourself enough to know what really and truly makes you happy can you decide which chopper completes you.

Exotic vs. Dependable

There are guys and gals out there whose chopper dream doesn't involve hitting the open road like Captain America. They want a chopper that looks so good that it is satisfying even when it is standing still.

Then there are people who couldn't give a hoot what the chopper looks like, as long as it can get them to where they are going with a respectable 0-to-60 time. You need to know which category you are in.

> **Wheelie World**
>
> Other than matters of personal taste, there is a good reason why those who ride American bikes and those who ride foreign bikes don't spend a lot of time swapping parts at swap meets. The reason is this: the metric system. If you are making a chopper out of a Honda, the parts you need must be measured in centimeters. If you are customizing a Harley, those same parts are measured in inches. Trying to put a metric part on a nonmetric bike is like trying to put a square peg in a round hole.

How Thick Is Your Wallet?

Someone who only knows about choppers from watching them built on the Discovery channel might think they need $100,000 of throwing-around money to own their own chopper. But nothing could be further from the truth.

If you want to start with a donor bike, or even if you want to start from scratch, the aftermarket world is growing larger every day. If you play your cards right, you can build your own chopper for as little as $5,000. That's only 5 percent of what you would need to purchase a Jesse James creation.

> **Wheelie World**
>
> Didja know that, according to the Motorcycle Industry Council, the number of motorcycles in the United States recently passed the 9 million mark. That represents an increase of 33 percent since 1998!

> **Flapping Lips**
>
> Says Discovery channel producer George Puckhaber, "You'll spend weeks poring over the custom chopper magazines for somebody to invite on an episode of *Biker Build-Off*, but they're sometimes very hard to find. Then we'll be taping a show at some small, second-rate custom bike show and you'll come across a motorcycle that just makes everybody's jaw drop and say, 'Who the hell built that?'"

According to cheap chopper expert Timothy Remus, a metric chopper can cost less than $5,000. However, if you want a Sportster Buell chopper, you are going to have to spend somewhere in the $7,500 to $10,000 range. If you have your heart set on a Big Twin, you will have to lay out somewhere in the neighborhood of $15,000 to $20,000.

Regional Differences

Be aware that where you live could greatly affect the type of chopper you should ride. Later on we discuss a concept that chopper owners like to argue about: old school vs. new school. To put it simply, old school is the way things were done back in the day, and new school is the way things are done today.

With the exception of Indian Larry, Dave Perewitz of Cycle Fab (Brockton, Massachusetts), and a few others, there was no old school on the East Coast. While bikers on the West Coast were living the old-school phenomenon, the guys in the East were watching it on TV or when they saw a biker movie. There is a simple reason for this, but it's nothing that a million years or so of global warming couldn't cure.

The Changing Seasons

Choppers caught on more slowly on the East Coast for the same reason that there are fewer motorcycles in general in the East: weather. With the exception of Florida and the rest of the Deep South, most of the United States east of the Mississippi River is a land of drastically differing seasons.

There are cold and snowy winters, rainy springs, brittle autumns, and scorching summers. The wet and the cold spell rust and corrosion for a chopper. One 200-mile trip in snowy conditions can do permanent damage to a chopper's running gear and front suspension.

Salty roads also take their toll—and potholes can quickly bust up springer forks and rear suspension. So the point is, the West Coast has the advantage when it comes to riding choppers—just as it does when it comes to motorcycles in general, or ragtop cars, for that matter.

Flapping Lips

"As historical birthplace of the chopper and launch pad of the custom motorcycle art form, there's little wonder that most notable motorcycle craftsmen still call the sun-baked West Coast their home. The long, straight roads, the seemingly endless summers, and a multiethnic youth culture have all helped make California the epicenter of the customized vehicle movement."—Mike Seate, Outlaw Choppers

Limited by Laws

Earlier we learned that exhaust pipes can be legal in one place but illegal in another. Well, in certain places east of the Mississippi, the same thing can be true of other parts of your chopper.

The District of Columbia, Pennsylvania, and New Hampshire—where politicians saw choppers as a threat to the civilized world—passed laws that limited the height of handlebars and the length of forks. That caused East Coast builders to turn away from apehangers and go with low handlebars. Wheelbases tended to be shorter in the East than in the West.

To be fair, almost every state has some sort of limitation on the height of allowable handlebars. The thinking is that if the handlebars are too high, only apes will be able to operate those apehangers and they represent a safety hazard. The most common legal limitation on handlebars is that they must be at the level of, or lower than, the rider's shoulders.

Show vs. Street

Perewitz remembers a time back in the 1970s when hardcore guys built choppers in the East that were neither practical nor legal: "The laws were so strict on what you couldn't do to your chopper, you had guys building bikes that could only be show choppers because they'd get impounded if we rode them on the streets. We started focusing on other things like crazy surface finishes and murals painted not only on the gas tanks and fenders, but air crushed on the frame rails, too.

"Guys in New England spent maybe three quarters of the year building their bikes, and they got three, four months of good weather to ride them in. They ended up coming to the shows in spring with these crazy, way-out customs. They'd spent all winter engraving these elaborate scenes in the chrome or wheels."

The good news is that the laws restricting custom motorcycle design today are a lot less stringent than they were 30 or 40 years ago. As long as you follow the laws that still exist, you can now ride your chopper just about anywhere without seeing those flashing red lights in your rearview mirror.

East Coast Practical Style

Because of the limitations, the weather, and legalities, choppers in the East tended to be more practical. Forks are extended, but sometimes only half a foot. In the desert, springer forks sometimes approach being 2 feet longer than their stock length.

In the East, fenders are usually not removed in their entirety, but are rather shortened and sometimes bobbed. A fenderless front wheel on an East Coast chopper is apt to fling mud into a rider's face.

Because of problems with bad roads, East Coast choppers tended from the start to have less-rigid frames. A West Coast bike ridden through the streets of Manhattan can be a bone-jarring experience. Harley-Davidson swingarm frames with telescopic shocks make a suitable backbone for an East Coast chopper.

Early attempts by East Coast builders to imitate the choppers they saw in Hollywood movies were usually short-lived and sometimes disastrous. To put it simply, East Coast choppers had no choice but to be more rugged than their West Coast counterparts. The 21-inch chopper front wheels popular in California would bend the first time they hit a pothole.

West Coast riders could allow their front forks to go naked. East Coast riders put *gaiters* on their forks.

This isn't to say that you can't build a West Coast–style chopper if you live in the East, just be aware that there are probably going to be many months out of the year when you will not be able to take it out on the road. Still, it'll look great in your garage!

def•i•ni•tion

A **gaiter** is a rubber protective sleeve that slides over a chopper's front forks and protects them from the elements. The term comes from England, where the weather greatly resembles that in the American East.

According to East Coast chopper builder Bill Steele of Oakdale Custom Choppers, the newer trends in East Coast choppers are less extension in the forks and stretch upward in the frame's forward downtubes, but with a drag bike's relaxed steering geometry.

"That's cool," Steele says, "because there's been a lot of obstacles to building choppers here (in the East), not to mention the cost. I think that's why choppers have caught on with younger riders. They want something that's going to be eye-catching, and you can easily throw $20,000 in chrome and performance upgrades at a stock Harley, but it's still going to look like everybody else's bike in the parking lot. It's a real challenge to build a chopper that gets noticed but is still good for everyday use on the roads."

Don't Be Afraid to Scrounge

About building a chopper on a budget, Steve Peffer of Steel City Choppers in Pittsburgh, Pennsylvania, says: "If somebody gave me $50,000 to build them a chopper, I honestly don't know what I'd do with all the money."

The secret to keeping the price tag low, Steve says, involves developing your fine sense of scrounging. Learn to love wandering around junkyards, picking up everything that looks like it might fit on your bike. Learn to love putting ads in the paper, begging for what you need.

"You can build a radical chopper out of the parts you find hanging around people's back rooms for next to nothing," says Peffer, who has been known to build a sissy bar out of the cold steel rods used to make security fences. "It just takes a lot of hard work."

Celebrity Bio

When most people think of the typical rebel chopper builder, they think of Jesse James, who has become a TV star in addition to being a respected creator of fine bikes. He claims to be the great-great-great-grandson of the outlaw Jesse James, and there isn't anything about his behavior that would lead you to believe that this isn't true. Today's Jesse James is an outlaw through and through. He was born in Long Beach, California, the son of an antiques dealer, and built his first bike when he was a freshman in high school. His dad's shop shared space with an aftermarket manufacturer of Harley parts. He played college football and had a short career as a bodyguard for rock stars before he began assisting hot rod builder Boyd Coddington. During the 1990s, he started West Coast Choppers, one of the country's top chopper shops.

Although it's true that most parts and accessories for just about any type of chopper—new or old—are available from aftermarket sources, some parts can still be found only by rummaging through junkyards with a cast-iron detector or kicking through the weeds in the backyards of abandoned houses.

Guys who like to build facsimiles of post-WWII Harleys know this to be true. The parts they need are antiques, which is another way of saying old and rare. Most of the parts that were originally manufactured are lost forever.

The parts that still exist are often in the hands of collectors who treasure them and won't sell them at any price—or, if those parts are for sale, the cost is prohibitively high. The choices are, assuming that the builder isn't a zillionaire, to either hope to find one in a widow's garage or put on the ol' welder's mask and try to fabricate your own.

The Least You Need to Know

- ◆ Unless you enjoy riding your chopper, it's not much of an investment. Those looking to get ahead by purchasing a product that steadily accrues in value should look elsewhere.

◆ Start your shopping process by reading all of the latest biker mags. Find out who is selling what, and then get on the horn and find out how much things cost.

◆ Building a chopper is a big responsibility. A flaw could get you hurt or killed—or sued! Know what you want and what you are capable of acquiring (or building).

◆ Make sure you have the space, tools, and time to complete your project.

◆ Keeping the price tag low on your chopper often involves some skillful scrounging.

Chapter **3**

Let's Be Practical

In This Chapter

- Only pretty, what a pity
- Reliability
- Usefulness
- Minipearls

Fantasy and reality often part ways when you're sitting at work dreaming of the open road. This chapter lists some things you have to consider before you customize the bike you already have, or buy or build a new chopper.

Quality of the Ride

Some chopper builders choose not to see the aesthetics of a good-looking chopper. Or they see the aesthetics as a secondary factor. These people do not think customizing a motorcycle is like creating a work of art. (Or their definition of "art" is drastically different.) They feel about the same as those guys on the drag strips of California in 1948. You make a chopper because you want to take a great bike and make it greater. Just as an overweight person goes on a diet, they want to reduce their bike into a leaner and meaner machine.

The tail end of Sonny Knighter's Big Dog.

(Barry C. Altmark Photography)

Among these builders is Blair Powell. Blair says, "I see these high-concept choppers and I think, 'Okay—who out there … doesn't realize that the original choppers weren't covered in corny murals or elaborate themes?' They didn't cost more than your mortgage."

Will It Get You There?

One of the key practical considerations when it comes to choppers is dependability. Will it get you to where you are going? Many a utility chopper has been begrudgingly transformed into a show piece because it couldn't get around the block without requiring some sort of maintenance.

Blair Powell—who paints all of his choppers the same color: black—says, "To me a 'concept' chopper means one that starts every time you hit the kicker or one that still has some oil left in the tank after a 200-mile ride."

Not for Millionaires Only

Powell points out that the original choppers were not for some millionaires-only club, but were built for and by working-class people. Powell fears that what was once meant to be a participatory sport is, because of the media, turning into a spectator sport. He feels that the Discovery channel TV shows, which create stars of the builders of high-end choppers, in the long run will alienate young people. He says that if he were a teenager again, he'd rather saw the mufflers off a stock Harley-Davidson 883 Sportster than try to build a chopper that in any way resembled those being made on TV. "A kid can build a whole bobber for half of what it would take to buy a single Jesse James part."

This 2005 Big Dog Chopper softail has a 40-degree rake.

(Barry C. Altmark Photography)

On the Cheap

Just because you want to build a chopper doesn't mean that you have to break your piggybank. You may want to take out a loan and put some money into your project, but it isn't necessary. There are economic options for just about every facet of the build, and I will point them out when we get to them.

One of the best excuses to pay attention to details is that mistakes inevitably cost money. The two best ways to save money on a build are as follows:

- ◆ Shop around so that you get all of your parts and components at the cheapest possible price.

- ◆ Plan out your build meticulously so that you get everything right the first time. Efficiency is the key to budgeting both time and money.

Seat

Just like snowflakes, no two butts are the same. Because of this, the seat that may be comfy under one person's bottom may give saddle sores to another's. Seats, like choppers in general, need to be test-ridden. In the *viva la difference* department, male butts and female butts are generally built by two completely different designers. If you and your mate plan to share the bike, make sure the seat is comfortable for both of you. Just because the seat is sweet to your cheeks, don't assume that the same is true for your significant other.

Make It Fit

I have to admit that I don't watch many of the chopper-building TV shows that are on now, mostly on the Discovery channel. But I did watch the show where Jesse James was building a chopper for Shaquille O'Neal. Shaq needs a huge bike. A person of normal size couldn't ride Shaq's chopper. He or she would not even be able to reach the handgrips. It is important to have a chopper that fits you.

Choppers come in different sizes. If you're purchasing one, make sure that when you straddle it your feet and hands are comfortable. If it seems even the slightest bit awkward—too cramped or too much of a reach—then this isn't the chopper for you. What seems a little bit awkward at first is going to seem a *lot* awkward over the long haul.

How Much Cargo?

If you're asking this question, maybe getting a chopper isn't for you. There are motorcycles, they're nicknamed *baggers*, that have a comfortable seat for the long haul and multiple compartments for your belongings. You can strap your bags on them; you can even hitch them up to a small trailer and pull your stuff around. It's a beautiful thing, but it doesn't have a lot to do with choppers.

def•i•ni•tion

A **bagger** is a motorcycle equipped to carry your bags. If you do not pack lightly and you want to go on vacation, a bagger is the right bike for you.

Choppers are almost exactly the opposite of baggers. They are designed to be slender and sexy, not thick and bulky. They are designed to be light and fast. Not slow but strong. Soccer moms (and campers) don't buy Corvettes.

Miles Per Gallon

Generally, fuel economy is not a major concern for chopper owners. Compared to automobiles and heavier bikes, choppers do very well in the miles-per-gallon department. But, like anything else, there is always room for improvement.

As Nervous Norvus used to say, "Put another gallon in the Allen!" But that was 50 years ago, and the price of gas is close to 10 times what it was back then. To make sure that you are getting the most out of every drop of fuel, you might install on your chopper a *digital fuel optimizer* (DFO). They cost less than $150.

def•i•ni•tion

A **digital fuel optimizer** modifies the outgoing signal from the ECU (electronic control unit) to your injectors, increasing the duration of the spray of fuel, thereby richening the mixture.

A DFO will optimize your fuel injection without the need for expensive dyno-tuning. With a DFO, you can quickly dial in your engine's fuel delivery. It doesn't matter if your powerplant is stock or if you've added a freer-flowing air filter and/or exhaust. It takes less than an hour to install a DFO. Adjustments can be made with a screwdriver.

RevTech makes a reliable DFO. The gadget is easy to mount because it is compact (3½" × 1½" × ¾"). It offers crisper throttle response and a three-range adjustable fuel-delivery curve—that is, adjustable pots allow you to add fuel where it is needed over three areas of the rev range.

A fourth pot allows you to set a transition point from light-load cruise to high-fuel performance mode. This allows both basic tuning and more sophisticated fine-tuning for specific racing situations. According to the July 2002 issue of *Ironworks*, a DFO that tried out "clearly made the bike a lot more pleasant to ride."

Good Investment

If you are looking to purchase a chopper as an investment, you might want to put your money somewhere else. Unless you want to be a full-time builder like me, choppers demand too much heart to make a good investment.

Customizing a Harley means designing a vehicle that becomes one with your personality. If you're just going to work on it and hope to sell it at a higher price, you might make a buck or two, but you won't get the soulful enjoyment.

There is one practical consideration that must be addressed. How big is the gas tank? And how far will the chopper go between stops at the gas station?

(Barry C. Altmark Photography)

And without customization, there can be no appreciation, only depreciation. At one time in the late 1980s and early 1990s, used Harleys sold for more than new ones—so anything you did to them increased the value. That's no longer the case. Bikes don't depreciate as quickly as passenger cars, but a used one is still cheaper than a new one and not the other way around. You'll be a happier person if you think of your chopper as an investment in making your life complete, and not as a way to turn a profit.

The seat and the tank can't be built independently, because, in the long run, they must fit together like pieces of a jigsaw puzzle.

(Barry C. Altmark Photography)

A store-bought chopper depreciates the second you drive it, but a plain-Jane custom-built bike depreciates, too. On the other hand, finely crafted bikes, such as those built at Precious Metal Customs and other professional chopper-building shops, don't lose value because they are used.

A bad-ass unique ride that has been built to turn heads from now until 10 years from now will only grow in value. Again, despite the fact that they appreciate in value, I do not recommend trying to make money by selling choppers unless you are building them, too.

Minichoppers

Dr. Evil needed a Mini Me to feel complete. Maybe your chopper needs a minichopper to be truly happy. Seriously, if you are small in stature, or if you have a kid who needs a chopper, minichoppers might be a serious option for you.

Wheelie World _____

Is the typical biker getting older? It depends on whom you ask. Perhaps it's time to add a touch of gray to those colors you're flying! According to one study, the average biker in the United States is getting older—much older. According to the Motorcycle Industry Council, in 1985 the average American biker was 27 years old. Today, they say that average has risen to 42 years old. Harley-Davidson, on the other hand, says that their research indicates the exact opposite, that one of the reasons a stock Harley has dropped is so that it would be more affordable to the ever-growing younger crowd.

Minichoppers—also called minimotorcycles, or scooters—have become increasingly popular over the past few years, and many of the major motorcycle companies now sell them. Even Harley-Davidson has one out.

Wheelie World _____

Ebay and other online auction houses are great places to buy new and used parts for your minichopper.

You remember minibikes, right? About 40 years ago, minibikes became a mini fad. The most popular minibikes were the Gemini and the Maverick, manufactured by Yamaha and imported to the United States from Taiwan. Minibikes were banned in a lot of places in the United States and eventually went the way of the eight-track tape player.

But now we have minichoppers, which are a cross between full grown choppers and the minibikes of yesteryear. As is true of regular choppers, you can buy a minichopper, or you can build your own. There is a wide variety of parts to choose from.

If you don't want to build your own minichopper, but you want your model to be individual to you, there are manufacturers who will build a minichopper specifically to your unique design concept. So you can, if you want to, make your minichopper identical to the chopper you already own, only smaller.

If you choose to build your own, remember these rules:

♦ Choose your parts wisely, because the quality of the parts will determine the quality of your ride.

♦ Take great care in choosing your frame because, as is true in any bike, the frame is the backbone.

♦ Determine your design, including the paint job, before you begin assembly.

A Word to the Wise

Building a super-long, super-radical chopper can be a lot of fun, but it could be very dangerous without the proper planning. If you're even the slightest bit unsure of yourself, do not hesitate to contact a qualified manufacturer for the correct information.

That said, do not be afraid of building the bike of your dreams for fear that it could be unsafe. Technology has come a long way since the 1970s. The builders of today don't just guess when it comes to peoples' lives. Engineering and mathematics are now applied to the chopper industry. Today, any reputable frame, rolling chassis, or bike builder should be able to lead you down the safest road to your dream chopper.

Wheelie World

Try a chopper with relatively short front-end extension—maybe 6 inches or less. Choppers with the best handling usually have frame rake dimensions of less than 38 degrees.

An ill-educated newcomer who tries to build any motorcycle will often produce a machine that, even if it looks freaky ill, can't be ridden. Either it becomes totally uncontrollable below a certain speed, or it wobbles above a certain speed.

Celebrity Bio

Born and raised in Miami, custom-bike builder Billy Lane holds an Associate of Science degree in mechanical engineering from Florida State University and a Bachelor of Science degree in mechanical engineering from Florida International University. According to choppersinc.com, Billy's father got him interested in cars and hot rods early on, so Billy had quite a bit of mechanical knowledge before going to engineering school. Then in 1989, he bought his first bike while in college. The bike was basically in pieces, so he had to learn how to put it together. But with the help of some old-timers, he learned a lot—and fast.

According to the website, "After college, Billy got a job with his brother working on bikes, then went out on his own. He started making custom parts as gifts for his friends when he was 'poor.' Eventually, a demand built up for these six-gun parts outside of his peer group, which led to the 1995 formation of Choppers Inc. in Melbourne, Florida. Billy credits his success to getting into the chopper scene ahead of the curve, before the motorcycle industry really started to recognize them as relevant. Now that chopper style is a huge industry, Billy is building a few high-quality bikes each year, which allows him time to develop new parts and ideas for new products and styles." Billy's bikes have been featured on many magazine covers and TV shows.

Make sure that you pick a suitable motor. More is not always better. More, in fact, can sometimes have extremely uncomfortable consequences—and might even turn your dream chopper into a nightmare. A bore of larger than 100 cubic inches can drop the reliability of the motor. Typically, on a larger stroker motor, the piston travels much farther up and back down the cylinders. This causes more vibration throughout the bike. The shorter the *stroke*, the less vibration.

def•i•ni•tion

The **stroke** of a motor is the distance the pistons travel up and down.

Can You Ride It?

Even if you can build it, can you ride it? Guys like me who build choppers are constantly aware of safety concerns. Does the gas tank obstruct the rider's vision? Is the response of the front wheel to the movement of the handlebars adequate to react to an emergency in traffic? That sort of thing.

Celebrity Bio

Most people recognize Rick Doss because of his ZZ Top beard. Since the 1970s, Doss has been building top-notch choppers without making concessions to fashion. A big believer in aerodynamics, Doss puts air dams on his lower frame rails. He is responsible for putting fat-tire chassis on street bikes. His frames are known for their flush-mount axle covers and internal fork stops.

If you're confidant that you can ride anything that can be built, then go for it. But if you are new to the world of motorcycles in general, you need some practice on a stock bike or a less-radical chopper before straddling a monster.

Enough with Practical!

There's only so far you can get into the mind of a chopper rider if you insist on staying practical. Eventually you have to say, enough with practicality! How cool is the bike? And, likewise, practicality cannot be the lone consideration when it comes to making your dream come true. People who never leave the world of practical end up driving to Daytona in an SUV. Eventually, you've got to let your imagination go wild.

This shot gives you a good idea of the space between the front and rear wheels of a chopper.

(Barry C. Altmark Photography)

In this book, we discuss choppers that are durable and choppers that are practical and choppers that are (shudder) legal, but when I set out to build a chopper, I don't think of any of those things. I think about making a one-of-a-kind chopper that is big, bad, and crazy. Whether it is me or someone else riding a chopper I built, I want the guy or gal astraddle that machine to get all of the attention. I want those spectators to be unable to blink as long as they are looking at it. I want jaws to drop and eyeballs to pop out and make that "ahhh-OOOO-gaaaah" sound. I want it to be unlike any chopper that anyone had ever seen before. If one of my designs seems too much like something I have built before, I scrap it and start over. Each of my bikes must have the "jaw-drop factor!"

For many chopper builders, it's the impracticality of their creations that make them so cool. A French chopper builder named Guy Van Der Beck once said, "When I set out to build a radical chopper, I think first about how the chopper will look and what kind of message it sends the world about my abilities as a craftsman. Later I think about how it will ride out on the highways."

How Fast Will It Go?

I really don't care about going fast. I just want to look cool at whatever speed. So many people build bikes with these ridiculously large motors. They seem to do it to one-up their buddies or maybe for resale value.

I'll tell you right now, I can build a bike with a stock Harley engine in it that will look better and sell for more than most large displacement bikes. For me, it isn't about the speed; it is about the image.

Is It *You?*

Remember, you want your chopper to be an extension of you—and I don't mean that in any kind of Freudian sense. You don't want to be a copycat. You aren't riding a chopper because you want to pretend you are someone else. Right? You are straddling the chopper in a celebration of being you.

Wheelie World

One of the reasons that the chopper phenomenon is back is that more and more bikers have the money to build or ride a customized motorcycle. According to the Motorcycle Industry Council, the average income for a biker was $25,600 in 1985. Today, that figure is up to $55,850.

As Stephen Peffer of Steel City Choppers in Pittsburg, Pennsylvania, put it, "Sometimes you spend too much time wondering how somebody else did something to one of their bikes, and you end up building a chopper that looks like everybody else's bike."

Putting your own stamp of individuality on your bike is the key to making your chopper dream become a reality. I think Greg Friend, editor of *Street Chopper* magazine, said it best when he offered this advice to up-and-coming chopper builders: "Do your homework, research history, and don't get caught up in the current trends."

To those who hoped to make a living, or a second income, out of building choppers, Friend added, "Keep your customers happy and build them what they want, but make sure you take the time to build bikes that show off your skills and innovative ideas."

A person's chopper is their fingerprint. So many people drop $35,000 plus on a store-bought custom. Tell me, how is some guy at an assembly-line factory 2,000 miles away, whom you have never even talked to, going to know exactly what you want?

I call it the puddle syndrome. You know, a guy has been looking at a bike and he is so anxious for the salesman to take his money that he has a puddle under his feet. We all hope it is drool, but chances are it isn't.

Celebrity Bio

Tommy Imperati, out of New England, is the founder of Tommy Gun Choppers, and has been building 'em since the 1970s. Although he has built many classic choppers over the years, he is perhaps most famous for the bike he made to look like a piece of World War II military hardware—sort of a Road Warrior meets Rat Patrol bike, built in tribute to his dad who fought with the 101st Airborne Division. There is a decommissioned .45 Thompson machine gun (a Tommy Gun) mounted on one of the frame's downtubes. A mural painted on the tanks and fenders depicts great moments in the 101st's campaign. Tommy built his first chopper at age 15 and today says, "I just like building motorcycles. I don't care if they're drag racers or choppers. It's just fun to see what we can come up with."

Customizing started with taking a stock Harley and changing it to fit your personality. Now these store-boughts are a dime a dozen. When you contact me, I spend a lot of time on the phone with you, and maybe you'll fly in to meet me. Precious Metal Customs can start you on your way to building your own chopper or we'll build it for you. Either way, Precious Metal Customs builds with you in mind.

Don't Forget the Paperwork

You need to be aware of a certain number of legalities before you build your own bike. Some of the paperwork that is all but taken care of for you—you usually just have to sign your name—when you buy a completed chopper from a chopper shop, you have to do for yourself if you are the builder as well as the owner/rider.

Manufacturer's Statement of Origin

The Manufacturer's Statement of Origin (commonly referred to as the MSO) is a document that legally demonstrates where parts of your chopper came from.

An MSO is necessary when you purchase a complete engine, engine cases, or a frame from an aftermarket supplier. The MSO is necessary to make sure that all of the parts you have purchased are legitimate (that is, not hot).

Road Closed

Do not do business with an aftermarket supplier who refuses to provide you with an MSO for your frame, engine, or engine cases. Also do not do business with anyone who provides an MSO that seems strange or bogus. There are folks out there who sell stolen parts. Steer clear.

If you are buying a used frame or engine, be sure that your MSO notes the previous transfers. Make sure that the form is filled out correctly. Without an MSO for your frame and engine, you won't be able to get the title for your home-built bike. (At least this is true in most states.)

Road Closed

To be on the safe side, make a copy of all receipts you get when you purchase parts for the chopper you are building. Another thing you can do to protect yourself against disaster is keep a photographic record of your chopper's construction, much like the photos that we took at Precious Metal Customs and are featured in this book.

Flapping Lips

"In South Dakota, you take the title for your donor bike, and the MSO for the new frame to the DMV station. The bike is titled as a rebuilt motor vehicle. If the new frame has a 17-digit 'vehicle-identification-number' (VIN) they just assign that number to the new title. You don't even have to have an inspection."—Brian Klock of Klock Werks

Title

After you have finished building your chopper, you need to obtain from your state a title to the bike. This is a document that legally proves that you are the owner of the chopper.

To obtain the title, you need to show receipts for all the parts you purchased, and the MSO for the parts mentioned above. This is to prove that you haven't purchased any stolen parts and that you have paid the appropriate sales tax.

Just showing the paperwork is not going to be enough to get your title in some states. In those areas of the country, officials are going to make you take your bike to everybody's favorite place, your local Department of Motor Vehicles (DMV), for an inspection.

All states are different. Call your DMV either before or during the construction process so you will know what paperwork and physical inspections are necessary in your area. If there is more than one DMV in your area, find out which one has the most experience with choppers and go to that one.

They want to make sure that the bike has been constructed properly before you take it out into traffic and possibly endanger yourself or others. (Some states don't necessitate an inspection at the DMV but run the same process through the state highway patrol.)

Insurance

Getting insurance for your newly built chopper can be tough. Insurance companies like to put motor vehicles into familiar categories. They know just how many Harleys crash compared to Hondas, they know how many of each make are stolen, and so on. But that creature you constructed, well, that's going to demand some original thought—and that's not the insurance company's forte.

Some insurance companies won't deal with home-built bikes at all. If you already have insurance on your house and car with one company, go to them and see if you can make the chopper part of your blanket coverage. If not, search around for a deal, but chances are you are going to pay more to insure your chopper. It's a definite downside.

Attorneys Who Ride

It's not something that you like to think about, but there comes a time in many chopper-owner's lives when they may need legal help. The legal troubles may come as a result of riding an outrageous and attention-grabbing bike.

Maybe you were injured while riding through no fault of your own. Or maybe your troubles have to do with the extra-curriculars of the biker lifestyle, which have been known to get out of hand. In any case, a lawyer might need to be called.

For the best legal representation, we suggest you contact the Law Offices of Richard M. Lester and his "Attorneys Who Ride" (1-800-531-2424). They have 110 law offices around the country so there is bound to be one near you. (They boast that they have at least one attorney in every state in the United States, as well as in every province of Canada.)

The Least You Need to Know

- In addition to how cool it looks, how comfortable a chopper is to ride is also a major consideration.

- A chopper should be built to fit its rider, like a pair of gloves or shoes.

- As minibikes were to motorcycles in the 1960s and 1970s, minichoppers are to choppers today.

- Newcomers beware. Get educated before building any bike.

Chapter 4

Old School vs. New School

In This Chapter

- ◆ Humble beginnings
- ◆ Birth of the aftermarket
- ◆ Safety concerns
- ◆ Today's limits: budget and imagination
- ◆ Mixing and matching

To review, veterans returning from World War II began customizing motorcycles in an attempt to make them go faster and look cooler. To increase the speed, they removed all the parts they deemed unnecessary. The increased ratio of power to weight gave them additional speed. Frames were elongated. Front wheels were extended. Sissy bars were added. The result was an unbelievably cool-looking bike.

Before long, people were customizing their bikes with little thought to extra speed, thinking rather of making a chopper that looked cooler than the other guy's. This resulted in what were called radical choppers, bikes that were outrageous for outrageousness' sake.

Many of today's chopper builders weren't even born yet. Is there a generation gap between the original chopper builders and today's enthusiasts? You betcha.

Old-School Elements

During the early days of choppers—"early days" including a span of more than 30 years—the customization of motorcycles occurred mostly in California. Almost everyone did his own custom job.

Riders enjoyed tinkering with their bikes and loved to alter the components and accessories on their motorcycles. Choppers during the 1960s and 1970s were a far cry from the gorgeous and expensive creations of today. There was no such thing as a shop like mine, Precious Metal Customs, that built choppers and sold them.

Starting in the 1970s, there were a few mail-order houses where you could buy chopper parts, but up until then everything had to be stock parts that were creatively used or altered. There was no *aftermarket*.

def•i•ni•tion

The **aftermarket** consists of shops of mail-order houses where you can buy parts and accessories different from the original factory equipment.

The Pioneers

The great majority of "old-school" choppers were born in someone's garage or yard, often on a tight budget and occasionally with limited expertise. I don't want to sound critical, though, because those guys (and a few gals, too) were pioneers.

Instead of having parts fabricated to create a coherent design, choppers back then were often a mishmash of parts, chosen more because of availability than for aesthetics. Although they looked rebellious as all get-out, and you could hear them coming from the other side of town, and they weren't pretty. Their lack of design was obvious.

The results were choppers that broke down frequently and were about as easy to ride as a bucking bronco with a burr under its saddle. When you had a severely steep rake with an outrageously long front end and an even more outrageous trail, riding without crashing was a real trick.

Flapping Lips

"Quick and agile is the key. The more stuff you pile on your bike, the more weight you add. A fat guy will use far more soap than a skinny one—that is a fact."—Jose De Miguel, Caribbean Custom Cycles

Every year the bikers of the world get together and show off their machines in front of a jury of their peers.

(Daytona Beach Area Convention & Visitors Bureau)

According to *Outlaw Choppers* author Mike Seate, "Riding and managing not to crash a radical chopper back in the day labeled a rider a hard man amongst men, the sort of guy who chases his tequila with Jack Daniels."

The forks themselves were part of the instability problem. Back in the 1960s and 1970s, the fork tubes being stretched into chopper forks were the same 38 mm telescopic forks that were stock on Harleys of the time. If someone wanted something different, he had to make it from scratch. Today all chopper builders have to do is open a book or thumb through a magazine to find the width they need. Now, builders can get more stability out of the same amount of stretch because fork legs are sometimes double the thickness. Some of these crazy front ends vary from an extremely modest (by today's standards) 41 mm to a whopping 73 mm.

Celebrity Bio

Have any chopper builders been at it for so long that they are both old school and new school? Sure. Some of those veterans built choppers back in the old days, stopped for a few dozen years, and then started again when choppers once again became fashionable. But there's one guy who has been building choppers right along: Eddie Trotta. Eddie runs a shop called Thunder Cycle out of Fort Lauderdale, Florida. My favorite Trotta chopper is designed to resemble the camel on a pack of Camel cigarettes. S-s-smokin'!

One thing that old-school choppers had that new-school choppers lack were bizarrely fat, tall, and ugly exhaust pipes. They often looked like bongs or Turkish hookahs tilted on their sides. Combine that look with a sissy bar tall enough to mount a basketball hoop on top and you've got one unfortunate old-school look.

Quite a difference from the sleek and sexy look today's builders go for. I should point out that creative tail pipes are still part of new-school designs. The only difference is that today's exhaust pipes look, uh, good.

Antique Components

As we've discussed, the appeal of old-school bikes is that they were very cool and the guys who rode them were genuine. The downside is that, because of their age and the way they were treated at the time, building a facsimile of an old-school bike using genuine parts can be tough. Those components are antiques now and very rare.

Some old-school parts are available from aftermarket sources. These include the following:

- ◆ Leather solo saddles
- ◆ Single-sided drum brakes
- ◆ Stock-length wide springer forks

But other parts are almost impossible to find. The solution is to make your own parts, or to adapt newer parts to fit the old-school bike. That sort of thing takes some expertise and is nothing we could hope to teach you in this format.

Flatheads

Old-school choppers are usually defined by their power plant as much as by their design. The most cherished old-school motor was the Flathead. Side-valve Flathead engines were the original Harley-Davidson motor. Today they are to choppers what a *Superman* #1 comic book is to comic book collectors, or a 1909S penny to coin collectors. Finding one is the find of a lifetime.

Wheelie World

Your typical Flathead displaced 45 ci and produced 22 horsepower.

Flathead engines were built between 1909 and 1974. They had no overhead valves. The valves ran alongside the engine and opened upward into a chamber beside the combustion chamber. The machine was simple because there were no rocker arms, no pushrods. The head was one casting with a hole on top for the spark plug.

But bikers, being who they are, have been known to put these found treasures—which had low compression but were reliable—on the choppers they were building, and then try to soup them up into something that could keep up with the more technologically advanced Harley engines that followed. God bless 'em, but it isn't something I would recommend. All too often these guys take their newfound treasure and blow it up. Finding a Flathead and then building a Flathead that rides like a Flathead is difficult and rewarding. Finding a Flathead and building a Flathead chopper that rides like a V-Twin is wacky—not that there's anything wrong with that.

Knuckleheads

We told you that the first chopper Indian Larry ever built was powered by a Knucklehead. The Knucklehead was the first overhead-valve Big Twin engine made by Harley-Davidson. The Knucklehead made its debut on Route 66 back in 1936. It was last sold in 1947. Now that's old school. The Knucklehead came in 60 ci and 74 ci models, which could produce, respectively, 40 and 45 horsepower.

When it comes to riding a Knucklehead in the twenty-first century, some feel that the aftermarket is for girlie-men. Old-school builder Brent Mayfield feels that builders are cheating if they purchase replica parts from aftermarket sources for their old-school bikes.

"Anybody can plunk down the cash for a replica seat to fit a 1938 Knucklehead, but to find an original steel seat pan and then have it reupholstered to meet the specs from the original owner's manual, there's a kind of rush in that," Mayfield said during a recent interview.

Panheads

The second-generation overhead-valve Big Twin engine, introduced by Harley-Davidson in 1948, was called the Panhead. Last sold in 1965, Panhead bikes usually featured black with red detail, scalloped paint, and lots of chrome.

Scalloped paint is a type of design, not a type of paint. These designs featured straight edges, and usually came to a point. Scallops were some of the first types of custom paint jobs because they could be accomplished with adhesive tape and a can of spray paint.

The Panhead engine came in 60 ci and 74 ci models, producing 50 and 55 horse-power. The Panhead, unlike the Knucklehead, had aluminum heads on the panhead, and the oil lines were interior rather than exterior.

Panheads were among the first bikes to be "bobbed," or chopped, to give them extra speed. Because of that, they are of special appeal to chopper aficionados. They are also very rare. Those original choppers were ridden about as hard as a bike can be ridden, so few have survived.

The second-generation over-head-valve Big Twin engine introduced by Harley-Davidson in 1948, called the Panhead.

(Jim A. Pearson)

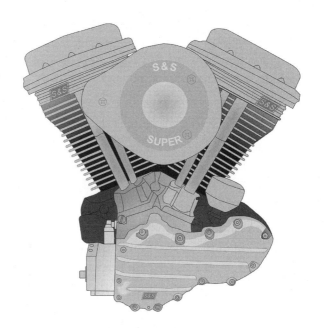

Today many builders are trying to build facsimiles of these aging beauties, using a conglomeration of found parts, bought stuff they got from aftermarket sources, or their own parts that they fabricated themselves.

Says Brent Mayfield, who built his own 1948 Harley Panhead bobber, "People told me I was crazy to build a chopper that looks and rides like the old-school bikes, but I really wanted to experience for myself what it was like back then."

If you want to build your own Panhead, you'd better be dedicated! Not only are they far more difficult to build than a modern bike, the difficulty of acquiring parts makes them equally difficult to maintain.

Mayfield's 1948 Panhead is indeed a labor of love—and that love has paid off. He has won many first-place prizes at custom bike shows all around the United States.

(If you're building a bobber but having trouble finding leaf-spring forks to fit, I recommend you get in touch with Kiwi Indian [4183 Fairgrounds Street, Riverside, CA, 92501, phone 951-788-0048, www.kiwimotorcycles.com]. They build leaf-spring forks that have that antique look, fit Harley frames, and can be customized per your specifications so they are the perfect length for your bobber.)

Rebuilding a Panhead

Even if you're lucky enough to find an old Panhead for sale in someone's garage, odds are you won't know until you get it home just how much work you'll need to do before it'll be ready to hit the road.

Tom Reiter, owner of Reiter's Garage in Worthington, Iowa, told *American Iron* magazine in 2005 about his adventures in fixer-uppers after purchasing a 1970s Panhead at a swap meet. He knew it was going to need a lot of work, but only after he got it to his shop and started to take it apart did he realize that the frame itself was bent.

He also discovered that the previous owner hadn't been overly concerned with being able to stop on a dime. The bike had no front brake and the rear brake was held together by a nail and a piece of wire. The lower legs had been welded on crooked. The head gasket was blown. It was all going to have to be re-done.

But Tom was well-equipped for this labor of love. He told his friends that he was on a mission to make the Panhead a bike to be proud of. Guys who had appropriate parts lying around offered them and soon Tom was well on his way toward riding around town on a 40-year-old bike.

Road Closed

Although motorcycle magazines are an excellent source for the latest and greatest in the chopper world, they're often not suitable for youngsters. *Easyriders* in particular likes to pose seminaked women with their bikes in their pictorials. Okay for adult readers, but not necessarily for kids. Parents, check out the mags before you let your kids read them.

Tom ended up keeping the same frame, although he did straighten it, and he kept the engine and transmission, which were in better shape than the rest. Bent shifting forks and the transmission bearings were replaced.

Tom didn't like stopping any more than the next rider, but he recognized the necessity of brakes. He installed two-piston caliper brakes on the front and a mechanical drum brake on the rear.

Wheelie World

Choppers got some early mainstream exposure a few years back when former NBA-star and overall bad boy Dennis Rodman rode one to the MTV Awards. That chopper was built by Todd "Top Notch" Kuntze, owner of TNT Choppers.

After a new paint job—a beautiful orange-on-black flame pattern—he was ready to go. But he didn't get very far. On the very first ride, the engine conked out—rust inside the mag. The carburetor, the original 38 millimeter Mikuni, blew soon thereafter, and Tom replaced it with an S&S carburetor. Eventually, Tom said, "every bolt, nut, and screw needed to be changed."

After many failed attempts, the bike now runs great. Tom says it was worth all the effort. He has ridden it thousands of miles and it gets 10 times as much attention as his old chopper, a 1990 softail.

Completing the History

To complete the history of the Harley-Davidson engine: the Shovelhead sold from 1966 to 1985. They were 74 ci with 60 horsepower. From 1984 through 1999, Harley built Evolution engines, with 81.8 ci in displacement and 70 horsepower.

Wheelie World

One advantage that today's chopper builders have is that they can order complete and very large engines. A 131-cubic-inch Merch, for example, is available with a phone call. Back in the old days, if a chopper builder wanted an oversized engine, he had to build it himself. And because being an engine builder is a specialty all its own (enough to fill another book), many of those engines blew up sooner rather than later, sending the rocket scientists back to the drawing board.

The Twin Cam 88 engine has been sold since 1999, so-called because it has two cams in the crankcase to activate the valves. Starting in 2001, the state-of-the-art Harley engine was the Revolution, which is water-cooled instead of air-cooled and has a *V* angle of 60 degrees rather than 45.

The Revolution displaces 69 ci but has a shorter stroke, enabling it to rev to 9,000 rpm and is equivalent to 115 horses.

The Harley Revolution: the state of the art since 2001.

(Jim A. Pearson)

Spoked Wheels

Other elements common to old-school choppers are springer front ends, cast-iron parts, and spoked wheels. In today's aftermarket, you can buy spoked wheels for nearly all motorcycles with a secondary chain or belt drive. And spoked wheels are safer than ever. Even wheels with 160, 240, and even 320 spokes can pass manufacturers' demanding tests, withstanding even more strain than required.

The steel hub can be made individual according to width, flange size, and bearings. The 80 or 120 spokes are made of 8mm stainless steel. The steel-made rim with its smooth design is available in diameters from 16 to 18 inches. The width depends on the diameter. All components can be purchased in a dull or polished finish.

"No Show-Queen Bikes"

In conclusion, let's quote the late, great Indian Larry who said, "If you go back and look at the old-school pictures of what people were riding when choppers first came out, there was nothing on any of these bikes that didn't help them go faster or lose weight.

"People tend to forget it these days, but the early outlaw choppers were like the sport bikes, the Ninjas and Ducatis, you see the kids riding today. The guys who built them wanted to ride a cool-looking bike that was different from what everybody else had, but they also wanted these bikes to be as fast as possible."

Flapping Lips _____

"Many motorcyclists these days are middle-aged guys or gals who might have ridden in the 1970s and really liked it but then had a family. Now that the kids are gone and they have more disposable income, they have motorcycles back on their want list," says the appropriately named Mike Mount of the Motorcycle Industry Council.

"Lots of guys drag-raced their custom bikes years ago and nobody wanted a show-queen bike that looked pretty but didn't run. That's why I still think choppers should be made without all that expensive *billet* stuff, and they should have skinny tires, small fenders, and motors that may not have these monster displacements of over 100 cubic inches, but because choppers are supposed to be lightweight, they don't really need all that."

def•i•ni•tion _____

Billet is another word for very strong yet light aircraft-grade aluminum.

The New-School Advantage

I don't want to sound like I'm bragging. It's true that the choppers of today are superior to those of yesteryear in just about every way. But a lot of that has to do with the advantages builders have today.

def•i•ni•tion _____

Roll your own, in addition to the more common meaning, means build your own chopper.

Whereas the first chopper builders had to make do with what they had, and what they had often wasn't a hell of a lot, today there are thousands of sources for parts. Whether you want to have an expert build your chopper for you or you want to *roll your own*, your only limiting factor is your budget.

Of course, when it comes to choppers, some things haven't changed much. Back in the old days, choppers were made to stop traffic, to inspire awe, and on occasion, to annoy. That has remained the same. Even though today's choppers have all the modern fixin's of their factory-stock counterparts—such as rear suspension, disc breaks, and electric legs—spectators are still just as apt to watch a chopper go by with their mouth wide open.

New-School Elements

Three elements of the new-school chopper distinguish it clearly from the old-school:

- **Long-stretched frames.** Many chopper builders today believe in the motto "the longer the better" when it comes to choppers.

- **Super-wide rear tires.** In the back only, of course, the ratio between the size of the front wheel (small, thin) and the size of the rear wheel (large, fat) lends to the outrageousness of a new-school chopper.

- **Billet parts.** As you learned earlier, billet is another name for aircraft-grade aluminum, and it is a standard material used in parts for new-school choppers. It is both strong and light. To be honest, it probably would have been standard material for old-school choppers, too, but for the cost. Until fairly recently, billet parts were prohibitively expensive because of the high cost of manufacturing components from single, forged blocks of alloy. Today production methods are cheaper.

Wheelie World

Billet parts have become almost a symbol of the difference between old and new school.

Here's a set of knuckle levers for stock Harley-Davidson and Performance Machine Controls, from Aeromach Manufacturing, Inc. (www.aeromach.net).

(Aeromach Manufacturing, Inc.)

Chrome levers will add some "attitude" to your bike. These aggressive levers are hand-machined from T6 extruded billet aluminum and mounted to all Harley-Davidsons for 1996 to 2004 with manual clutch, except 2004 Sportster. They also fit Performance Machine and Jay Brake hand controls. Also available from Aeromach are floorboard cruisin' pegs, flame mirror and arm, raptor mirror and arm, and die-cast mirrors.

Only for the Rich?

There was a time, not that many years ago, when "new-school" choppers cost an arm and a leg, and those living on modest means couldn't afford one. But that no longer is the case. Things have become more economical.

The recent chopper craze has been similar to the original craze back in the 1960s, only in reverse. Back then, when things first started, cheap bikes and foreign bikes were commonly customized into choppers. Then came *Easy Rider*, and everyone had to meet a certain number of expensive preconceptions.

Celebrity Bio

Vince Doll, owner and operator of a bike shop called Redneck Enginuity in Liberty, South Carolina, got his start building hot rods. Well known along the East Coast and in parts of the Midwest, Vince pushed his reputation all the way to the Pacific Ocean when he bought vendor space at the 2003 Laughlin Run. There he showed off a stretched-out, rigid 250 chopper with a New Skool Springer front end. The frame had 6 inches added to the backbone and a single downtube. There were 48 degrees of rake in the neck. The bike's only suspension was a 16-inch-over New Skool Springer held in place with a set of triple trees. Traditional hot-rod graphics completed the look. Now Vince is known from coast to coast.

In the new-school world, things started out being very expensive but, as time goes on and our concepts of what is and isn't allowable in the world of choppers loosens up, choppers have become cheaper. Not across the board, but today there are many cheap and acceptable alternatives.

Mixing and Matching

Author Timothy Remus, in his book *How to Build a Cheap Chopper*, calls old school "the Phaze One Craze." He calls new School the "Phaze Two Craze." That's his spelling, too. He points out that old-school bikes can now be built in a new-school fashion.

Remus writes: "Hardtail frames designed to accept a 750 Honda engine, built during the good old days, can often be found at swap meets or on the ever-growing number of chopper websites. There's currently enough interest in this emerging old-school way of doing things that a limited number of reputable shops are once again building frames designed for the metric chopper market."

That number of reputable shops is growing larger every day. So no matter how old or how new you want to go, there are options open to you.

Old school and new school are fun terms, and they describe a real phenomenon, a division among chopper people that resembles the familiar differences between fathers and sons. It's a generation gap—and, like many gaps, it is bridged by love. Old-school riders and new-school riders often are often more alike than they realize.

The Least You Need to Know

♦ There is a generation gap between the original chopper builders and today's enthusiasts.

♦ Many old-school choppers broke down frequently and were difficult to ride.

♦ Elements that distinguish new-school from old-school choppers are long-stretched frames, fat rear wheels, and billet parts.

♦ New-school choppers don't necessarily have to cost an arm and a leg.

♦ It is okay to mix old-school and new-school elements in your chopper. There are no rules.

Part 2

To Potential Owners (and Builders)

In this second part of the book, we address the needs of you readers who may be in the market to purchase or build your first chopper. Before you go out shopping for a chopper, or a chopper kit to build, you should have a strong sense of who you are and what you want.

Then we take a quick tour of the workspace, whether you have a shop, work out of your garage, or got desperate and converted a room in your house into a workspace. Here are a few simple rules about which tools to possess and how to set up your space for maximum efficiency and flexibility—because you never know when you might be in a hurry or trying to adapt to something that has gone wrong.

I show how a chopper is built, step by step, starting with a rolling chassis and parts choice, and finishing with a completed chopper. Hopefully, this will give those of you considering assembling your own chopper from a kit an idea of whether the job is for you. Some people build, and some people have things built for them. They pay. Hopefully, you know which you are.

5

The Workspace

In This Chapter

- ◆ Perfect for beginners
- ◆ Setting up shop
- ◆ Filling your toolbox

Let me start this section on getting ready to build a chopper—or repair one if you purchased one—by talking directly to you first-timers. This is for those of you who are seriously contemplating building a chopper for the first time, either from scratch, from a kit, or by customizing a donor bike.

Get a Kit

Here's a quick tip, a word from the wise. If you have never built a motorcycle before, and you want to construct your own chopper, I suggest you work with a kit. A chopper kit means that you are purchasing all at once the parts you need for your chopper. All fabrication and painting has been done for you. All you have to do is put together the pieces. Sounds easy—unless, of course, you've never done it before.

Kits are a relatively new phenomenon. You can buy a kit just for one component of you chopper (for example, rolling chassis kits), or you can buy a complete kit that contains just about everything you need.

Wheelie World _____

A rolling chassis kit comes with the chassis and the wheels already assembled. You can see what your finished product will look like after the engine and other parts are added. This is perfect for the kit builder who doesn't look forward to welding his or her own mounts. That has been done for you.

And face it, for a lot of you, building a chopper from scratch is a matter of biting off more than you can chew. Building from a kit is something you can chew. We discuss kits in greater detail in Chapter 6.

Be True to Your Shop

For best results it is advisable to get the help you need from someone you know. If you have a chopper shop in your town or city that you like, go there regularly. Buy all of your stuff there. Try to avoid a situation where you are getting your bike stuff in 50 different places and you are a stranger at all of them.

Celebrity Bio

Joshua Ford is the owner of Killer Choppers in New Hampshire. He is of the cool-is-more-important-than-practical school. His bikes are super-long and great to look at, but taking one for a spin around the block can be an adventure. One of his bikes had a 113-cubic-inch motor with supercharger, 14-inch overstock forks, no front brake, and a rear fender composed of black skeleton fingers over a 250 mm tire. Perfect if you're dating Wednesday Addams. Top speed: 130 mph—if you dare.

Of course, some of you live out in the middle of nowhere and have to order everything over the net. You can befriend your UPS guy if you want. For the rest of you, be true to your local shop. You are more apt to get quality help if you need it, and you are also most likely to catch a break every now and again on price.

Setting Aside the Time

Even though building a chopper from a kit is relatively easy, it is still time-consuming and a lot of hard work. You are going to need to set aside large chunks of time if you hope to ever finish the project.

Custom billet parts make the chopper look just like you—attractive and dangerous at the same time.

(Barry C. Altmark Photography)

For most of us—those who are not independently wealthy, that is—buying a chopper kit is a major investment. It would be a shame to waste that money because you had underestimated the time it would take to build your bike. Don't be the sort of person who can't seem to finish a project.

Just as the only important lap to lead during a race is the final one, the only really important part of building a chopper is the last step, the one that let's you say, "Ahhhhh, I'm going for a ride." Until you get to that point, all of the money and time you have spent is in vain.

Road Closed

There are a lot of flammable liquids in any chopper shop, so be sure to always have a functional fire extinguisher handy. Do not attempt to put out an oil or gasoline fire with water. You will only spread it further.

Building the chopper may end up being rewarding in the long run, but there is no way it is going to be the most fun part. The most fun comes when you ride the chopper, and you can't do that unless you finish what you start.

Prepping the Workspace

In this section, we discuss ways to prepare your workspace so that you can most efficiently build your chopper. The workspace, for our example, will be a one-car garage with the car removed.

A well-kept and well-used workspace.

(Barry C. Altmark Photography)

Although you can get away with slightly less, for the sake of this guide, we figure a space that is 300 square feet, 12 feet wide, and 25 feet deep.

A Hard Bottom Without Bounce

One of the most important things in a good workspace is an appropriate floor. It should be hard, or else it will end up getting gouged and uneven very quickly from dropped tools and parts, kickstands, and other wear and tear.

Wheelie World

A couple of the top companies selling chopper kits are Biker's Choice, home of the E-Z Choppa; and Custom Chrome, where you can buy the Hard Core, Nemesis, or Goliath chopper kit.

The floor should be reasonably level. Slopes are the enemy of stability. And it should be strong. A weak floor has bounce, and you want your chopper to be rock-steady when you are working on it. The best floor is concrete. Linoleum is too soft, and has a tendency to tear. A no-slip paint is best on your concrete floor. And make sure you use a light color.

Beige is perfect. The reason is small parts are easier to find if you drop them on a light-colored floor.

It is important to keep your floor clean. If the floor gets too dusty, every step will kick up microscopic dust particles that can get inside the moving parts of your chopper and cause problems.

"A Place for Everything"

Benjamin Franklin said, "A place for everything and everything in its place." He might not have been working on his chopper when he said it, but he knew what he was talking about. When you have decided where everything in your shop goes, make sure it stays there. After you are finished using something, put it back where it belongs.

It doesn't make any difference how well you organize your shop if you don't maintain that organization. Every second spent saying, "Where did I put that?" is a wasted second, one you could be spending making your chopper great.

Cleanup Time

Just as keeping everything in its place is essential to maintaining an orderly shop, so is regularly cleaning it. You can't let trash pile up on the floor. I suggest ending each day in your shop with a little cleanup time.

Because cleanup is against the nature of many bikers, I also suggest keeping a trash can handy. Instead of throwing that torn-up packaging material on the floor, can it. There will be less to clean up at the end of the day.

Road Closed

Asbestos tile is appropriately hard for your shop floor, but tends to crack if you drop a wrench on it.

Celebrity Bio

Stephen Peffer runs Steel City Choppers in Pittsburgh, Pennsylvania. He got his start building choppers when he was in high school. His first donor bike was a Honda CB 450. By the time he got out of school, he had learned to do his own fabrication, finishing work, airbrushing, and bodyworking.

Wheelie World

It's best if your workspace has a lot of convenient electric sockets. There should always be a plug handy. I'm not suggesting that you rewire your garage, but a few extension cords might be in order. It's easier to move the electricity close to the thing you are working on than the other way around.

Workshop Essentials

Here are some of the key things you need in your shop:

◆ A workbench. It should be somewhere in the neighborhood of 3 feet by 8 feet. The perfect top is plywood topped by stainless steel. That way you can use it for welding. The space under the workbench can be used for storage. Mount a vise on the front edge somewhere near a corner. Have a six-outlet strip mounted nearby for plugging things in.

◆ A shelf unit with five shelves.

◆ Metal storage cabinet, also with five shelves. Large items—gas tanks, drain pans, seats—can be stored on top of the cabinet.

◆ Tool chest.

◆ Open storage area. This is where you put your frame and tires, etc. when you are not working with them. This is usually in the back corner of the garage.

◆ Free space covered with a rug. You need the rug because the concrete floor can scratch painted and chrome parts.

◆ A stool. To sit on. Preferably one with adjustable height.

◆ Parking spot in the center for your chopper. Place scatter rugs on either side, where you spend most of your time. You, like chrome parts, can be easily scratched.

◆ Good lighting. You have to be able to see what you're doing. Paint the walls white and use a 15-watt or stronger light bulb. Also have a droplight handy to brightly illuminate the thing you are working on.

◆ Air conditioning and heat. Unless you live in a place where it is exactly 72 degrees all of the time, your workshop is going to tend to get too hot or too cold. Even if it's just a fan and a space heater, have a way to warm things up or cool things down.

This stand was built specifically for working on a Sportster engine.

(JIMS Performance Parts and Tools)

This is the stand you'd need if you were working on a five-speed transmission.

(JIMS Performance Parts and Tools)

Tools You Need

You need these basic tools:

◆ Hammers (ball-pein, soft-faced [rubber or plastic], and carpenter's claw)

◆ Phillips screwdrivers (the kind with the cross-shaped tip)

- Slot screwdrivers
- Hex drivers
- Nut drivers
- Pliers (in varying sizes, including the needle-nosed variety)
- *Combination wrenches*
- Socket wrenches
- Adjustable crescent wrenches
- Allen wrenches, regular and ball-end (also known as hex keys; they are designed to fit socket-head cap screws) (Warning: Do not get hex key sets that fold out of a jack-knife type handle, because these often lack the strength to do tough jobs.)

def•i•ni•tion

A **combination wrench** has a box-end wrench on one end and, in the same size, an open-end wrench on the other. The most valuable American sets will range in size from ⅜ inch to 1 inch. Best metric sets span 8 mm to 19 mm.

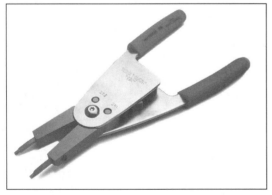

It's always good to have a variety of pliers handy for any chopper project.

(JIMS Performance Parts and Tools)

WheelMate

Some maintenance or repair tasks make it necessary for the wheels to rotate. Cleaning the chain comes to mind. Since rolling the bike back and forth across the floor of your usually too-small work space can get to be a drag, one alternative is setting the bike on two roller stands, which allow the chopper's wheels to rotate without the bike actually going anywhere.

The best of these is the WheelMate (made by Aerostitch, 1-800-222-1994, www.aerostitch.com). This device is ramped so it is easy to get the bike up onto it. The rollers are made of nylon and accommodate all wheel sizes.

Working on the Motor

If you are going to be working on your motor in your new shop space, there are some additional items you will require. Here's a list of the bare essentials:

- A clutch-spring compressor
- A compression tester
- A ½-inch drive socket set with assorted sockets ranging from $\frac{7}{16}$ inch to 1¼ inch, a ratchet, a 2-foot breaker bar, a 2-inch drive extension, a 6-inch drive extension, a torque wrench, assorted drive adapters, and universal joints for each drive size
- A deep socket set
- A machinist's scale
- A scratch awl
- An impact driver set
- Retaining ring pliers
- Bits and sockets for unusual drive patterns
- Compressed air
- An electric drill with variable speed
- A cylinder hone

A clutch spring compressor is an essential for any chopper workshop.

(JIMS Performance Parts and Tools)

The Temporary Workspace

Not everyone is going to be like me: build a chopper, get hooked, keep building choppers forever. Some people (maybe most?) who build a chopper will build only one. The project temporarily takes over their home, and upon completion, is never repeated. The home returns to normal, except now the builder gets to ride his chopper.

Point is, the workspace will be temporary. If you're really willing to uproot your life for the build, then a lot of otherwise unthinkable spaces become potential workspaces for your project. In addition to building in their garages, one-time builders have also been known to use the living room, kitchen, basement, or any small space.

I have talked to guys on the phone who have literally built their bike on the kitchen countertop. Sometimes people just make do with the space they have. You really don't need a big space to build; you just need to be organized. When in a tight space, it is crucial to keep things organized!

Here are three tips to keep you organized:

◆ **Have a table or even a rack that you can lay your parts out on.** This also allows you to keep everything clean and organized, as well as take inventory of your parts with ease.

- **Consider using a tool tray.** It never fails; without a tool tray, you will misplace your tools. I can't tell you how many times I've set a tool down and forgotten where I put it. If you set it in the tool tray, it will always stay in the tray.

- **Keep your fabrication separate from your final assembly.** That means welding and grinding need to take place somewhere else. The worst thing you can do is have your nice, new, clean parts 2 feet away from the dirtiest area during the job. Try to keep these things in mind while building your bike. It will only make your life easier.

The Least You Need to Know

- Working from a kit is perfect for a first-time chopper builder.

- A well-organized and supplied workspace is key to building a chopper.

- For many people, the chopper workspace will only be a temporary disruption of an otherwise orderly household.

- You gotta do what you gotta do. If a tabletop is the only available workspace, then so be it!

Chapter 6

Building From a Kit

In This Chapter

- ◆ Don't fly solo
- ◆ Tools you need
- ◆ Tasks you face
- ◆ Places to shop

We touched on the subject of building a chopper from a kit back in Chapter 5, while discussing setting up a workspace, whether it be permanent or temporary. Now we are going to look at the things you need to have and do to build from a kit, and have a look at some of the kits that are available.

In addition to the text, you'll find a series of photos of me building a bike. The photos will show, and hopefully make it easier to understand, the installation of the internal fork stop, triple tree, bearings, legs, axles and gas tank. There will also be photos to show how to center the rear wheel.

No Changing Your Mind

For starters, let me say that you should spend at least as much time determining which kit to buy as you spend actually building it. Kits are

Road Closed

Don't be fickle. After you make up your mind, stick to it. Changing design in the middle of a project is a luxury that only a millionaire can afford.

not flexible. You use the kit, and you will get a chopper that looks just like the one in the picture on the box.

You don't change your mind about what you want your chopper to look like midway through the building process. You should be locked into the "what" right from the git-go. That way you can focus your concentration on the "how."

Because of this, you had better be darned sure that you like the outcome of the kit. When you buy the kit and start building it, you are committed. Either you finish the project or you don't, and not finishing is stupid.

Wheelie World

The other advantage to a kit is economic. When you buy all the parts together they are cheaper than if you buy them one at a time. Chopper kits will run you between $14,000 to $25,000.

You don't need a lot of fancy tools to build a chopper from a kit. The items you see here will get the job done.

(Precious Metal Customs)

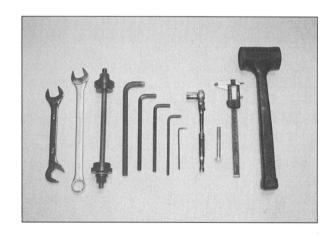

Getting Help

Do not undertake any portion of kit assembly if you are uncomfortable with it, or if you think you lack the necessary skill. Maybe you have a friend who can help out. If necessary, hire professional help. Make sure the job is done right. That's the only way to be sure you have a safe ride when you are finished.

After installation, the internal fork stop kit will sit here.

(Precious Metal Customs)

Decide before you start what aspects of the assembly you are going to need help with and schedule that help. Some aspects of putting together a kit can't be done last (the wiring, for example), but must be done at the appropriate point in the process.

Russ installs the internal fork stop kit.

(Precious Metal Customs)

Creating a Budget Sheet

To help you determine how much your chopper build is going to cost, you should compile a Custom Motorcycle Build Budget Sheet, just like the one we use at Precious Metal Customs. It should look something like this:

Custom Motorcycle Build Budget Sheet

Frame _____
Front/rear suspension _____
Wheels/tires _____
Rotors/pulley _____
Brakes _____
Hand controls _____
Foot controls/pegs _____
Handlebars/risers/grips _____
Headlight/taillight _____
Gas tank _____
Front/rear fenders _____
Engine _____
Transmission _____
Primary drive _____
Starter _____
Carburetor _____
Intake _____
Ignition _____
Charging system/battery _____
Hydraulic/manual lines _____
Wiring _____
Harness/switches _____
Engine _____
Transmission _____
Bolt kit _____
Polishing _____
Powder coating _____
Paint _____
Misc _____
Labor _____

_____

Total _____

Russ installs a triple tree and top bearing.

(Precious Metal Customs)

Here's how the triple-tree stem and bottom bearing look once installed.

(Precious Metal Customs)

You install the top triple tree by threading the triple-tree stem.

(Precious Metal Customs)

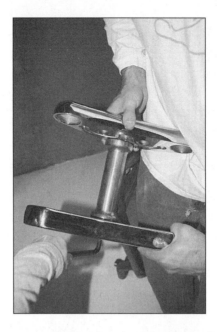

Russ installs the spreader bolt onto the bottom triple tree.

(Precious Metal Customs)

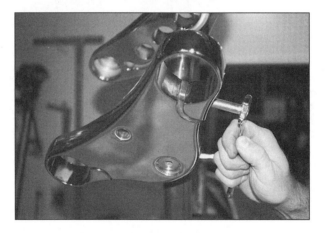

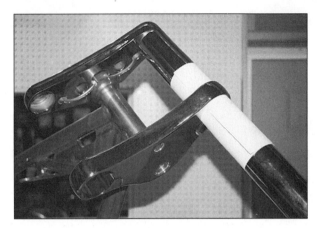

Russ screws in the leg of the front end. Notice how he has wrapped a piece of paper around the leg to protect it from scratches. The spreader bolt is removed and the clamping bolt is installed. After the leg of the front end has been screwed in, Russ repeats the process with the opposite leg, starting with the installation of the spreader bolt.

(Precious Metal Customs)

Kit Assembly Steps

Here's a list of the steps you can expect to take while assembling your kit chopper:

- ◆ Assemble swingarm and shocks onto the frame. (Not applicable if you are building a rigid chopper.)

- ◆ Install and align the engine and transmission. (Do it correctly or you destroy your drive train.)

- ◆ Shim the engine and transmission to protect your inner primary cover.

- ◆ Install the front-drive sprocket.

- ◆ Assemble and align the primary components.

- ◆ Assemble the front fork and front end.

- ◆ Install brake calipers.

- ◆ Shim and bleed the brakes.

- ◆ Install the front and rear axles and wheels.

- ◆ Assemble forward controls.

- ◆ Set proper rear-belt tension.

♦ Install sheet metal: oil tank, gas tank, and fenders (if you're doing fenders).

♦ Assemble clutch basket and clutch cable.

♦ Install clutch ramp, coupler, and rod.

♦ Wire the bike.

♦ Install ignition system components.

♦ Install oil hoses.

♦ Assemble and set up the carburetor.

♦ Install the intake manifold.

An installed axle and right axle spacer.

(Precious Metal Customs)

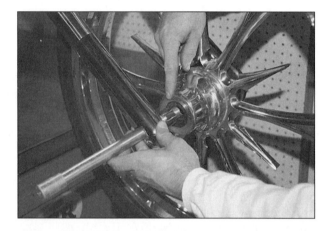

The left axle spacer is installed and the axle is threaded into the opposite leg.

(Precious Metal Customs)

Wiring

Here's a list of the essential tools you need to wire your chopper kit:

- Test problem set

- Wire cutters and strippers

- Multimeter

- Soldering iron and electronic solder

- Crimping tool and assorted crimp connectors

- Lighter (as in Bic lighter)

- Needle-nosed pliers

- Heat-shrinkable tubing

Celebrity Bio

The Martin Brothers, Joe and Jason, have been producing some of the top choppers in the Lone Star State for 10 years, and their work keeps getting better and better. Martin Brothers Bikes, out of Duncanville, Texas, has been featured on the Discovery Channel series *World Biker Build-Off*. Joe and Jason have been in partnership ever since they finished high school, although they did stints as musicians in a band, and as builders of hot rods before they settled down in the world of custom motorcycles. Joe conceives of the bikes and is the head builder. Jason is the money guy. His job is to make sure that they spend less than they bring in, so that there's something left over for the kitty. The Martins have customers who are willing to pay for a top chopper, so one gets the impression that the kitty is doing all right. Mark Juarez, who Joe and Jason call the "third Martin Brother," is the crew chief at the shop. The shop specializes in long-forked choppers.

Stage 1 and Stage 2 Kits

Like Precious Metal Customs, some companies sell rolling chassis, which we call rollers. Part of the assembly has already been done for you. Starting with a roller is the best way to get the ball rolling for a first time builder.

For example, Precious Metal offers a complete roller package. Our Stage 2 roller consists of everything that a home builder would need to build a bike minus the drivetrain, hoses, cables, electrical, and paint.

That pretty much makes us a one-stop shop. We have spent hours and thousands of dollars doing research to find out which components work best for our customers. We guarantee when buying our rollers that your bike will be safe, and the build will flow much easier than a compilation of odd parts.

We feel our job isn't done until you have cranked the bike and are riding down the road. Everyone building a bike needs someone to turn to for help and we hope we will be that someone to you. Check us out at www.preciousmetalcustoms.com.

If you are going to build your own chopper, from a full kit or partial kit, you still have some decisions to make. All kits are not the same, so you need to make up your mind what you want. Here are your first four steps.

1. Choose your rake and stretch.

2. Decide on a style of wheel.

3. Pick a gas tank.

4. Call me, Russ Austin, at Precious Metal Customs—678-494-4150.

I sell rolling chassis kits in two stages. Which you buy depends on two things: how much you want to spend, and how much work you want to do. Stage 1 kits include a rolling chassis with Avon 250 mm for about $9,000 or with an Avon 300 mm for about $500 more. That kit also includes the following:

- Our PMC spoon-style frame

- 63 mm inverted front end with wheel spacers: #2 (upgrades available)

- Internal fork stops

- Your choice of one of our wheel sets with tires

- Your choice of gas tanks

The Stage 2 kits cost $13,499 with the Avon 250 mm and $13,999 with the Avon 300 mm. With the Stage 2 kits, you get everything that comes with the Stage 1 kit, plus the following:

- Matching rotors and pulley

- Four-piston front and rear HHI brakes

- Set of PMC drag handle bars and built-in risers

- Our EL hand controls

- Billet throttle housing

- Our EL forward controls

- PMC billet headlight with bulb

Available Kits

The market today offers a wide selection of chopper kits. Almost every part on the entire bike involves options. What style would you like those footpegs in? Spokes or billet for the wheels? Of course, none of the kits they offer are quite as good as the ones I sell, but there's something for everybody, I'd like to think.

Besides, I know a lot of people like to deal with a shop that is close to home and, because you just may not live in the Atlanta area, here's a geographically diverse sampling of shops that sell kits, beginning with Biker's Choice.

Installing the set screw.

(Precious Metal Customs)

(Precious Metal Customs)

Installing the rear axle prior to cutting the axle spacers.

(Precious Metal Customs)

To center the rear wheel, Russ uses a straight edge on the inside of the frame. He measures from the straight edge to the outside of the rim using a micrometer, and then verifies that all sides are identical.

After the wheel is centered, measure for your right-hand axle spacer.

(Precious Metal Customs)

Biker's Choice

One of the most popular complete chopper kits comes from Biker's Choice. It's called E-Z Choppa. You get a frame with a 38-degree rake, 5-inch stretch in the front legs, and a 3½-inch backbone stretch.

There is also a 6-inch over-wide glide front end with chrome billet triple trees and chrome legs. Comes with a 96 ci S&S engine, steel oil tank, Sportster-style fuel tank, shotgun exhaust, and Corbin seat. To learn if there is a Biker's Choice outlet near you, call 1-800-343-9687, or visit www.BikersChoice.com.

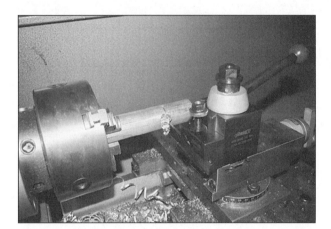

Russ uses a metal lathe to cut each individual axle spacer. Precious Metal Customs will cut axle spacers for you after your measurements have been taken. Russ then does the same thing for the other side, taking into consideration that there are different braking applications. This particular bike will have a drive side brake set up; therefore no additional brake bracketing will be required.

(Precious Metal Customs)

Russ installs the rear axle into the right side of the frame. He slides the axle spacer over the axle and pushes the axle through the wheel and out the other side. He then installs the left-hand axle spacer over the axle as it protrudes from the wheel.

(Precious Metal Customs)

Be sure to hold the nut into the end of the axle while turning the right side of the axle with your Allen wrench.

(Precious Metal Customs)

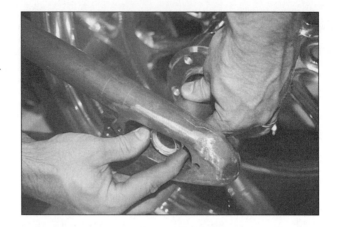

Install four rubber tank grommets and metal sleeves onto the tabs that have been prewelded onto the frame.

(Precious Metal Customs)

Set the gas tank on the frame. Install the four mounting bolts.

(Precious Metal Customs)

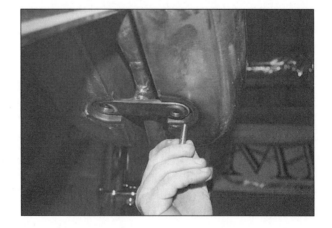

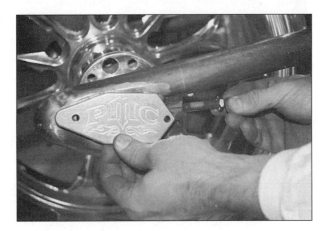

Install the axle adjusters and axle covers.

(Precious Metal Customs)

California Customs

At California Customs Cycles, in Mountainview, California, you can choose from rigid, hidden shock or rubber mount. You get a 250 tire.

If you fret over having the proper paperwork for your chopper, this place is for you. They take you step-by-step through all of your unwanted clerical obligations—registration, insurance, etc.

Custom Chrome

For the hardcore rider, Custom Chrome offers the Hard-Core II Bike Kit. You get a rigid single downtube frame, and a 100 ci motor with a RevTech six-speed transmission. It also comes with a Jesse James Villain gas tank and a Jesse James–designed rear fender.

Midwest Motorcycle

Midwest Motorcycle Supply (there's a local outlet near you, if you live in the Midwest) offers what they call the "Fat Bastard Build-a-Bike Kit."

The kit is manufactured by Ultima Products. You get an 86 ci or 96 ci Ultima engine, and 200-series tires. There's a one-piece gas tank and Chrome Horse billet calipers, triple trees, forward controls, and frame.

Cautionary Tale

Here is a cautionary tale about arrogance. I don't know the dictionary definition, but I think an arrogant person is unaware of what they don't know. They have a limited idea of their limitations. Therefore they tend to give expert opinions on things they know little about and attempt to do things they are unqualified to do.

Take a guy I know. We'll call him Jack. Jack had assembled bikes before but never completely fabricated a bike. Being kind of a know-it-all, Jack never took advice.

A good builder does a rough assembly prior to the complete build. Did Jack do this? Nooooooo! Jack dismissed it, because he "knew what he was doing." Jack started in on the chassis fabrication. He did some modifying to the frame, built a custom tank, and worked in a lot of sheet metal.

He was ready to send it all to paint. I popped in the see how he was coming. The bike was beautiful. As I looked closer, though, it looked to me as if there might be some clearance issues. I asked him if he mounted the drive train in the frame to see if it fit. He disregarded my question and even got a bit offended that I asked. So I shut up; it *was* a beautiful bike.

A couple of weeks went by and I get a phone call with a frantic Jack on the other end. He said, "I need you to come by *now*!"

As soon as I got there, I saw a beautifully painted chassis. That was the only good thing I saw. We compiled a list of things we would have to correct. Here is that list:

- Remake the oil bag (did not allow room for the starter) and get it painted.

- Reorder forward controls (mounts were for an FXR, and that wasn't what he wanted).

- Reorder new triple trees (frame required external fork stops).

- Reorder handle bars (Jack once again had not checked for clearance).

- Make somewhere for the battery to go. (He forgot about the battery!)

- Remount the rear fender. Jack did not account for tire growth. (Rubber, like just about everything else, expands in the heat.)

- Drill for wires. (Mr. Know-it-All forgot to drill prior to painting.)

- Touch up the paint on the entire bike. It is impossible to fabricate on a painted chassis without damaging the paint job at least a little bit.

So the moral of the story is: don't be arrogant. Be aware of your limitations. Be aware of what you don't know. And realize that common-sense rules designed for mere mortals probably apply to you as well. All of Jack's problems could have been solved by mocking up the bike prior to paint and final assembly.

But no, he knew better.

The Least You Need to Know

♦ Spend at least as much time determining which kit to buy as you spend actually building it.

♦ Before starting, make sure you know someone who is an expert and who can help you when you need it—and you will need it.

♦ The market today offers a wide selection of chopper kits. Almost every part on the entire bike involves options.

♦ Of course, Precious Metal Customs' kits are the best, but great chopper kits are available in shops around the country—and the world.

Part 3

Anatomy of a Chopper

The third part of this book is the "Visible Chopper," to show you the chopper part by part. The frame and the engine are the skeleton and heart of the chopper. Because everything that moves has to eventually stop, we spend a chapter looking at wheels and brakes. From there, we look at the controls, lights, and electronics of a chopper. Wiring your own bike is another task you shouldn't attempt yourself if you don't know what you're doing.

It's no coincidence that many of today's top chopper builders started out in metal work. Assembling a chopper is a skill. Designing the metal parts for a chopper is an art. Unless you can bend sheets of metal into flowing, smooth-lined sculptures, you probably shouldn't fabricate your own metal parts for your chopper. After that we examine different methods and beautification effects possible today through the wonder of paint—then finally, the chrome and the pipes.

7

Frame and Engine

In This Chapter

- ◆ Skeleton of a chopper
- ◆ Not just stiff—rigid!
- ◆ Controlled burn
- ◆ Riding on air

Okay, ready for Chopper Biology Class 101? In this chapter, we look at the frame and the engine. Some may argue for the wheels, but the frame and engine are probably the most important parts. Argue among yourselves.

Whichever, they are pretty important. Without the frame, there would be no way for the other parts to stick together; and if you don't have an engine, you will be pushing the chopper along with your feet like Brick Fonda on *The Flintstones*.

And interesting setup in Daytona.

(Andy Wyzga)

A rear view of the same bike.

(Andy Wyzga)

The Frame

The frame is the skeleton of the bike. Builders begin with the frame, and then they attach the parts of the bike to the frame, or to pieces that are attached to the frame. Choppers simply have less flesh than other bikes. Some riders believe their bike should be both their transportation and their apartment. They don't own choppers. The frame provides cohesion for the bike, and also determines its size and shape.

Appearance

The practical reasons that the frame is there are boring compared to its importance to the bike's design. I'm all in favor of pushing the envelope when it comes to shaping the frame of a chopper. The frame, as any skeleton would, defines the shape of the bike. If you want to be compact or long and sleek, it all depends on the shape of the frame.

Wheelie World

It was a chopper designer named Roger Bourget who mass-produced the first drop-seat frame. He did this by removing the oil bag from under the seat—where it typically goes on a softail frame—and by putting oil in the frame. His shop in Phoenix, Arizona, still produces choppers with this ground-breaking feature. A softail frame, introduced to the chopper world in 1984, looks like a rigid frame but offers hidden rear shocks and springs.

In the beginning, the frame was nothing more than a series of tubes designed to hold the bike together, but chopper culture changed all of that. Bikes could be curvaceous and sexy, like a slender, pouncing cat.

Here's a good look at how a chopper's frame determines its inevitable configuration.

(Barry C. Altmark Photography)

Handling

In the 1970s, bike designers realized they could affect the handling of the bike by altering the stiffness of the frame. Hardtails with rigid frames were the ultimate culmination of the stiffer-the-better frame philosophy.

Stiff? We're talking about rigid.

Flapping Lips

"I want my choppers to look cool, but the people I build for, they want to ride," says Michael Ballew of Ballew's South Central Customs in Poplar Bluff, Missouri.

Today's aluminum frames, if you know a good metal bender, can take chopper design almost anywhere an imagination can go. Choppers handle comparably to stock bikes these days. We've come a long way from the frames of yesteryear.

Suspension

Built into the frame is much of the bike's suspension: the forks and the shocks, if any; the cushion that makes sitting astride it a tolerable ride. It's called suspension because this is the system that keeps the frame suspended off the ground.

> **Road Closed**
>
> When designing your chopper, remember that it is illegal in most states to have handlebars that are higher than the rider's shoulders.

Shocks are a matter of taste for chopper riders. Some want all the modern conveniences with an outlaw look. Others are willing to let the fatness of the rear tire be the only thing to cushion the bumps. We talk about suspensions a little later in the chapter.

Durability

On the East Coast, durability becomes a concern. Today many frames and frame kits are made of thick steel tubing with internal reinforcement and TIG welded junctions. The frames are designed to stay solid no matter how hard or far the rider pushes the bike.

> **Flapping Lips**
>
> According to *Easyriders* magazine reporter Cheese Puddin', the best thing about a great chopper is "a powerplant that humps like a hippo on steroids."

TIG stands for *tungsten inert gas*, a form of welding that became an instant hit in the 1940s for joining magnesium and aluminum. Using an inert gas shield instead of a slag to protect the weldpool, the process largely replaced gas and manual metal arc welding. TIG has played a major role in the acceptance of aluminum for high-quality welding and structural applications.

Tires have made great strides in terms of durability over the past 40 years. Tires today last three times as long as they did in the 1970s. In the old days, you couldn't cross the country then cross back on the same set of tires. Now you can cross the country, east to west, five times without changing tires.

Diggers

One of the innovations in chopper frames came with the design of the first low-rider chopper. A low rider is sometimes called a *digger*, I guess because it looks like the riders "dug into the bike." The low-rider style first became popular in the 1970s. Many say it was invented by West Coast chopper builder Arlen Ness.

Diggers typically were steered with low two-piece welded-together handlebars mounted to the top triple clamps. Because the handlebars were so low, riders sat bent over, or dug into the bike.

def•i•ni•tion _____

Described by Mike Seate, a **digger** is "characterized by goose-neck frames that combined the stretch chopper's radical 38- to 40-degree rake dimensions with telescopic front forks that were often shortened, rather than lengthened, for dramatic effect."

Know Your Geometry

To design a chopper from scratch, you have to know a little about geometry, and a touch of trigonometry, too. Remember sine, cosine, and tangent? Your front-suspension geometry is determined by six factors:

1. The offset, which is the centerline of the top steering neck to the centerline of the top of the fork tubes

2. The *rake*

3. The fork length, or the distance between the top of the fork tubes to the centerline of the axle

4. The diameter of the front tire

5. The *trail*, normally between 2 and 4 inches

6. Raked triple trees, if needed to bring trail figures back into line

def•i•ni•tion _____

A chopper's **rake** is the angle in degrees of the steering neck from the vertical cord. The **trail** is the distance defined by the vertical line from axle to ground and the intersection of centerline of the steering neck and ground.

The first step in designing a chopper is to choose the proper rake and trail. There is a specialized CAD program that helps determine the rake and trail. CAD means computer-aided design. The program helps the designer do the complicated math involved in determining the chopper's rake and trail, and allows the designer to view the chopper under design in three dimensions. Designers who previously sketched out the choppers they were designing now "sculpt" them.

You input the rake, diameter of the front tire, and height of the neck (from middle of neck to the ground). The program then figures out the best and safest trail for the setup and gives the dimensions for the front and rear legs as well as rockers.

> ## Road Closed
>
> It is very important to make sure that your chopper has sufficient trail. Too little, or negative, trail, and the bike will handle great at low speeds but develop a potentially disastrous wobble at high speeds. Too much trail can make a bike sluggish at high speeds and difficult to balance at low speeds.

Backbone and Downtube Stretch

Stretching a frame at one time meant cutting the downtube and/or backbone, repositioning the neck where you want it, and adding in tubing to fill the void. Those were the old days. That's not how it happens anymore.

> ## def•i•ni•tion
>
> **Stretching** means that the tubing in the frame is longer than the stock length. For example, if you were to have a 5-inch stretch in the backbone and an 8-inch stretch in the downtube, that would mean the neck position on an X.Y axis has been moved up 8 inches and out 5 inches. Always discuss these measurements with your frame manufacturer. Unfortunately, there is no documented standard that everyone follows, but most take their measurements—for both the backbone and the downtube—from a Harley Softail Standard's dimensions.

Today it is rare for someone to cut up a frame. Stretching now occurs at the time the frame is created. Why cut when it is so much easier to pick up a catalog and choose the frame of your dreams?

Wheelie World _____

If you are outsourcing the stretching, be aware that at a lot of places you have to pay extra if you want extra backbone or downtube stretch. In some places, there is an additional $10 charge for downtube stretch past 5 inches and another $10 for each inch of backbone stretch past 3 inches.

The Motor

This is a quick overview of how the parts of a chopper engine work together. It is the story of "controlled burn," of up-and-down motion being transformed into circular motion, of how kicking an engine starts the wheels going 'round.

The V-Twin motor from a black 2005 Texas Chopper.

(Barry C. Altmark Photography)

Most chopper engines are four stroke—that is, there are four strokes of the piston moving up and down for each power cycle:

1. The piston moves down with the intake stroke and draws in the fuel charge—the intake stroke.

2. It then moves up for the compression stroke.

3. The ignition and burning of the fuel-and-air charge pushes the piston back down with the power stroke.

4. Finally, the piston moves up and pushes out the burned gasses with the exhaust stroke.

This bike was built for zoom, but looks good standing still.

(Andy Wyzga)

Today's engines are a far cry from the single-cylinder engines that powered early bikes, including some choppers. It terms of their cubic inches, these engines were huge. The advantage of the one-cylinder engine was that it did not break down much. The disadvantage was that it didn't produce adequate power. Their exhaust system made a thumping noise and so they were called thumpers.

Increasing Engine Power

The key to getting more power out of an engine is to increase the amount of fuel/air mixture that is burned over the piston. There are five ways to do that:

- Bigger bores
- Longer strokes
- Hotter cams
- Better pipes
- Trick headwork

Don't worry about it if you aren't sure what some of those things mean. They are all customizations designed to increase the airflow into your engine. That's the tough part. Increasing the fuel-flow is comparatively easy and involves installing bigger jets/needles.

Crankshaft and Primary Drive

The primary drive is a drive chain or belt connecting the engine's crankshaft to its transmission. The crankshaft is connected with connecting rods to the pistons. The pistons, propelled by internal combustion caused by the controlled burning of the fuel, move up and down inside the cylinders.

Celebrity Bio

Max Friz was a German engineer who, in 1923, invented the Boxer-style motorcycle engine, elements of which are still in use today. It was an opposed-twin engine with the pistons thrusting outward like fists—thus the name, Boxer. The pistons opposed each other, which had the effect of canceling out primary vibration. The engine also, because the pistons were on the sides, came with its own cooling system: the airstream created by the bike in motion. Friz's invention caught on worldwide. During World War II, Harley-Davidson bikes built for the war effort had the Boxer. Boxers created abundant torque and could travel at high speeds for extended periods.

That controlled burning of the fuel comes in the form of fuel charges, created when the carburetor mixes fuel with air to create the explosive concoction. The top portion of each cylinder where the explosions occur is called the combustion chamber.

The SS117 displaces 1,918 cubic centimeters.

(Barry C. Altmark Photography)

The crankshaft turns the up and down motion of the pistons into a circular motion. (You've heard of rpms, right? Revolutions per minute? Well, it is the crankshaft—not the wheels as is sometimes assumed—that is revolving.)

Engines that use a system that forces the fuel charge into the combustion chamber with an electronic or mechanical pump are said to have fuel-injection systems. Fuel-injection systems first appeared on motorcycles in 1984 in Germany.

Transmission

The circular movement created by the crankshaft setup is transmitted to the transmission (sometimes called the tranny) through a series of gears or by a chain or belt. In many motorcycle engines, the crankshaft and the gearset live next to each other in what is called a unitized transmission. In Harley engines, however, which power most choppers, the engine and transmission are separate, connected by a primary drive.

This 2005 Legend Softail runs on a 111 motor that displaces 1,818 ccs.

(Barry C. Altmark Photography).

Many cars have automatic transmissions, but you never find any such thing on a chopper. Choppers have manual transmissions that consist of the gearset. Going through the gears enables the bike to get up to speed.

Gears are interlocking wheels with cogs (teeth) on their outer edges. The gears vary in size and the cogs interlock, so that the turning of one gear automatically turns the others. A large gear turning slowly can make a smaller gear turn more quickly.

The characteristics and capabilities of your chopper's powerplant are determined by the diameters of the gears in your gearbox. Those diameters are determined by complex mathematical equations. Very complex. That's why there isn't a chapter in this book about building your own transmission. You should buy your transmission whole and be satisfied with installing it all by yourself.

The clutch is a series of spring-loaded plates that when pressed together disengage power from the crankshaft to the transmission so that the rider can change gears. The gears within the gearset are moved with devices within the tranny called shifting forks.

There was a time when motorcycles did not have clutches. Early bikes had a leather belt transmitting the power from the engine to the back wheel. The rider could tighten the belt with a pulley mounted on a lever. The clutch replaced that system. It is a series of spring-loaded plates that, when pressed together, transmit power from the crankshaft to the transmission. Early American bikes had a foot pedal that operated the clutch. Then European bikes came out with hand clutches and foot shifts. Now that system is considered best.

The shifting forks are normally operated by a lever near the rider's left foot, which is connected to a shift linkage rod and shifter arm. These in turn are connected to a shaft that controls the forks.

Celebrity Bio

Edward Turner, another motorcycle genius who preferred to work alone, was the inventor of the innovative speed twin engine. He first made a name for himself by building a 350-cubic-centimeter single-cylinder motorcycle engine in 1927. Ten years later, he was the general manager and chief designer at Triumph Engineering Company. In 1937, Triumph introduced the 500 cc Speed Twin, a 27-horsepower parallel-twin engine. It remained the engine of choice on Triumph motorcycles up until the 1980s. The engine vibrated less than a V-twin but more than a Boxer. In Japan, they still use modified versions of the Speed Twin, with a redesigned crankshaft and counterbalancers to reduce vibration.

This softail has four triple trees.

(Barry C. Altmark Photography).

Atop the cylinder block rests the head. Inside the head is the valve train, valves that let fuel in and exhaust out. Valve trains are composed of either overhead cam systems or pushrod systems. With an overhead cam system, the most common, the cams are above the valves and connected with rocker arms. The rocker arms are levers. The cam lobes push one side of the rocker up; the other side of the lever pushes down and opens the valves. In this way, the engine breathes.

Types of Suspension

Whether you are purchasing or planning to build a chopper, one of the main decisions you have to make concerns what kind of suspension there should be. You hear a lot of terms thrown around, like hardtail or softail. "What the hell is hard and soft about the tail?" you might ask. These terms refer to the construction of the frame and whether it has rear suspension. Believe it or not, suspension is not a necessity.

There are three main types of suspension:

- **Swingarm suspension.** It usually has the most travel, around 4 to 5 inches. This is usually identified by the two outer shocks, one found on either side of the bike. A swingarm-style rear end is found on many of the Harley-Davidsons today, such as the Dyna Glide or Road King.

- **Softail.** It is also a suspension rear end only with less travel, around 2 to 3 inches. However, it has two struts or shocks that are mounted beneath the transmission. These bikes can appear to look rigid due to the lack of exposed shocks.

- **Hardtail, or what I call rigids.** On these choppers, there is no suspension. Some people may believe that this would be a harsh ride. I beg to differ. Rigids can be very harsh, depending on how the frame is built. However, each frame manufacturer fabricates them differently.

Road Closed

Don't believe everything you hear about rigid-framed choppers! I have been riding rigids for some time, and the biggest problem I see is the gross misrepresentation of the frames. Most of the time, a guy has heard a horror story or two from his best friend. Then when the best friend is asked, "Have you ever ridden one?" He ever so quietly says, "Well, uh no. But I had a friend …." Don't listen to anyone unless he or she speaks from experience, and about that particular frame. Not all rigid frames are the same. Ask around before you buy and find out if a rigid frame is right for you.

Choppers have long been known for their lack of durability because of the weakness of their front suspension systems. On a perfect road and in perfect weather, choppers do okay, but this is not a perfect world. Hardly.

A Canadian parts manufacturer named Rich Goldammer invented front forks with an electronically activated air-ride suspension system capable of extending or contracting 5 inches of travel.

Air-ride suspension is basically an air bag inserted in place of a traditional shock. The traditional shock has a coil over spring setup usually with an oil-filled damper inside. An air ride is a balloon that is inflated or deflated to get the desired ride or look.

Although such a thing might be a great gadget for a bike show, I wouldn't want to ride a chopper that has one. To change the length of your forks while riding would change your trail in a possibly dangerous manner.

Choppers, to be blunt, are not supposed to have great suspensions. It's as simple as that. If you were worried about the suspension, you wouldn't chop your bike to begin with. There was a time when no suspension at all, rigid bikes, were the norm in the chopper world but today so-called "improvements" have been made, but nothing a chopper purist would approve of.

Flapping Lips

Describing a 113-cubic-inch Shovelhead that he had just built, Tommy Imperati of Tommy Gun Choppers said, "I used a springer front end and they used to be hell on guys' bikes for all the flex and frame damage that can occur, but Paughco now makes one with a single shock up front that looks like the old one did, only this one really works. You can get aftermarket rebuild kits now for Shovelheads, Panheads, and all these old engines that actually make them run better than when they were new. Everybody likes to talk about how choppers are old school now, but without some of the new parts, they wouldn't be as popular."

Oil Cooler/Outer Cover

Biker 1: "It's an oil cooler!"

Biker 2: "No, it's an outer cover!"

Biker 1: "It's an oil cooler!"

Biker 2: "No, it's an outer cover!"

Biker 3: "Wait a second. You're both right! It's two, two parts in one!"

An SS111 with a six-speed tranny, and right-side drive.

(Barry C. Altmark Photography).

The guys at Tauer Machine (1-888-345-2135; 1041 Southbend Avenue, Mankato, MN, 56001; www.tauermachine.com) have come up with a new and improved lubricating system for the chopper owner who wants to both look good and ride hard.

According to *Easyriders* tech reporter John Sullivan, "To overcome high engine oil heat they came up with a primary drive that has an oil cooler built into its outer cover. They also made it so that the oil filter fits into the inner primary/motor plate. Now you can build a super-clean bike, ride it hard, and keep your oil cool." At the fifth annual V-Twin Expo, the cover/cooler won the New Tech Product of the Year award.

The Least You Need to Know

- The frame is the skeleton of the bike. The parts are organs and flesh. Choppers have all the organs as other bikes—just not as much flesh.

- Today's most durable chopper frames are designed to stay solid no matter how hard or far the rider pushes the bike.

- Using a "controlled burn," the chopper engine makes an up-and-down motion that is then transformed into circular motion. The pistons going up and down make the wheels go around.

- Modern technology is helping the chopper lose its reputation as a vehicle with a weak front-suspension system.

Chapter 8

Wheels, Brakes, and Wires

In This Chapter

- ◆ Rollin', rollin', rollin'
- ◆ Fat in back, skinny in front
- ◆ Simon says stop
- ◆ Getting wired

In the preceding chapter, I said the frame and the engine were the most important components of a chopper. But I did admit that there is a case for the wheels being in that category, too. After all, without the wheels, friction would keep the bike from going very far.

In this chapter, I also discuss the brakes, without which coming down the other side of the Rocky Mountains would be a lot more of an adventure. Without brakes, riders would wear out their shoes in a hurry.

Then there is a discussion of the chopper's electrical system—with just enough explanation to convince you that you should probably consult an expert if your bike has electrical problems. But first, the wheels.

Going 'Round and 'Round

Technically, the wheels are part of the suspension system—the parts that keep the frame and, by implication, your butt—off the ground.

Wheelie World _____

Wheels are not just available in forged aluminum. You can also get chrome or steel custom wheels.

With the thriving aftermarket, competition is hot and designers around the country are working to come up with wheels that are just a little bit better and more imaginative than the next guy's. Those technicians and designers are seeking to create superior forged aluminum wheels.

Front End

When picking your front wheels, you not only have to decide on diameter, you have to think about design. Wheels come in thousands of different designs. It has always been cool to keep the front wheel of a chopper large in diameter and small in thickness.

Road Closed _____

Do not purchase a rear wheel for your chopper that is wider than that recommended by the manufacturer of the frame.

Back in the old days, the "bicycle wheel" look in the front was impressive but not particularly long-lasting. Those wheels looked fragile, and they were. Today, because of new technology, and the strength of forged aluminum, front wheels can be thinner and smaller than ever before, while remaining durable enough to do the job over the long haul.

Rear End

Although the rear wheel has the clever designs in its spokes that will give your chopper its own individual look, the rear tire on a chopper also serves as a shock absorber that helps keep the bumps from slamming directly into the rider's spine.

The latest trend in back wheels can be described in one word: fat! Any self-respecting twenty-first-century chopper has a rear tire anywhere from 8½ inches to 1 foot thick. You could do thicker, too. Tires for wheels of that thickness are in the 240 to 300 series.

The front wheel on many choppers is not much thicker than that on an all-terrain bicycle.

(Barry C. Altmark Photography)

This 2005 Legend Softail has a 250 rear tire.

(Barry C. Altmark Photography)

Spokes or Billet?

The design of your wheels often is a matter of: How many spokes? Some chopper builders believe in this motto: "The more spokes, the better." Pat Kennedy, a veteran chopper builder from Arizona, has been known to build 120-spoke wire wheels. I've seen several wheels with more than 300 spokes! That's radical!

The 280 rear tire on a 2004 LSC Hardtail.

(Barry C. Altmark Photography)

Spoke wheels come in three basic parts:

- Hub, the center piece with a hole in the middle through which the axle goes

- Rim, the outer circle piece

- Spokes, which are attached to the hub on one end and to the inside of the rim on the other

Don't confuse spokes wheels with billet wheels. The companies that make billet wheels often use spokelike designs, and they may call the style "spokes," but if it's made out of billet, it's not a real spoke wheel. Performance Machine, Inc., for example, has a billet wheel called the Tantrum that starts in the center as a three-spoke tire. Those 3 split into 6, however, and those 6 into 12, before the spokes reach the outer rim.

Performance Machine, Inc. also makes a billet wheel called Torque. That wheel has nine-arced spokes, each terminating in a knifelike profile at the rim. The Roulette, so named because it resembles a roulette wheel in a gambling casino, has 10 multi-faceted spokes, each of which splits into two dagger-like spars before they reach the rim.

> **Flapping Lips**
>
> "As a custom bike builder, I tend to create product that no one else can. I look at a product and often see a need to design something totally fresh and new," says Roland Sands, head designer for Performance Machine, Inc.

*There's a 280 tire mounted
on the rear of this 2004
LSC Hardtail.*

*(Barry C. Altmark
Photography)*

You get the idea. You can get your wheels in just about any design you like. They
aren't just the round things that help your chopper roll. They are shrewd displays of
aluminum sculpture!

Celebrity Bio

Jesse James, whom I discuss in greater detail elsewhere in this book, got so into designing wheels for his custom cars and motorcycles that he formed his own company just for
that purpose: Jesse James Wheels.

Tips on Wheels

Here are some things to keep in mind if you are choosing the wheels for your new
chopper. If you're building a chopper from a kit, your wheels come as part of the
package. But if you're building a chopper from scratch, or if you are having a pro
build your chopper for you, here are some things to think about:

♦ The size of your chopper's wheels and tires is determined by the size and style of
the frame.

♦ If you are purchasing a chopper used, examine the wheels and tires to see if they
need to be replaced. Older tires, obviously, may be worn bald, and new tires are
often safer and look better than old ones.

♦ If you are working on an antique chopper, always do your homework before
buying wheels or tires from an individual. A lot of people who are looking to sell
something will say anything to get your cash.

♦ When purchasing appropriately sized wheels and tires, make sure you factor in a clearance for the width and diameter between the rim and the tire. Again, do your homework. The clearance is necessary because tires will swell after a few hundred miles of the rubber meeting the road.

♦ Find out ahead of time if a wider tire might have a bad effect on your chopper's steering and handling.

♦ Take into consideration the part of the country you live in. Remember that a tire that might be perfect for the long, straight roads of the plains states might be all wrong for the changing conditions and rough road conditions found in the Northeast. A hard-track tread in a tire is perfect if you will be riding on hard, dry surfaces. A soft-track rear tire is preferred if you will be navigating over irregular surfaces.

Road Closed

Do not purchase wheels and tires for your chopper without getting a warranty.

Sometimes a simpler design in the front wheel is desired.

(Barry C. Altmark Photography)

Brakes

Nostalgia being what it is, people are more apt to remember the good old days than the bad old days. The early days of chopper mania were a lot of fun, but those bikers had a lot of problems that we're lucky not to have today.

That said, it can now be revealed. Bad brakes were a part of chopper heritage. Those bikes were built to go. Stopping, not so much. It's not like tailgating is ever the smartest thing to do on a bike, but you no longer have to make sure the vehicle in front of you is a dot on the horizon to be safe in case they stop short.

This hardtail has Performance Machine brakes.

(Barry C. Altmark Photography)

Two types of brake systems have historically been used in motorcycles: disc brakes and drum brakes. Both types are operated by the rider through hand controls on the handlebars or foot controls on the frame.

Disc brakes slow your chopper by squeezing pistons inside a caliper. The caliper is attached to your frame or fork. To slow the chopper, the pistons push against a disc that is attached to the wheel, thus slowing the wheel down. (If you have disc brakes, remember to regularly change your *brake pads*.)

The drum brakes work by expanding stationary, horseshoe-shaped devices inside your wheel hub known as brake shoes. The expanded brake shoes push against the inner surface of the hub, which is part of the rotating wheel, slowing the wheel down.

Chopper brakes have evolved over time, and each change has made the chopper a little bit safer. There was a time when a drum brake on the back and no brake at all in the front was the norm. Then choppers with disc brakes in back but none in the front were in vogue. Now disc brakes both front and rear are more and more common.

def•i•ni•tion

Brake pads are metal-backed fiber pads located at the ends of the pistons in the calipers.

Wheelie World

The chopper is the most prevalent type of customized motorcycle in the United States, but that's not necessarily the case in other parts of the world. In Europe, for example, most motorcycle customizations involve the creation of café racers and streetfighters.

Now it may rub the hardcore rider the wrong way, the guy who wants to chop everything but the bare necessities off his bike. Today, however, just about all riders—those who ride choppers as well as those who ride other types of motorcycles—agree that the ability to stop quickly and safely in an emergency is a necessity.

Wiring

In the anatomy of a chopper, the wiring system is comparable to the human bloodstream and nervous system. The lights and ignition on your bike operate on electricity, which is supplied by the bike's battery.

If only one thing goes wrong with your chopper, it will probably have to do with the electrical system. Though leaps and bounds have been made in today's electrical systems, it's still the part a chopper that's most apt to malfunction.

Good lights are essential for any chopper. A run, like a ballgame, should never have to be called on account of darkness.

(Barry C. Altmark Photography)

The chopper needs electricity both to provide current to the ignition to start the fuel-burning cycle, and to provide power for all of the parts of the chopper that function on electricity (the headlight, for example).

The electrical system consists of a battery, where electricity is generated, connected by wires to the ignition system and other necessary places.

Be strongly aware that you should not undertake wiring a bike yourself for the first time without someone who really knows what they are doing nearby at all times. Even then, take care, go slow, get it right.

The Charging Circuit

Every chopper will have one of two types of charging circuit. They will either use an alternator or a dynamo. An alternator produces an alternating current, or AC power. A dynamo produces direct current, or DC power.

Any time you attempt to fix something regarding your chopper's electrical system, make sure the lights work when you're finished.

(Barry C. Altmark Photography)

Because the electricity needed in a chopper has to be of the direct current variety, an alternator needs to come with a rectifier that will convert the power from AC to DC. (AC/DC! That would be a great name for a band!)

Dynamos do not need rectifiers because the power they produce is DC already.

Permanent Magnet

A permanent magnet setup begins generating electricity as soon as the magnets start spinning. This type of setup may not require a battery. Some need a battery—the less-effective ones. Others may need a capacitor, which stores up enough electricity to start the engine.

Using a battery even with a permanent magnet is recommended to avoid overheating the regulator. Avoid using an older electro-regulator in a custom job, because it might overcharge a battery that is smaller than the one it originally came with.

The regulators for permanent magnet setups tend to get hot. That is because they convert extra electricity into heat. Because of this, it's a good idea to put the regulator in a place where there is good airflow, so the heat will have a way to escape.

Electromagnet

Electromagnets are used in a field-effect charging circuit. A field-effect system requires a battery to activate the magnets before the thing will generate any electricity. All bikes with field-effect charging circuits require a battery.

The problem with alternators overheating is not as extreme with electromagnets because most switch off or reduce the current to the electromagnets if there is surplus electricity.

The best way to learn how to wire a charging circuit is to find a copy of an original wiring diagram. Teaching you how to do it is beyond the scope of this book.

Ignition Switch

The ignition switch for a bike has more in common with the one on a boat than it does with the one on a passenger car. It has to be able to function even after getting wet. So keep that in mind when you shop for an ignition switch. A boatyard might be the best place to look.

You need a switch with four terminals on the back. You won't need one that has more than three positions: On, Off, and Start. Mount the key switch on the left side of the bike, convenient to your left arm. (If the bike has a kick-only start, you only need a switch with two terminals: On and Off.) To help keep the key switch from turning, mount it in an oval hole. To the "BATT" terminal on the back of the switch, connect a thick wire and a 30-amp in-line fuse.

The Starter Motor Solenoid

The next step is to mount the solenoid for the starter motor. This connects to the battery's "+" terminal and the starter motor using a cable the same size or larger than those designed for the stock setup. If the solenoid only has one wire, the earth comes through the solenoid's body. If this is the case, you must provide a separate earth lead from the body.

The wire from the solenoid is connected to the "START" terminal on the back of the switch. When the key is turned to the "START" position, the solenoid is activated.

If there's a black wire, that's usually the ground (called the "earth" in some places). Temporarily fit the ground cable to the battery and check if the motor turns over when you turn the key to the "start" position.

Mounting the Coils

When mounting the coils, connect the plus terminal to the switch's "IGN"; connect the minus terminal to the points wire. If there are no terminals on your coils, just two wires, the female connector goes to the points wire, the male connector to the feed.

After you have reconnected the ground cable, verify that your installation is correct by making sure power flows to the cables when the switch is "on," and no power flows when the switch is "off." (To install an electric ignition, either get an expert to do it or supervise you.)

Road Closed

Some riders like to use their throttle to slow down when they are in traffic. This can be quite effective, but it could cause safety concerns, for a reason you might not have thought of. If you do this at night, you will be slowing down without your brake lights coming on, and the car behind you might not notice.

Fuse Box

Your fuse box must have three or more fuseways, each capable of taking about 20 amps. Connect the fuseways on one side of the fuse box together so that power flows to each fuse, and then connect that group to the key switch's "ACC" terminal. Power should now flow to those fuses when the switch is on "on." Because so much power is needed to turn over a motorcycle engine, some key switches are configured to go dead when the key is turned to "start" so that the lights and such don't compete for power when you are trying to start the engine.

Connect one of the fuses to about a 20-amp rating toggle. Again, get one from a boat shop if you can; it's important that it doesn't mind getting wet. The toggle switch has two feeds, one connects to the dip or dimmer switch, the other to the rear light. With a dip switch, the central terminal on the switch body is often the feed. The terminals on either side of the dip switch are the dip and main beams. Connect the side terminals to the headlight bulb and the ground to the frame.

Custom Cables

We close this chapter with an example of how the aftermarket keeps getting better and better. Here's an example of how the options available to chopper builders keep growing in number. Because there are so many different shapes of handlebars, and risers come in sizes ranging from 1 inch to 12 inches high, it can be very difficult to get a set of cables that perfectly fit your one-of-a-kind chopper.

To design a chopper from scratch, you have to know a little about geometry, and a touch of trigonometry, too.

(Barry C. Altmark Photography)

Now, finding custom cables is easier because of Barnett Engineering (2238 Palma Drive, Ventura, California, 93003-5733; 805-642-9435; www.barnettclutches.com), a company that has been making quality clutches and cables for more than 50 years. Barnett offers builders the option of custom-made cables for both clutch and throttle applications.

Cable Installation Tips

While we're on the subject of cables, here are a few quick tips for those of you who may one day attempt to install your own cables in your chopper:

♦ Before you purchase cables, know exactly what you are going to be attaching to what, where those endpoints will be, and the route the cable is going to take to get from one end to the other.

♦ To measure the length of a cable over a meandering course, use a wire hanger. Bend it to simulate the path of the cable, and then straighten it and measure to determine the length of cable you need.

♦ When designing the path of your control cable, do not put in too many sharp turns. The cable should have long and sweeping bends, nothing that might cause friction or increase lever effort. Most mistakes in bending the cable too sharply are made in the top half, as the cable moves from the adjuster into the handlebar lever mount.

♦ Successful design is in the details. Choose a housing that goes well with the overall design of your chopper.

♦ Before installing a cable, make sure the bike is ready for it. Move your front end from side to side to make sure there aren't any places where your new cable will be stretched or pinched.

So there you have it. There are a thousand different things to keep in mind if you want to own a chopper. If you're not good at memorizing things, make a lot of lists.

The Least You Need to Know

♦ Technically, the wheels are part of the suspension system.

♦ No matter the size and shape of your frame, there are wheels and tires to fit it.

♦ Along with your frame, your wheels and tires also need to be compatible with your riding style and your geographical location.

♦ Although it's true that bad brakes are part of the chopper heritage, today an adequate braking system is a necessity for even the hardest of hardcore riders.

♦ If only one thing goes wrong with your chopper, it will probably have to do with the electrical system.

Chapter 9

Hanging the Sheet Metal

In This Chapter

- ◆ Give this a theme
- ◆ The Teutul effect
- ◆ Paying homage
- ◆ Crazy tank

This is the chapter about *hanging the sheet metal*. Now that we've looked at the bones, the organs, the legs, and the heart, let's take a look at a chopper's skin. In other words, the sheet metal.

The Well-Dressed Chopper

One point of choppers is that they have less skin than other bikes. Stock bikes have sheet metal designed to protect the bike and the rider from the elements. Chopper riders pity the elements! We like to fly with our machines naked, their organs and muscles showing.

Still, it is through the sheet metal that the builder most often expresses the identity of the bike—its name, its theme, whatever. There's that word: *theme*. Don't get me started. Too late ....

def•i•ni•tion

Hanging the sheet metal means fabricating and installing a bike's metal parts—usually the gas tank and the fenders.

Sheet metal dominates this chopper's design.

(Andy Wyzga).

The texture of this tank changes depending on your point of view.

(Andy Wyzga).

No Themes!

Today it is customary (because it makes for entertaining television) to give your bike a theme. Conventional thinking is that your bike should be a tribute to something you respect—an homage! It only goes to show that choppers have come full circle since the post-WWII days when they were born.

I do and I don't believe in this. I believe that every chopper I build should have a cohesive look, but I also think it's okay to build a chopper just for the chopper's sake. My bike, the Pimp, for example, is not a tribute to those guys with feathers in their hats who debase women. My bike, 24K, is painted gold, but it isn't a tribute to anything that is actually made of gold. You get the idea.

Today it is all about building—creating. In the beginning, it was all about removing, chopping. Taking a too-heavy bike and slicing off the unnecessary parts. If you want to be like those guys drag-racing on dry riverbeds in California, that's cool.

Road Closed

Think twice before attempting to fabricate a gas tank that has no flat spots. The idea of a completely rounded gas tank is very cool, but in reality very difficult to work with because it tends to roll away while you are trying to work on it. You spend all your time saying, "Get back here!" And other things.

The Teutuls

You can't discuss theme bikes without talking about the Teutul family and the *American Chopper* show on the Discovery Channel. First, I need to thank the Teutuls. Whether other builders like it or not, they have boosted the public interest in choppers. The fact that they exist and are as famous as they are will probably result in this book selling more copies than it would have in a world with no Teutuls.

I like them. I like what they stand for. They work for charities and they pay tribute to fallen heroes, and things like that. Super stuff. I just want to put the rest of what I have to say in context. Nothing against the Teutuls, but ….

I do not like their bikes. I hate "theme" bikes. If you need to have a theme to make a bike look cool, the bike is not cool to begin with. Look at Matt Hotch or Joe Martin—they don't build theme bikes, and every bike they do is cool.

I understand the Teutuls have a niche and it works for them. Big companies get lots of advertisement from it. That's great. I say if you're an individual, drop the theme and build a cool bike. As for the Teutuls, I sure hope you guys keep it up. You are helping everyone's motorcycle business flourish.

Paying Tribute vs. Personal Signature

We wouldn't be here today if it weren't for the old-school guys. I would have to say a tribute is great, but a knockoff is just another way of saying the builder isn't talented enough to come up with his or her own idea.

> **Road Closed** _____
>
> To hang your own sheet metal and make it look anything other than amateurish, you better have gotten an A+ in metal shop in high school. Unless you are comfortable heating, bending, and welding metal, your best bet is to get a pro to construct your metal parts.

Of course, to some extent, all chopper designers are paying homage to the pioneers who came before. On the other hand, each chopper designer should develop his or her own style.

Everyone has a style. Look at Exile choppers. Their bikes are black and satin. All of them. That's their thing. You want another color, you have to go someplace else. But their bikes don't look identical. Each one is different.

At my shop, Precious Metal Customs, we specialize in solo fenderless choppers. We manufacture our Spoon-Style Rigid frame and build every bike off of it.

Stick to Your Guns

After you come up with a design, stick to your guns, no matter how many people tell you that your scheme is impractical, or worse—impossible. In 2003, I had an idea once for a chopper called 24K. I had people telling me that my design couldn't be done, so I knew I would have to do all of the blueprinting myself. The only help I would need was to get someone to bend the tubing.

The frame I had in mind was completely ill, but I got the guys at Gambler to do it for me. When it was done, the frame had the following:

- Eight extra inches in the downtube
- Five extra inches of backbone stretch
- A rake of 45 degrees

The seat rail was dropped 6 inches, which meant that it was only 17 inches off the ground. The chopper's only suspension was a massive 73mm inverted Mean Street front end with 22-inch over legs held by 5-degree Mean Street triple trees.

When I first designed this bike, called 24K, some "experts" told me it couldn't be done. Here's proof they were wrong.

(Precious Metal Customs)

The powerplant was a RevTech 100-cubic-inch polished engine.

(Precious Metal Customs)

The wheels were Beach City—a 21-incher in the front and an 18-incher in the rear. The tires were Metzeler, with a 240 in the back. I matched the wheels with Beach City rotors and finished the braking setup with P.M. calipers.

Celebrity Bio

Billy Lane, from Melbourne, Florida, is the founder of Choppers, Inc. He isn't just one of the world's most famous chopper builders, thanks to his appearances on the Discovery Channel's *Monster Garage* and *Biker Build-Off*, he's also the author of a great book about choppers called *Chop Fiction*. It's a tabletop book with excellent photography by Michael Lichter. At Choppers, Inc., you can get everything you need to be a full-fledged chopper rider. You can even get Choppers, Inc. sunglasses, T-shirts, baseball caps, hoodies, posters, Zippo lighters, and boots.

I added on a Mikuni carburetor and a set of Martin Brothers pipes. The transmission was a Baker six-speed right-side drive with a built-in oil tank.

(Precious Metal Customs)

For power, I picked a RevTech 100-cubic-inch polished engine. Then I added on a Mikuni carburetor and a set of Martin Brothers pipes. The transmission was a Baker six-speed right-side drive with a built-in oil tank. The tranny received its power via a BDL 3-inch open primary and clutch assembly.

The Gas Tank Must Be Crazy!

The tank must be the strongest expression of the bike's design motif. Because it is at the heart of the bike, it is often the visual focal point. The color and the graphics on the gas tank, in addition to the tank's shape, individualize each chopper.

With that big frame, I wanted a crazy gas tank. I did the fabrication for the tank with the help of master metalworker Dave Wright. It was gigantic. It had to be to match the frame and the front end. There were no fenders and the seat pan was incorporated into the tubing. A nose cowl was molded into the frame, which hid the battery and regulator.

The top of 24K's gas tank. It's huge! Looks a little like the head of a cobra, huh?

(Precious Metal Customs)

Fabricating a Gas Tank

Let's start with the gas tank. Every chopper needs one. To fabricate your own tank, you need to start out with four pieces of 16-gauge cold-rolled steel—two large and two small. The two large pieces become the body of the tank. The smaller pieces will eventually become the end caps.

> ### Road Closed
>
> To fabricate and weld a brand new gas tank is one thing, but fixing a used gas tank can be a lot more complicated. If there is any old gas or gas fumes inside the tank, the last thing you want to do is start pelting it with sparks and flame from a welding torch. We heard of a repair man once who wouldn't do torch repairs on a used gas tank until the owner took the tank out to the parking lot and stuck a lit match in it. To lessen the possibility that you'll blow yourself to smithereens, always (ALWAYS!) thoroughly rinse out the gas tank with water, then blow it out with compressed air. When you think there couldn't possibly be any gas fumes inside the tank, do the whole flushing process one more time just to be safe. Only then attempt to weld a break on the tank.

Wheelie World

If you are working from a kit, installing the gas tank is a breeze. Tank mounts should already be welded onto the frame. To install the tank, screw in the petcock and run the bolts up through the frame mounts—with a rubber insert in each mounting point—into the bungs welded into the bottom of the tank.

Hot-rolled steel is formed under heat. It tends to be more brittle, and has a shale-like finish. Not good for fab work. Cold-rolled is formed at room temperature under direct pressure. Cold rolled is more expensive but easier to work. Perfect for fabrication.

To bend the large pieces into the shape you want, you need a sheet metal brake. The two large pieces will be bent into half tanks, one identical to the other. Then the two halves are welded together. Tack weld the piece first. Finish weld last. This helps prevent warping during the final bead.

Fenders

In addition to the gas tank, the shape of which goes far toward communicating the chopper's personality, the other sheet metal some builders will need to hang is the fenders. I can't say much about that; as I said, I build fenderless bikes. We build our frames such that fenders are rendered useless. That's *our* thing. But not all Precious Metal bikes look the same. Every builder has something that they love deep in their heart and they carry it throughout each bike.

Wheelie World

You can buy kits of sheet metal. The gas tanks come in "weld yourself" or fully assembled. The former item comes in two halves, and the latter costs about three times as much. One company that offers this option is Metal Monsters, Inc. (www. metal-monsters.com). Their gas tanks have names like Chopper Tear, Chopper John, Franken Tank, and The Bomb. They also sell front and rear fenders.

Go for the Gold

I had the paint job done by Randall Rutledge, who applied layer after layer of a paint called Gold Rush (made by House of Kolor). A logo, "24K" (as one might see engraved on the inside a ring), was painted onto the underside of the gas tank.

After everything was painted, the chopper was reassembled. I bolted on a set of Joker Machine risers to hold the PMC handlebars with Excel Components hand controls. I used foot controls by Excel and pegs by PMC.

The headlight was by Ness and a taillight/license plate combo by Cyril Huze. The last step was the wiring. Eight wires were run internally, keeping the chopper as clean as possible. Beautiful, if I do say so myself. And they said it couldn't be done.

The Least You Need to Know

♦ I don't like theme bikes. I believe that every chopper I build should have a cohesive look, but I also think it's okay to build a chopper just for the chopper's sake.

♦ Although it is okay to give a tip of the hat to great builders of the past with your chopper design, I believe that each bike should have some element that is unique to its builder.

♦ After you come up with a design, stick to your guns, no matter how many people tell you that your scheme is impossible.

♦ To fabricate your own tank, you need to start out with four pieces of 16-gauge cold-rolled steel—two large and two small.

Paint Job and Seat

In This Chapter

- ◆ Gas tank as canvas
- ◆ Mist from a tube
- ◆ Back in the saddle, again
- ◆ Softening cheek shock

This chapter is about aspects of your chopper that admittedly do not make it go faster. These are parts that have to do with how cool the chopper looks, and how good you feel when riding it: the paint job, all-important when it comes to self-expression; and the seat, also a potential "statement" of design—but all-important when it comes to your butt. This chapter is a guide to keeping all of your parts happy: from top to bottom, with an emphasis on the bottom.

Visions of Color

But first we are going to talk about the paint job. Some folks believe that all bikes should be painted midnight black, and that's that—but most builders have a more colorful vision than that. Most agree that the paint job is one of the most important aspects of a cool-looking bike.

Stare too long at this wildly decorated gas tank and you might dazzle your eyeballs.

(Barry C. Altmark Photography)

Paintwork is sometimes highly personalized. This sheet metal, painted by Jay Moody's HotRodPaint.com, belongs to a professional guitarist.

(Jay Moody's HotRodPaint.com.)

Bike painting and tattooing are similar in the sense that you can do it yourself, but it's going to look a hell of a lot better if you hire a real artist. In this chapter, we go over some painting options so you can determine what's best for you.

This Tucson, Arizona, bike, featuring some of the local wildlife, was painted by Jay Moody's HotRodPaint.com.

(Jay Moody's HotRodPaint.com.)

Choosing an unusual paint scheme, a design that is not "trendy," such as this design by Jay Moody's HotRodPaint. com, will keep your bike from going out of style.

(Jay Moody's HotRodPaint.com.)

Some paint jobs feature designs that are simply designs (psychedelic patterns, for example). Others are designs that represent something real to life, such as flames. Some artists depict fancy logos. Some paint objects and people on the tank of a chopper.

Chances are, no matter what your vision is for the paint job on your chopper, you will be able to find an artist who can do it for you. If the right artist isn't local, you just have to mail the artist your sheet metal, along with a check. When he or she is done, the painted metal back is mailed back to you.

This paint job depicts a three-dimensional lightning bolt, spiky pitchfork design in red, yellow, and purple.

(Barry C. Altmark Photography).

Sophisticated artwork by Garry Williams. This tank has been painted to look like the cover of Penthouse *magazine.*

(Garry Williams/Hammond, Indiana.)

Steps to a Successful Airbrushing

Today's best custom paint jobs are done by airbrushing, a process whereby the paint is applied in a fine mist blown onto the surface with an air tube. The best airbrushers use House of Kolor and Dupont products.

The new kid on the block, when it comes to airbrushing products, is Lectra Finish, which gives a crystallized look resembling frost in any color combination.

According to Rick Corgan of Be-Unique Airbrushing (www.be-unique.com), these are the nine steps to a successful airbrushing:

- Strip all metal parts down to bare metal. Clean and prep them for prime.

- Use only the best primer, HOK epoxy-based (five or six coats). This allows high build for smooth sanding and a smooth base.

- Apply an HOK black or white sealer, depending on base color, for easier base coverage and to seal the primer.

- Apply base coat. Add a few coats of *Klear* to protect the base while sanding for proper adhesion of artwork and topcoats.

def•i•ni•tion

As its name implies, **Klear** is a transparent paint that helps to seal in the color you've already laid down.

Another masterpiece by Garry Williams. Here's the perfect artwork for those of you whose favorite color is skull.

(Garry Williams.)

- Sand the clear and tape out the flame pattern with ⅛-inch 3M blue fine line, followed by ¼-inch blue fine-line tape.

- Mask the base coat to expose only where the flames will be.

- Spray the flames. Pull tape. Apply a few coats of Klear.

Wheelie World

When you are getting your new chopper painted by a pro, why not give the painter your helmet, too. You know, if you wear one. Matching flame effects on your gas tank and helmet can look pretty cool.

Examples of the artwork of Marc W. Osmun.

(Marc W. Osmun)

- ◆ Wet-sand to remove any flame edges. Then apply three more coats of Klear. Then more wet-sand.

- ◆ Buff and polish.

The yellow, orange, and red highlights in this paint job appear to be the very essence of flame.

(Andy Wyzga)

"How to Paint a Chopper," by Marc W. Osmun

We sought out an expert opinion on how to paint a chopper, and received a whole education in the art from Marc W. Osmun, occupation freelance airbrush artist/ illustrator/fine artist/animator. He has been doing custom automotive painting for six years.

Osmun also sells his fine art paintings in various galleries and to private individuals. "I have done works for celebrities, made animated commercials in New York City, and designed concept art for many animation and film companies. I am founding Blue Fire Studios as my home base for various creative projects," Marc says.

He was kind enough to write this text, which we print here with his gracious permission:

Before we even touch on paint, we must briefly discuss the processes prior to application. You can be the best custom painter in the universe, but if your welds aren't clean and ground down and your body work and primer applications aren't flawless, the base paint and the artwork will look like garbage.

An artist always makes sure his canvas is ideal before applying anything to its surface. If you are painting on fiberglass or plastics parts, make sure there are no pinholes or gouges. On tins, everything should be perfectly straight and smooth. Your gas and oil tanks must be pressure-tested to prevent any leaks that will completely ruin your paint down the road. Any screw and bolt threads should be masked off. Not until all of these processes are flawless and checked off your list will you be ready for primer.

If you are not sure how good the bodywork is by this point, the uniform color of the primer will pull out any imperfections you may have missed. It is entirely up to you what you choose to overlook; however, always keep this in mind: choppers have become the epitome of high-end motorcycles. Big money is usually thrown into the production of these one-off projects which express the individuality of the owner and the builder. Due to the pure nature of the project, not to mention your own reputation, I advise that you spare no expense or amount of time to do the job right the first time. Any shortcuts will always cost you more in the long run. Now, you don't necessarily have to possess these bodywork skills yourself as long as you have a trusted body guy who is as meticulous with his work as you should be with your own. Which brings us to what you are reading this chapter for....

Fabricators and mechanics create the monster, but the painter usually gets the glory. Paint is the icing on the cake, the clothes on the person, the magician's illusion. Above all, it is an art form which can be broken down into four main categories.

- ◆ Basecoat painting
- ◆ Graphics and effects painting
- ◆ Mural art
- ◆ Pinstriping

Basecoat Painting

Basecoat painting is just what it's called, the application of the base foundation color that will cover most parts of the bike. Many people tend to overlook the importance of this stage of the process, particularly if there are wild graphics or artwork on top of it. But the fact is, a nice basecoat color can give a chopper a classy and clean look.

However, the simple appearance of basecoat is deceivingly difficult. First it is necessary to understand color. Most times a client wants a completely original color, and the painter must possess a thorough understanding of various color theories to mix his paints properly. It is indeed a science that should be studied by all custom painters, particularly if color scanning is being relied on too heavily at paint distributors who charge for this service. Entire books are written on the subject, so we don't get into specifics here.

After your color is chosen, you apply it. There are paint guns and airbrushes of various sizes on the market, and it is in your best interest to purchase the best one you can afford. Before spraying your paints, it is important to be informed of its dilution ratio and psi range. All paints are different from brand to brand and type to type, so you won't spray a pearl at the same psi as a flake or a flat base.

Because choppers tend to consist of curved surfaces, you must use proper technique to ensure a proper and uniform application and avoid heaviness or spottiness in any one area. To make sure the application of paint is uniform, it is important to keep your paint gun or airbrush at a consistent distance from the piece you are painting and at a steady airflow particularly when painting tri-coats such as candies. The best way to learn these techniques is to attend a vehicle body and paint program through a college, seminar, or with someone in the business. Remember, there is no substitute for constant practice.

In addition to choppers, Marc also paints beautiful and sometimes bizarre helmets.

(Marc W. Osmun)

Graphics and Effects Painting

Graphics and effects painting is the first major leap into getting more creative and artistic with custom chopper painting. Examples of this range from two tones, flames, scallops, and multilayered wild shapes to marbleizing, organic textures, metal rips, etc. Everyone has his or her own methods of achieving these various looks, but there are a few things that remain constant.

The first is that you will be doing more taping off and cutting than actual painting. Again, the best materials will minimize the potential disasters you could encounter while performing these stages. So make sure you have quality fine-line and masking tapes of various sizes appropriate to automotive painting. Cheaper or incorrect kinds will not give the correct adhesion and flexibility to ensure tight lines that will leave a clean edge and not lift the paint. Also whether you are using masking tape, masking paper, or spray frisket, make sure that you are always using a sharp razor blade.

Second among the constants is the need to better your basic artistic abilities. To make your work look good, you must understand composition, color, light and shadow, and so on. Without this, your work will look cluttered, confusing, and downright gaudy.

Finally, you must allow proper drying and curing time between layers. You can put the piece in the sun, under a heat lamp, use a heat gun, or just let it sit in a room with low or no humidity. Regardless of method, paints dry at different rates. If you don't allow the paint to cure properly before applying another coat, the result can be lifting, bubbling, spottiness—whatever. Either way spells disaster and the magic word in custom painting is clean. Spraying intercoat clear between layers will also save you from various potential disasters.

A tank and fender, freshly painted by Marc Osmun, attached to their frame.

(Marc W. Osmun)

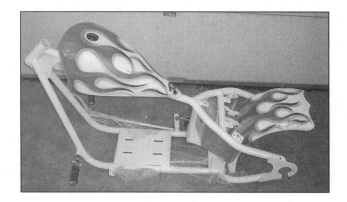

Rule 1: It's Art!

The first and most important point to make before becoming an airbrush mural artist is to emphasize the importance of the word art. Before even getting involved in painting a chopper, educate yourself in as many techniques and theories in art as possible. All too often, "airbrushers" and "tattooists" jump into these fields before becoming an artist first and foremost. I studied fine arts at the School of Visual Arts in New York City, animation at Sheridan College of Animation in Toronto, and had apprenticeships under master artists in various fields before I even began painting choppers. I didn't even seek out a profession in custom bike and hot rod painting; I happened to fall into it.

There is not enough room in this book to discuss the range of techniques and theories that exist in art that apply to custom chopper painting. The simple advice is to educate yourself (either formally or informally) and practice your butt off … then practice some more. Regardless of public perception, there are only a handful of great automotive mural artists in the world. If you have the ability, desire, and discipline to be one of these people, there is a huge demand for you.

If, as is probably the case, you're simply a consumer in search of this particular talent, I have some advice for you, too. First, remember that just because you're not capable of it yourself, what you're looking at isn't necessarily good. You should not only look at as many portfolios and photo albums as possible; it is vital to look at actual pieces. Artwork always looks better in a photo or in print, and those images won't show the texture or cleanliness that may or may not exist in the artist's work.

When you're fortunate enough to find the right artist, arrange for appropriate business conditions that are fair to both parties. Decide if they will work in-house or as an independent freelance contractor. Make sure they get paid what they're worth.

If you're a garage owner, hang on to the real artists for dear life. They may be a bit more spoiled than you are comfortable with, but the bodywork business and reputation they'll bring to you and your garage will be invaluable. Both equal more business in the big picture.

Marc has painted a devil of a gas tank!

(Marc W. Osmun)

Pinstriping

Pinstripers tend to be in a class of their own and, as a result of vinyl-cutting machines and other technologies, are becoming a dying breed. Most pinstripers come from the sign-making field and as a result possess an ever-so-steady hand for lettering and pulling lines. They are also as invaluable as an airbrush artist; most tend to do both.

Good pinstriping will always pop out a flame, graphic, or lettering and is an advisable technique to learn. You can go classic with some scrolly striping, or edgy with jagged striping. The beauty of good pinstriping is that it always looks good and is fast to execute.

As with base painting and airbrushing, proper materials are key. The most popular striping brushes on the market tend to be the Mack brushes and are made of squirrel hair. However, pick through any striper's box and you will see all sorts of brushes in various shapes, sizes, brands, and hair types.

Regarding paint, most stripers are adept with One-Shot Enamel Paints, which are great for sign painting and quick striping on automobiles and the like—as long as it is done on top of the clear coat. If used on top of any sort of basecoat then cleared over, it will lift. It is advised to use a urethane-based striping paint if you want to bury it under clear.

Clearcoating

Which leads us to the final process in custom chopper painting. Again, different brands and systems operate differently, so make sure you check compatibility before mixing systems of paint and clearcoat. A good three to four coats is generally advised and should be cured between layers.

After a minimum of 24 hours, before the clear fully cures, the piece should be wet-sanded (or color-sanded) and buffed to a mirrorlike shine. This will eliminate any runs, orange peel, or unwanted textures and give your paint incredible depth and intensity. It is advised not to wax your newly painted and cleared project for one to two months after its completion to ensure full curing and breathing.

As with the bodywork process before painting, clearcoating and buffing are equally important in the post-painting stages. Why ruin a great paint job by getting impatient or lazy at the end? If paint is the icing on the cake, the clearing and buffing are the cherry on top. Remember that a piece of art is only as good as its worst part. That is why each stage of the process needs proper attention.

Safety

Through science and technology, automotive materials are getting safer and easier to use. We have moved from lacquer paints (which by the way, will always make the others peel up) to enamels, and currently have two- to three-stage urethane processes dominating the market.

Whether spraying paint, clear, primer, or spreading and sanding body fillers, always wear a proper, approved respirator and dust mask, protective clothing or a body suit, and eye protection. Over a prolonged time in unsafe conditions, these materials will give you breathing diseases, be absorbed into your skin and organs, and poison you or cause cancer. Many custom painters die young out of stubbornness and no respect for the materials they are using.

So get into these good habits early in your painting career. Fortunately, manufacturers such as Auto Air Colors are developing great water-based paints that are as vibrant and mesmerizing and easy to use as urethanes. With zero percent VOC, they can be sprayed with nothing more than a dust mask. Until all painting materials get this safe, please practice safe painting.

You can reach Marc W. Ormun in Fulton, New York, at 315-593-2797 or at mosmun@hotmail.com.

Seats: Looking Good

As you can see, the gas tank on a chopper is much more than a receptacle for fuel. It is a canvas upon which artists paint their masterpieces. The same thing came be said for chopper seats. They still serve as a fine resting place.

If you've ever gone on a long run on a bike that has an uncomfortable seat, you know what a pain that can be. A poorly constructed seat can even be dangerous. The unmuffled vibrations of a chopper running directly into your coccyx? Have mercy! In fact—with foam rubber or synthetic equivalents, air, or gel to absorb cheek shocks—they are more comfortable than ever. But they are also canvases for artists who work in leather.

Some seats seem to best suit riders who are a little bit broad in the beam, and you know who you are.

(Barry C. Altmark Photography).

Custom Stitch Graphics

Chopper seats come in a wide variety of shapes and looks. You can get a seat that looks just like the seat on your Stingray bike when you were 9. You can get them made out of leather, or customized with an exotic skin.

Celebrity Bio

One of the top chopper seat designers today is Will Cascio, who founded Heavy Magic Fine Leather Customs of Austin, Texas, in 1995. He grew up in the Southwest with a rock-and-roll gypsy mom and a cowboy dad. Before turning full-time to working in leather, Will spent 9 years as a rodeo cowboy, 4 years as a jockey, 8 years as a professional graphic and web designer, and 13 years as a pro actor/stuntman. Cascio's most famous onscreen roles were as stunt double for Michael J. Fox on the *Back to the Future* films, and playing "Raphael" in *Teenage Mutant Turtles III*. Although building chopper seats is his primary and most lucrative expression of his art, he is also a master leather craftsman, does wax carving for bronze sculptures and silver jewelry, and acrylic hand painting and airbrush on canvas.

Designs are placed in the leather in a couple of ways. The old-fashioned way is through custom-stitch graphics, the leather equivalent of embroidery. Designs are sewn into the leather, in other words.

Inlay Options

The more modern method of decorating leather is through inlay. In this process, the seat maker actually carves sections of the leather out and replaces them with other material, usually colorful. This other material may also be an animal skin of some sort. Interesting skins that have been used on chopper seats include snake, elephant, shark, alligator, giant African bullfrog, crocodile, hippopotamus, stingray, and ostrich.

Wheelie World

The motorcycle is the modern horse, and the seat is, of course, its saddle. Therefore it should surprise no one that a lot of seat makers also made saddles for horses.

How a Seat Is Made

Here are the steps to making a chopper seat:

- A pan style is selected.
- The pan is created out of fiberglass. A mold is made.
- Brackets and hardware items are installed.

- Foam or gel seat is molded to rider specifications.
- The foam is attached to the pans.
- Skins are cut and sewn.
- The cover is put on seat.

Complementary Seat and Tank

When a chopper builder designs a bike, he cannot think of each part separately. The chopper is like a jigsaw puzzle. The pieces have to all fit together perfectly for the whole to be functional.

This is even true when it comes to the seat and the gas tank. Many beginners think the only thing they need to determine when designing a seat is what is going to be the most comfortable on the rider's butt. But the seat also has to complement the gas tank. The nose of the seat must be a perfect fit to the recess in the rear of the gas tank.

Tank with eagle design by Terry McCall, using PPG black with in-house mixed colors.

(McCall Colors, Mccallcolors@ aol.com)

This RHR helmet was painted by Terry McCall, using a PPG black base with one of many styles of free-hand flames out there now. The graphic colors were mixed in-house.

(McCall Colors, Mccallcolors@aol.com)

Flapping Lips

Says chopper seat artist Will Cascio, "I really love the leatherwork. I was fortunate enough early on to be allowed into the shop and to learn the basic ropes and some advanced techniques from a man I look up to and consider to be the absolute best of the best in the world of leather, Bill Wall. Leather to me is all-consuming, to the point where I would not eat if I did not need the nutrition because I feel there is not enough time, only time to create, and as many hours of the day as possible. I am obsessive, driven, and dedicated. Consistently reaching a particular level of physical endurance while creating is where the magic is for me. When I sit down to a piece for 17 hours, there comes the hour when life, problems, basic distractions all melt away. It is here, in this area of purity, creation is set free and my world begins. This is where great leather work becomes Heavy Magic. When you give a piece this much attention in one setting, something changes; it's no longer just a job, it becomes a part of you, and you become a part of it. Sometimes it's really hard to let some of the pieces go when they turn out better than you could have dreamed. You just want to say 'I'm keeping this one,' but of course it has to go, and I get a real kick when the client is really happy with their piece. Makes it all worth it."

Terry McCall painted this grim reaper design with PPG black base and all in-house mixed colors.

(McCall Colors, Mccallcolors@aol.com)

The stars and stripes design was painted by Terry McCall using House of Kolor candy red and candy cobalt blue over silver with PPG platinum pearl over bright white.

(McCall Colors, Mccallcolors@aol.com)

The seat and the tank not only have to be compatible in terms of shape. Color and design between the tank and the seat should be complementary, too. I've seen guys who got a great painter to do their tank and a great seat maker to do their seat, and both were great on their own. But when they were placed next to one another they looked ridiculous.

Your Butt's Future

Bikers are like cowboys, in that neither are likely to be the campers with the happiest cheeks. Riding a chopper can be tough on your butt, so it understandable that seat technology is becoming quite advanced.

The Carolina Butt Buffer

There is available today a product called the Carolina Butt Buffer, which is actually a series of seat cushions and inserts in a multitude of styles. They "absorb the road conditions that you encounter while riding."

> **Wheelie World**
>
> You know that the drop-seat craze has really caught on when guys who have never built a bike with a drop seat before, start to do it. It's like when the Rolling Stones recorded a disco song. One guy who just built his first drop-seat chopper is Frank Oddi of Oddi Cycles in Hamden, Connecticut. His drop-seat debut was called "Drop 2004." It took three months to build and had a 113-cubic-inch R&R engine, with S&S cam and carb. The rake was 42 degrees, and the stretch was 6 inches. The transmission was a 2004 Baker six-speed. Frank, as usual, did his own fabrication and assembly. He built his own handlebars, risers, fenders, taillight, foot controls, pipes, and did his own electrics. Performance Machine provided the wheels and the brakes. It was painted with an intricate graphic design in various shades of orange by Billy Streeter using House of Kolor paints.

The technology was not originally developed to aid bikers' butts, however. It was originally designed to prevent bed sores for the bedridden. It was a happy coincidence that it also served as a balm for bikers' bottoms.

Never Fully Compressed

The secret, they say, is the Butt Buffer's dry polymer core, which is both supportive and flexible. In other words, it is never fully compressed; when it is not compressed it returns quickly to its original shape. It doesn't leak or spill out if it is punctured, either.

Road Closed _____

Be aware that a lot of high-tech modern choppers seats may not protect your butt in cold temperatures as well as they do when it's warm. Below 50 degrees or so, a lot of them stay hard. With you sitting on it, the seat warms up fast enough, but—depending on what the thermometer says—it might take a few minutes before the seat's shock-absorbing capabilities are optimal.

Wheelie World _____

Believe it or not, there is a product out there that is designed specifically for the backside distress a rider experiences after a long ride. It's called, and I kid you not, Anti Monkey Butt Powder, and it works great.

The hypoallergenic Butt Buffer evenly distributes heat and weight, reduces shock and dampens vibration, can't freeze, is easily repaired, is unaffected by water and hydrocarbon oils, doesn't support bacteria, is fire-rated as self-extinguishing, does not absorb fluids, and is—thank heavens—fungus resistant.

It comes with a nonslip bottom, so you can just put it on top of your seat and go. All of the Butt Buffer cushions come with adjustable Velcro straps and clip that can be secured to your seat.

Other Side of the Coin

What can I say about painters? I want to first say that there are some great painters that are great businessmen. They keep to their schedule and turn out great quality. We have talked to and about a number of extremely talented and reliable guys in this chapter. Those are the guys that are booked all year round.

Below that first tier of quality there is a major drop-off. When I was first starting in chopper-building, I had to deal with the painters I could afford, and I was rarely, if ever happy with the results.

In fact, thinking back on it now, I cannot remember a single time when one both stuck to a promised schedule and gave me the quality that I wanted. I hate to generalize, and I know a lot more about the situation in my neck of the woods than I do about, say, the American Northwest, but I would say that the majority of the chopper painters out there are unreliable.

If you are a talented and reliable painter and disagree with my generalization, don't get mad. Instead, please give me a call. I am looking for *you!*

My first bad encounter with a painter turned out to be the best thing that could have happened. I started building my dream bike. The painter was slow but his quality was very good so I was patient. He kept pushing my paint delivery back. The bike was almost finished except for the gas tank and rear fender. I was trying to get ready for a big bike show. The show was one week away. The painter delivered the tank to me with *no rear fender*. He forgot the rear fender.

"No big deal," he said. He promised I would have it on Friday.

Friday came, *no rear fender*. He couldn't get it to me for another week! I had to get the bike cranked and test ride it now. I had to come up with a solution.

I made a billet bracket that held my seat up away from the rear tire as I rode it. I took it to the show. People loved it! I won first place, with no rear fender. Go figure—the painter's screw-up actually helped me.

I decided that from then on I would start building bikes with *no rear fender*. I guess I liked the sound of it. Here I am, several years later, fenderless. And why? Because without a rear fender, *there's less to paint!*

The Least You Need to Know

- You can paint your chopper yourself, but—as is true with tattoos—it's going to look a hell of a lot better if you hire a real artist.

- Chances are, no matter what your vision is for the paint job on your chopper, you will be able to find an artist who can do it for you.

- Artists who work on sheet metal and leather are just as talented and dedicated as those who use more conventional canvases.

- Riding a chopper can be tough on your butt. Luckily, seat technology is becoming quite advanced.

Chrome and Pipes

In This Chapter

- Chrome, sweet chrome
- Etch-n-sketch
- Cut to the long side
- Legal beagles

Chrome is short for chromium. When we talk about chrome parts, it means that these parts have been plated with a thin layer of chromium alloy, creating the most shiny and silveriest of all surfaces.

Some folks can't get enough chrome, and it's easy to see why. It's shiny and clean and allows the eye to appreciate curvaceous lines. And that is a good attribute to have when you are dealing with something as curvaceous as a chopper. In this chapter, we take a quick look at what chrome is, how to find a chromer to do your chopper, and how to etch designs in your chrome. Then we are going to move on to another subject.

Some folks can't get enough chrome!

(Danny Sutton at MarkKings Custom Metal Etching)

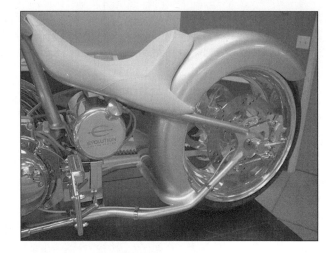

The exhaust on this black 2005 Texas Chopper is by D+D Exhaust.

(Barry C. Altmark Photography)

Finding a Chromer

You could go on the Internet and find the chromer closest to you. Or you could pick up a phone book, turn to the Yellow Pages, and pick the chromer whose name comes first. But I don't recommend it. It is smarter to use your contacts within the biker community when searching for someone to lay down your chopper's chrome. Ask around. What's the scuttlebutt?

If you see a hot custom bike and you like the chrome work, do not hesitate to ask the owner who did the job. As you probably know, a rider's favorite subject is always his or her bike, so getting the info shouldn't be hard.

The billet grips pictured are chrome-plated and have a unique tribal flame pattern. The caps at the end are threaded and can be removed to add a mirror to the end of the left grip. To add a mirror to the end of your grip, simply remove the threaded cap from the left side and thread on the grip end. Then attach the mirror of your choice to the end of the grip.

(Jeff Schwen at Aeromach Manufacturing)

According to Jeff Schwen at Aeromach, the small oval, large oval, classic round, and street fighter styles of mirrors look the best.

(Jeff Schwen at Aeromach Manufacturing)

Of course, give greater credence to the riders you trust and respect than those you don't. Some folks, if they say more than two sentences in a row, they're lying. If possible, get a second opinion. Ask the guy you trust if he knows any other of the chromer's clients you can talk to.

Some chromers are known for the quality of their work, but are difficult to work with and expensive. Another might be cheap and easy to work with, but his work was shoddy. Take all of the factors into consideration before making a choice.

Road Closed _____

If you are fabricating a piece for your chopper that you are later going to chrome yourself or have chromed by a professional chromer, be very careful that the metal remains perfect. Any imperfection in the metal will be magnified by the chroming process.

The seductively curved pipes for this chopper were built by Martin Brother's Pipes.

(Barry C. Altmark Photography)

Doing Your Own

Unless you have had some schooling in chroming or have worked as an apprentice chromer, I don't recommend that you do your own chrome work. Let's make it a rule. Outsource your chroming. Buy chromed parts or have parts chromed by a professional.

Celebrity Bio
One reliable chromer is Ronnie Brown (Brownsplating.com), whose family business has been chroming since 1968. Brown's Plating Service, Inc. started as a one-man operation in Paducah, Kentucky, and grew to be one of the largest chrome businesses in the country. Their motto is, "No one lays down chrome like Brown's."

Do you remember when the Three Stooges tried to wallpaper a room? That's how amateur chromers feel. And you end up looking like the Tin Man in the *Wizard of Oz*. "Oil can! Oil can!" Don't do that to yourself or your bike.

Exhaust pipes, when made by experts, never travel in a straight line.

(Barry C. Altmark Photography)

Chrome Etching

Back in the 1960s and 1970s, it was popular for chopper builders to engrave designs into their chrome parts, just as you might have a piece of jewelry engraved. (And, as you recall, that chopper/jewelry analogy is near and dear to my heart.)

Wheelie World _____

Aeromach Manufacturing (www.aeromach.net) makes custom chrome parts for choppers. As you will learn, I have issues with rearview mirrors, but the custom mirrors Aeromach makes are cool. You can get a mirror shaped like a Maltese cross, or one shaped like flame! Aeromach started making chrome billet parts for Harley-Davidson in 1992 and Metric Cruisers in 1996. Since then, they have created a line of aftermarket parts for H-D, Honda, Road Star, Royal Star, V Star, Vulcan Classic, Nomad, Drifter, Valkyrie, Aero, Ace, VTX, and the Intruder.

Today builders are still decorating their chrome with intricate designs, but they no longer use engravers, whose work, though beautiful, was slow and all-too-often cost-prohibitive. Nowadays, chrome is etched, and one of the top chrome etchers today is

Danny Sutton of MarkKings, a metal etching company in Mesa, Arizona. He uses a machine he adapted from defense contractors, originally designed to etch serial numbers on military hardware.

State-of-the-art etchers such as Danny Sutton can put any design onto any surface on your bike.

(Danny Sutton at MarkKings Custom Metal Etching)

The machine used to etch chrome is based on one developed by the army. The prototype was used to etch serial numbers on military aircraft parts.

(Danny Sutton at MarkKings Custom Metal Etching)

Flapping Lips

"Chop till you drop."— XsSpeed, reporter for *The Horse* magazine

Sutton started out using the machine to etch designs into knife blades, Zippo lighters, and other small items—but over the years he moved on to bigger and better things. Today Danny has developed the technology to the point that he can etch just about any design onto any piece of chrome or polished metal.

Danny didn't start out etching parts for motorcycles. He began on a smaller scale, etching intricate designs on knife blades and Zippo lighters.

(Danny Sutton at MarkKings Custom Metal Etching)

Danny's etching is an homage to a gluttonous donkey.

(Danny Sutton at MarkKings Custom Metal Etching)

Etching a logo onto chrome, or another surface, is a lot like tattooing your bike!

(Danny Sutton at MarkKings Custom Metal Etching)

Your artwork is attached to the part the image is to be etched upon. That part is then electronically charged and painted with a special etching chemical. The process remains the same, but the chemical changes depending on what surface you want etched.

(Danny Sutton at MarkKings Custom Metal Etching)

The tech writer for *Easyriders* magazine known as "Wordman" explained the process this way: "It all starts with the artwork. Could be a logo from a business card, a photo, literally anything."

Danny's process places the image into the chrome as opposed to burning through it.

(Danny Sutton at MarkKings Custom Metal Etching)

"After deciding on the basic dimensions of the artwork," Wordman continued, "the customer gets to see the proof to allow for last-minute corrections. From there, it's something similar to tattooing."

"The artwork is attached to the metal piece which is then electrically charged and a special etching chemical is applied which varies on the type of metal used. From this weird science, the image is then etched into the metal. Chrome parts are treated with what is called a surface etching which places the image into the chrome as opposed to burning through it. This process preserves the integrity of the chrome which prevents damage, peeling or other unsightly messes. The result is a cool, clear, knock-your-socks-off image."

Let your imagination go. Danny is always looking for new design ideas.

(Danny Sutton at MarkKings Custom Metal Etching)

An extra set of wings will help this chopper fly.

(Danny Sutton at MarkKings Custom Metal Etching)

Chrome vs. Chrome

Warren at ChoppersRule.com has a thing for chrome, and like a Discovery Channel show, likes to pit bike builder against bike builder. In 2005, he pitted a chopper built by Dan Newman—a 1999 Special C&C Softail with 42-degree rake, a Tolle front end, a Murch 120 horsepower engine, a Baker six-speed transmission, American Steel stretch gas tank, Legend Air suspension, and all chrome done by Brown's of Paducah, Kentucky. The bike was built for Dan by Chaz O'Neill of Shreveport, Louisiana.

Chrome sweet chrome.

(Andy Wyzga)

In the other corner was the chopper of "Doc," that's the Doc who works for Rough Rider Motorcycles. His all-chrome beauty passed the endurance test when he took it 2,400 miles (to California and back) in 5 days. "And I was taking my time," Doc bragged. Doc described his bike as, "FXR with 5 inches of stretch in the backbone and 6 inches of stretch in the up tubes. It has adjustable trees with 10 degrees of rake and a neck rake of 45 degrees. It has a 2-foot over-wide glide. The powerplant is a 98-cubic-inch EVO motor with a 3-inch primary going to a stock transmission, then a belt final drive to a 180 rear wheel. Her name is Nina!"

Who was the winner? Everybody, that's who.

Pipes: More Skill Than Tools

When it comes to building a chopper, some tasks are made much easier if you have access to the latest automated equipment. If you are fabricating a steel gas tank, for example, it is much easier to shape the metal with a pneumatic pounder (you just hold the metal while the machine pounds the bejeepers out of it), than it would be if you just had a hammer.

But when it comes to making pipes, the secret is not in the tools. It's in the mastery of those using them. Just as a great artist uses the same brushes and paint as a house painter, the pipe artist uses the same simple tools as the guy who doesn't know what he's doing. Most pipe jobs can be done with just a set of torches and maybe a set of circlip pliers.

After you have designed the exhaust pipes you want to build (and have checked with an expert to make sure they work), the first step is to analyze the difference between the stock system and the one you have designed. In other words, to get from here to there, you have to determine precisely where "here" and "there" are.

Cutting Pipes

Because we are making analogies that the parts of the chopper are like those of a human body, you know what part the exhaust pipe is. True, humans only have one— unless, of course, they've had a new one ripped for them lately—and choppers have more, but the exhaust pipes on a chopper are still the hole from which the waste leaves. With choppers, however, we try to make the waste system as attractive as possible—often using chrome.

Wheelie World

The old carpenter's axiom, "Measure twice, cut once," is also applicable when cutting pipe for a chopper exhaust.

Cutting pipe for a chopper is a lot like giving someone a haircut. There's an old joke that says, "I keep cutting and cutting and it's still too short!" The point is, always cut toward the long side.

Pipe design often compliments the V shape of the powerplant, and then goes on to simulate wildly writhing human forms—or something like that.

(Danny Sutton at MarkKings Custom Metal Etching)

If you're off, you can always cut off a little more. If you cut the pipe too short, you either have to …

- Redesign the pipe you want to put on your bike.
- Add a new weld.
- Get a new pipe and start all over again.

> **Road Closed** _____
>
> Your exhaust pipes must work. If they don't, you've got a museum piece on your hands. Looking cool is important, of course, but all that coolness is for naught if the exhaust system isn't functional.

Installing Exhaust Manifolds

When you are installing the exhaust manifolds, keep in kind that one day you might want to take them off. Nothing is forever. You want to change the design or a road mishap may have changed the design for you and you want to return the pipes to their previous glory. Whatever, put them on, keeping the idea of taking them back off one day in mind.

When you are fitting your manifold tips, make sure they are secure. Tighten them securely but not so tight that they can't be turned. Be aware of your wrench angles, so you (or the next guy) can get at the manifold nuts if the need comes up.

Compatibility

The next consideration is compatibility. Just as you had to design your seat and your gas tank in conjunction with one another, because they had to fit snugly against one another and compliment each other visually, you have to design your pipes with the rest of your chopper also in mind.

It is not unheard of for great-looking new pipes to be bent and ready to put on the chopper when the builder realized (for the first time) that the pipes interfered with the footpegs. It's a puzzle. Make sure all the pieces fit on the drawing board before they are fabricated.

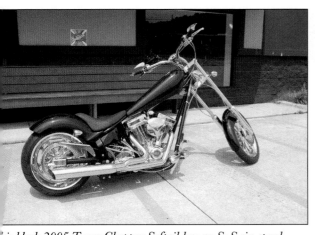

his black 2005 Texas Chopper Softail has an S+S six-speed
_insmission, a 280 rear tire, tear drop mirrors, a progressive
_pension, and double caliper brakes.

_rry C. Altmark Photography)

Big Red is a hardtail. It has a rigid frame, which is about the
same as having no suspension at all.

(Barry C. Altmark Photography)

_is 2005 Legend Softail has a 42-degree rake, and a 38 frame
_ke.

_rry C. Altmark Photography)

Some folks don't go for intricate graphics and
effects in their paint jobs. They like solid colors
on their bikes, like this blue for example, just
because it looks great when it reflects the sky.

(Barry C. Altmark Photography).

Sonny Knighter calls this chopper Big Dog.

(Barry C. Altmark Photography).

Barry C. Altmark's photograph clearly shows how curvaceous a chopper can be.

Here's a 2005 Big Dog Chopper Softail with a six-speed transmission and Performance Machine Brakes.

Here the motif is yellow-to-orange flame with indigo and black plumes woven through.

(Barry C. Altmark Photography).

Big Red comin' atcha!

(Barry C. Altmark Photography).

A 2005 Texas Chopper Softail.

(Barry C. Altmark Photography).

This paint job looks like smoke through seawater at midnight.

The idea for many designers, is to get the seat as low as possible and the handlebars as high as possible.

This paint scheme is a subtle interweaving of maroon and black.

An AIH Hardtail with right-side drive.

The orange-and-blue color scheme looks great with the D+D exhaust system.

This 2005 Legend Softail is designed to look like it comes with its own bloodstream.

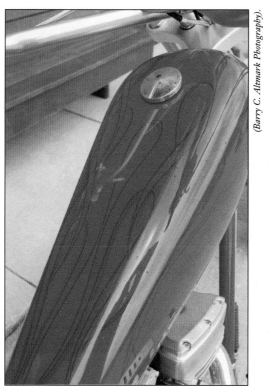

Ready for a Fantastic Voyage?

Anthony Matano's Ultra Chopper!

The Ultra Chopper has a 113ci S+S polished aluminum motor.

Legality

As I've said before, and I'll say again, knowing the local laws of your community regarding choppers (in this case specifications regarding your pipes) is not enough. You have to know the local laws of every place you go, too.

Again, word of mouth will keep you pretty well informed as to where you can't go if you have pipes that don't meet their standards. I recommend some legal research outside of the biker world, too, because—as you know—guesses and assumptions often become facts when it comes to word of mouth.

Also be aware that when you are traveling on a hot chopper, you will be pulled over, yanked around, and sometimes ticketed by local cops not because of the specifics of any local ordinance, but because the patrolmen found it fun.

The laws regarding chopper specifications here in the United States may seem too stringent to a lot of bikers, but they are nothing compared to those in Europe. A guy on a chopper in Europe gets pulled over and checked every time he goes out.

Licensing and inspection regulations are also far more stringent. In Germany, the laws regarding choppers are so tough that they should just simplify matters and outlaw the customization of motorcycles altogether.

The Least You Need to Know

- Use word of mouth and the biker network to find a trustworthy and talented chromer who is in your price range.

- Today chopper builders decorate their chrome with intricate designs that are etched rather than engraved.

- The first step in customizing existing pipes is to determine the difference between the stock pipes and the pipes you envision.

- Some pipes are legal in some places and illegal in others—so know the laws in all localities you plan to visit.

12

Finished Choppers

In This Chapter

- ◆ Building on a tight schedule
- ◆ Indian-powered chopper
- ◆ $100,000 means "I love you!"
- ◆ Shovelheads and TV shows

We have looked at choppers piece by piece. Now let's take a look at some of the finer examples of the whole. In this chapter we talk about some award-winning choppers built by some very different builders under very different circumstances.

Some are masterpieces of design, others of engineering. Some are not masterpieces at all, but are noteworthy for the obstacles the builder overcame. Some were built fast, some slow. Some with deep pockets, some on a budget.

One of the great things about going to rallies—along with the fact that it's almost always one hell of a party—is that you get to see some of the great choppers in the world. The builders and owners of today's state-of-the-art choppers are inevitably eager to show off their artwork, so they love to go to rallies and park in a spot where they'll get maximum exposure. We'll learn more about rallies in Chapter 17.

Less Is More

One of the chopper shops in Florida that believes, as I do, that the less you have on your chopper the better, is Ultimate Cycles of Hialeah, Florida. The three builders who work there—Ariel Alfonzo, Sal Baez, and Isaac Velazquez—all agree that the minimalist approach is best. The trio took four months to build a 2005 Pro-Street for like-minded purchaser Ernesto Padron of Miami Lakes, Florida. The chroming was done by Atlantic Coast Plating of Pompano Beach, Florida. The chopper was painted "ultimate blue" with silver graphics by the Ultimate Cycles crew, who also did their own polishing. "Ultimate blue" was a custom-mixed color, with a touch of midnight in it.

The bike was powered by a 2005 TP Engineering engine that displaces 124 cubic inches and, coincidentally, produces 124 horsepower. There's a Barnett clutch assembly, a Baker five-speed gearbox, a chain-drive primary. The result is a reliable powerplant designed to keep its owner off the side of the road.

Ultimate Cycles started with a long and low Pro-Street softail-style frame built by War Eagle. It combined a 42-degree rake, a 5-inch stretch, and a rake of 5-degree in the tree. The forks came from Perse Performance. Redneck Engineering supplied the handlebars and risers. Mirrors and pegs came from Paul Yaffe Originals. Arlen Ness, "The King of Choppers," provided foot controls. The levers and hand-controls were from Performance Machine. There are RevTech Doom wheels on the front and back. The brakes are by Hawg Halters.

The best thing about this bike isn't the way it looks, but the way it rides. Here's a fine example of a bike with a kicked-out front that any biker would be eager to ride cross-country on. Talk about a bike with a dream attached. There was a time when that sort of thing only happened in the movies.

Dem Bones

Remember when I said that the frame of a bike is its skeleton, and that all of the other parts are the organs and connective tissue that turn the chopper into a living, breathing thing? Well, here's a story about a guy who took that chopper/human body analogy literally!

Do people call you goth? Do you believe that the finest customized car of all times was the Munster-mobile? (*The Munsters* was an old 1960s black-and-white TV show about what would have been an average American family if dad hadn't been

Frankenstein, Grandpa a vampire, and Eddie the kid a werewolf. Their car was half-hearse and half-dragster.)

Well, have we got a chopper for you. John Farr at Crypt Custom Cycles of Opelika, Alabama (www.thecryptcycles.com, or call John at 334-705-0283), has designed a chopper that features, as an integral part of its frame, a solid titanium human skeleton.

It's a facsimile, of course. Real bones would be too fragile. But it looks real. The skeleton comprises the entire top half of the frame. It's not for decoration. The frame's backbone is the skeleton's backbone. The frame's legs are the skeleton legs. It comes as a rigid only.

Because the upper frame is what it is, a hollow framework, the gas tank has to be moved from its customary spot. Instead it resides under the rear fender/cowling houses. It can be set up for just about any drive-train configuration and tire size. It can be built for one or two riders and airbags are optional.

Lucifer

David Covington grew up around motorcycles, so designing great custom bikes comes as a second-nature to him. His forte is building bikes that look great but can also tear up a quarter-mile track.

He is a second-generation designer, after working for his dad at Covington Cycle City in Woodward, Oklahoma. David's latest creation, built upon a drop-seat frame, is a hot-rod Harley painted pagan gold and called Lucifer.

Covington's goal was to get both Old School and New School bikers to equally gawk, and he has pulled it off. Surprisingly, the inspiration for Lucifer didn't come from the motorcycle world at all, but rather from an automobile: the 1931 Ford, to be exact.

The exhaust has flared tubes and tips that give the bike its hot-rod look. Dave has combined a 103 cubic-inch panhead with Stromberg 97 carburetors. Perhaps the best example of the bike's combined new and old elements is the gas tank, which has the overall shape and feel of an old Sportster tank, yet has been stretched and streamlined brilliantly to keep it in sync with the bike's magnificent stretched curves.

As of the fall of 2005, Covington was already planning his next creation, which would probably be called Lucifer II. This one, he was thinking, might combine a knucklehead engine with the Stromberg carbs.

The James Dean Bike

In the tribute and homage category comes "Little B------," a chopper built to re-semble the Porsche Spyder sports car that James Dean died in on September 30, 1955. The car was silver and curvaceous with the racing number "130" painted on the side. The chopper's tank matches the color, and also has the identical racing number painted on its side. The flip-up gas tank cap is modeled after that on the Spyder, and the wheels, exhaust pipes, and headlamp are all similarly derivative.

James Dean was a young movie star who only made three movies before he went out on California Route 466 in a blaze of glory. But he still had a strong following of intense fans, and among them is chopper builder Brian Hatton. His chopper made its public debut at the 2005 James Dean Custom Car Show in Fairmount, Indiana. Hatton (www.brianhattonenterprises.com, 615-731-2983) can build you your own James Dean-style chopper. Price tag: about $75,000.

Hit the Switch

A best-in-show chopper from John "Head Gangster" Dodson and Gangster Choppers (www.gangsterchoppers.com) is the "Hitman," a rigid that boasts 14 inches-over-stock tapered legs, but is best known for its electric start attached to a Baker six-speed transmission. To fire it up, you just hit the switch.

The powerplant is an 80 cubic inch shovelhead. The carb is an S&S E. All of Dod-son's choppers are red, and this one is the color of glossy lipstick. The paint job was done by Chuck Whitlock of Greenville, South Carolina.

The tranny/shovel combo is very effective—so much so that there is virtually no pun-ishment to the rider or the bike even when cruising 75 m.p.h. The wheels were made by Gangster Choppers and have 60 spokes. The seat was supplied by Darren Nash Leather, and electronics by Larry Mann.

Simply Psychedelic

Some chopper builders have a sense of aesthetics that seems firmly implanted in 1968, when Peter Max black-light posters were in vogue, and all fashion was brightly colored to simulate the effects of then-popular psychedelic drugs.

One such builder is Rick Fairless who owns and operates Strokers Dallas in Texas.

You may know Rick from the TV show he hosts on the Speed Channel called *Texas Hardtails. V-Twin Motorcycles* magazine says that Rick's TV show is more of a spoof of reality shows. They call it "some sort of Beverly Hillbillies of the 21st century."

Sometimes Rick builds his bikes for private buyers. On other occasions, companies commission the building of choppers to use as part of an advertisement campaign.

The Wrong Side of Dallas

Since 1995 Rick Fairless has been the owner of a chopper shop in Dallas, Texas. Rick grew up on what he called "the wrong side of Dallas." He started riding when he was nine, and began tinkering with bikes two years later.

When he was 11, his uncle was smart enough to give young Rick a bike that wouldn't run. Rick had to fix it. By the time Rick got that old Sukuki up and running, he was hooked on tools and grease. The rest is history.

Rick's Shop

Originally known as Easyriders of Dallas, Rick's shop was a franchise based on the popular biker magazine. When the mag folded their franchise business, Rick carried on, changing the name of his shop to Strokers Dallas.

Next door to the shop, Rick opened the Strokers Ice House Bar and Grill. Although as a dealer Rick has sold thousands of bikes, he has built far fewer on his own.

Each Bike Unique

Rick says he builds 10 bikes in a good year, but there have been years when he has built as few as four. He knows he could build more if he were willing to build the same type of bike over and over again, but he wants each of his creations to be unique. The challenge of always trying something new keeps Rick's building skills sharp.

Rick has become well-known for the psychedelic paint jobs he puts on his bikes. His initial fame came when he built a Triumph chopper for an episode of the *Biker Build-Off* TV show. Based on that appearance he got his own show, *Texas Hardtails*, which appears on the Speed Channel.

FatBook Chopper

The latter was the case with Rick's latest chopper, which was commissioned by the folks at Drag Specialties. They wanted Rick to build a chopper solely out of parts that were available in the Drag Specialties catalog, which is called *The FatBook*. The resulting bike would be used in future catalogs to show potential customers what could be accomplished by ordering from the *The FatBook*.

Rick likes his choppers to jar the senses and the chopper built from *FatBook* parts was no exception. The incredibly busy paint job, by master painter Vince Goodeve, features Ratfink-type cartoon characters, scantily clad women sitting atop pairs of dice, a flying eight ball, and other peculiar details. The words "Drag Specialties" appear on the sides of the gas tank. The colorful paint job couldn't clash more with the black and white seat which resembles the markings on a Holstein cow. As Rick likes to put it, sometimes he adds design elements "because they are wrong." The parts Rick chose from the catalog included: a single downtube frame, a 36-inch tapered leg, a TP Engineering 124-cubic-inch motor, a Baker right-side drive six-speed transmission.

The King, Back When He Was a Prince

If, after reading this book, you decide you want to know more about choppers, one of the guys you should research first is Arlen Ness, the King of Choppers. There is plenty out there. Just about everything Ness does these days is covered by the motorcycle press.

But one thing you might not see is Ness's very first chopper, which he built in 1964, based on a 1947 knucklehead. The chopper, which is still around and sometimes makes appearances at shows, is called Untouchable, after *The Untouchables* TV show about Elliot Ness that was popular at the time.

Classic—Yet Still Contemporary

The chopper is one of the most innovative motorcycles ever. Back in 1964 there were many things on the bike that had never been done before. It was so far ahead of its time that it still looks contemporary now, more than 40 years later.

For one thing, it has a 100-cubic-inch knucklehead motor. Back in 1964, an 80-inch knucklehead was considered huge. Ness accomplished the additional displacement by adding a stroker comprised of a set of flathead 80 flywheels.

Smoothing Out the Tranny

Knuckleheads back in those days were not known for the smoothness of their transmissions. Ness took care of that by mating a Sportster tranny to the knuckle motor, then attaching everything to a custom frame made of ⅞-inch tubing.

The springer front end was made of thinner than usual material so it would go with the "spindly" look of the frame. He put oil in the frame, also unheard of at the time. Superchargers were new back then and Ness put one on this bike.

Cops and Robbers

Since *The Untouchables* was a TV show about cops and robbers during the Prohibition era, the paint job—done by Arlen Ness himself—shows flapper women sitting in martini glasses and men in suits with guns in their hands.

Compared to the bikes Ness builds now, this one is small, but back in the day he used to love riding it, taking it on trips where it proved to be dependable transportation in addition to being a real jaw-dropper.

The 30-Day Chopper

One advantage an amateur chopper builder has over a pro is usually time. The amateur builder is almost always building the chopper for him- or herself. The pro has a customer who needs the chopper yesterday. Here's an example of a pro chopper builder who built a hot and unique chopper under severe time constraints.

How quickly can a chopper go from concept to road? It has been done in as quickly as 30 days. According to *American Iron Choppers* magazine, a guy named Matt Burris (also known as Dragon Matt) did it in 2004. A top-notch custom job like the kind Matt builds should take five months of design and building, but Matt had a customer named Bert Baker from Michigan who needed a chopper, and he needed it for Daytona. So Matt went to work.

> **Celebrity Bio**
>
> Matt Burris is the designer, chief executive, and production manager for a chopper-building company out of Indiana, called Dragonbilt. Dragonbilt is Matt's second job. He's a full-time firefighter.

Dragon Matt Works Alone

Matt didn't have the advantage of delegating a lot of tasks to his staff—because he doesn't have a staff. He fabricates, welds, and assembles by himself. He finds that doing as many of the tasks as he can by himself is the best way to maintain quality control.

Having a huge staff you can trust absolutely is the best way to do business for a lot of people, of course, but that is a luxury very few chopper builders can afford. Some builders started noodling with cars and motorcycles in the first place because they wanted to be alone. The builder and the bike gets to be a love story.

> **Flapping Lips**
>
> "Once I start on a bike, I don't use drawings or mock-ups. Instead I work with the metal and visualize how it's going to look when I'm finished. It's a technique that works well."—Paul Teutul Jr. of *Orange County Choppers* and *American Chopper* on the Discovery Channel

> **Wheelie World**
>
> Another of Dragon Matt's choppers, called Scalliwag, turned some heads when it made its debut. It was a pirate-themed chopper with a super-low seat, a doorknob gas cap, a flintlock motor count, and a "rum keg" oil tank.

Matt was used to working fast, but a 30-day chopper? Whew! That was going to take some tenacity and determination—and did I mention that he had to do it all in his spare time, because he's a full-time firefighter? Matt felt the pressure. He'd only been building bikes for a few years. His buyer was taking a risk. He didn't want to disappoint him.

Although Matt was a relatively new chopper builder, he was already gaining a top-notch reputation. His most notable chopper was called the Devil's Cadillac. It won the 2003 Bike-of-the-Year award at the VQ Biker's Ball in Daytona. That same chopper also won First Place Best-of-Show at the 2003 Easyriders Bike Show Tour, Franklin County Veterans Memorial Facility in Columbus, Ohio.

At their meeting, Matt and Bert discussed Bert's desires, and they went over a list of suppliers Matt thought would be able to deliver what they needed fast. One advantage of being a respected chopper builder is that suppliers give you special treatment if you want it.

Right-Side Gearbox

Matt's 30-day chopper wasn't going to be a clone of anything. On the contrary, it was going to be one of a kind —the first motor vehicle with a production six-speed right-side gearbox. The innovation was Bert's idea. He wanted the right-side six-speed to be the focal point of the chopper. The transmission would have the serial #1.

Matt thought that the advantages of having a right-side drive were threefold:

- Bigger tires without mounting problems

- No overhang

- Better balance

Matt began the build the day after his meeting with Bert. He started with an assembled engine, a *massive stroker* 131-cubic-inch Merch. The engine included 10.8:1 pistons, inlet valves that were slightly more than 2 inches in diameter, and a Merch .650-inch lift camshaft.

def•i•ni•tion

A **massive stroker** is a really big engine. In this case, it displaces 131 cubic inches. Truly massive.

The innovative gearbox was built and delivered by Baker Drivetrain, whose specialty was building prototype transmissions, so they weren't thrown by the fact that nothing like this had been built before.

Low-Mounted Headlight

The engine and transmission were coupled with a Karata belt that was 5 inches wide. The frame and forks came from Rolling Thunder. The 11-inch over-springer front end, with gas-charged shocks mounted inside the springs, usually come triple-chrome plated, but Matt ordered this set as raw steel—that is, without the chrome.

He wanted to further customize the custom parts before the plating went on. Matt likes a low-mounted headlight and machined clearance before having the chrome applied. And everything had to be done right away because the clock was running—tick, tick, tick.

Celebrity Bio

Dave Winthrow is a publisher with the Primedia Group, which publishes 10 motorcycle and truck magazines. His entire life consists of traveling from bike show to bike show, from rally to rally. He used to live in California's Orange County but recently moved to the Black Hills of South Dakota—not far from Sturgis, naturally—to open up his own chopper shop closer to where the action is. Among the magazines he publishes are *Hot Bike, Hot Rod Bikes, Dirt Rider,* and *Motorcycle Cruiser*.

Chrome Frame

Another aspect of this chopper that made it unusual was its chrome frame. There is a lot of chrome on a lot of choppers, but very little of it usually goes on the frame. With this chopper, the entire frame was to be chrome. The chroming was done by Paw Paw Plating of Paw Paw, Michigan.

Road Closed

Be aware, when you're on a tough deadline like Matt was, the toughest part of the build to get done on time is the paint job. Matt's friend Brad Bole is not only talented but quick, too. The bike was painted "organic green," which looked hot with all the chrome.

Chromed frames on choppers were more prevalent 35 years ago. If you see a chopper on the old *Starsky and Hutch* TV show, the frame is liable to be chrome. These days it's a rarity. The reason: cost. Powder coating is cheaper.

Matt built the headlight, the sharkskin seat, and the rear fender himself. He got the risers, handlebars, and taillight at Choppers, Inc. The oil tank came from Rolling Thunder. Matt came this close to running out of time. At the end, he had to break his usual rule of working alone, and a good friend came over to help with the build. The chopper was moved down to Florida for its Daytona debut before it was fully assembled. Matt did the last of the assembly in Florida, and Bert rode it to the rally. Final cost to the customer: $47,000.

Since the building of the "30-day chopper," Dragon Matt has split the Midwest and has gone closer to where the chopper action is: Sturgis, South Dakota. His new shop there is called Black Hills Choppers.

This Titan Sidewinder belongs to Anthony J. Matano.

(Barry C. Altmark Photography)

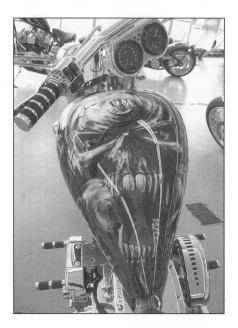

The Sidewinder's gas tank is graced with a blue skull.

(Barry C. Altmark Photography)

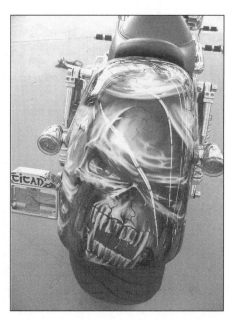

The Titan chopper has a 250 rear wheel, and a fearsome fender with another blue skull.

(Barry C. Altmark Photography)

The Titan has a 120 front wheel.

(Barry C. Altmark Photography)

Matano's Titan Sidewinder has a six-speed JIMS transmission, rubber-mount motor, and inverted forks.

(Barry C. Altmark Photography)

Indian Chopper

Bobby Maione of Apache Cycles in Stuart, Florida, got credit for building the first Indian-powered chopper when he rode his to a Daytona Bike Week in 2004 and no one had ever seen one before. His Indian chopper can't be certified a prototype, but it certainly can't be called derivative, either. Maione once told *American Chopper* reporter Adrian Blake that he didn't know of anyone else even working on one. His Indian chopper was unique. Like Dragon Matt, Maione was still working on the new chopper, right up until he got to Daytona. He was working days, nights, who needs sleep? He calls the bike Tomahawk.

The Monster Engine

Maione estimated that the bike took 60 total hours of work, spread out over 3 months. The chopper's obvious focal point is the 100-cubic-inch Indian Powerplus motor. It's a 45-degree V-twin, long stroke—the biggest engine built by the American OEM motorcycle company.

The engine's designer pays homage to Indian motors of the past by using:

- Serrated, billet-aluminum rocker boxes,

- Polished push-rod tubes,

- Rounded cylinders, and

- A Mikuni 42 mm flat-side carburetor.

Even the Indian Vintage air cleaner is built in a retro manner, visually recalling Indian air filters of 50 years ago.

Flapping Lips

Bobby Maione says, "Tomahawk is a cool name for the bike, something like Tomahawk cruise missiles. I guess you could say this bike is kind of a weapon against all those mainstream choppers!"

Matching Frame to Engine

He matched that powerplant to an appropriate frame. The frame is softail-style, with a 40-degree rake and 6 inches of up-stretch. Even though the frame and engine were going to look great together right from the git-go, truth was, they didn't quite fit. The original frame interfered with the exhaust and transmission. That was taken care of. There was also difficulty with the mounting of the engine itself. The frame had to be further modified. He custom-fabricated the engine mount, coil mount, and the key switch mount.

Retro Feel

The whole design of the bike has a retro feel. The steel gas tank, based on the Harley Sportster tank, holds 2.8 gallons. The tank has a 25½-inch raised tunnel stretched along the backbone. The stock electronic ignition module was pulled by Maione and replaced with a Thunder Heart standard ignition. The exhaust system is the Hell Bent system from West Coast Choppers.

Maione told *American Chopper* magazine that he'd seen another bike with a set of Hell Bent pipes, and had really liked the look of them. The look was radical, just as he'd wanted it. The engine was, as intended, very powerful.

"Out on the highway, there's incredible throttle response and torque throughout the rpm range," Maione said.

The front and rear brakes are RevTech four-piston calipers with 11½-inch matching drilled discs. The chopper is stable, with its Avon 250 in the rear, and turns easily at low speeds considering that there's 80 inches between the rims.

Wheelie World

One of the things people like best about Maione's Indian-powered chopper is what he did to the trademark Indian headdress on the tank. He got on his computer and added flames to the headdress and gave the Indian a more fearsome expression.

No actual cows were harmed in the making of this chopper. The seat has extra padding and is covered with fake leather. *Pleather*, they call it. The seats were built by the ironically named Dead Animal Seats, also of Stuart, Florida.

The handlebars are minimum-rise with a radical pullback. The hand controls are contoured. The forward controls are billet. The headlight is teardrop shaped. The dealership painted the bike black. The engine was powder-coated in California.

The $100,000 Bike

Michael Ballew is the owner of Ballew's South Central Customs in Poplar Bluff, Missouri. He is a second-generation motorcycle man. Dad Gene owned Ballew's Harley-Davidson from 1972 through 1991, so Michael grew up in a shop.

Gene Ballew says he knows of builders who make bikes just for show. That's not what Michael is about. He says his son does not want to just make pretty bikes: "He wants them to be functional and tough." Then he added, "When we spend this kind of money on a motorcycle, we don't want it just sitting in the corner collecting dust."

Michael customized his first bike in 1998. By the time he was done with it, that bike had a 113-cubic-inch engine, a six-speed transmission, and a 200 mm rear tire. Today, he is an experienced chopper builder whose bikes are regularly featured in motorcycle magazines.

Oriental Blue

Michael says he tried to incorporate everything he thought custom bikes were missing into this bike, the Blue Bike. The generically named bike took half a year to build and cost Ballew $100,000.

The Blue Bike is a 2003 Merch Stage Three that Ballew built himself. It got its name because of its simple but stunning oriental blue paint job, which was done by Danny Morgan, the in-house painter at Ballew's. The rockers, lifters, and pushrods were by JIMS. The chroming was done by S&H Chrome Plating of Madison, Tennessee.

Oil Tank Under Tranny

The Blue Bike's design was innovative. The oil tank was designed to fit under the transmission, and the air suspension was mounted flush with a rock guard. This enhanced both the bike's sleek look and increased the quality of the ride.

Ballew points out, "The pivot point of the swingarm is raised so that under acceleration, it can't cam over center or collapse the suspension, which in turn would loosen the belt."

"Cam over center?" you may ask. Well, I've never heard it put quite that way, but I know what he means. You have to keep the pivot point of a softail swingarm in line with the rear axle and transmission output shaft. When a swingarm flexes up, if the pivot were too low the belt would get very loose and pivot down would be too tight. Vice versa if the pivot point were too high. Look at Harleys or Hondas. They always keep the pivot in line.

Ballew kept repairs in mind in his design, too. The rear cam belt can be replaced in a half hour, as opposed to the six hours it would take you to do the same repair on a stock Harley.

The trickiest part of the build, says Ballew, was the fabrication of the gas tank. There were no flat parts in the entire tank. Everything was rounded, and it "kept rolling away."

Supercharger Optional

The powerplant was the most awesome aspect of this chopper—a Stage Three Merch engine that displaces 120 cubic inches and produces 140 horsepower. The MagnaCharger *supercharger* is optional, but if installed can boost horsepower to 200!

Ballew was asked if he'd ever had the Blue Bike out on an open road to see what she could really do.

def•i•ni•tion

A **supercharger** is a device that increases the power produced by an internal-combustion engine by increasing the air charge beyond that drawn in by the pumping pistons.

Again, where are we getting this material? This chapter is being digested from magazine articles from the last couple of years. The articles are all credited in the bibliography. "I don't know if there is a road long enough to try it out," Ballew replied. Ballew says he once passed a buddy on a bullet bike. The friend later said that he was showing 130 mph on his speedometer when Ballew blew past him— then shifted into sixth.

So, the Blue Bike might be an animal—but it is a beautiful animal. It earned third place in the Unlimited Class at the Metzeler Custom Bike Contest in Rapid City and the Best in Show at the Pyramid, both during 2004 Sturgis Bike Week.

Canadian Shovelhead

Of course, great choppers are not just built to the United States. They come from north of the border in Canada, too. Dave Green of London, Ontario, is proof of that.

Most of Dave's mechanical and artistic expertise comes from his dealings with four-wheeled vehicles. He only switched to motorcycles a few years ago, because two-wheeled projects didn't take up as much room in his garage as his Pro Street and vintage muscle car experiments.

Wheelie World

Although the riding season is sadly abbreviated by the cold weather, chopper builders from the Great White see that as just more time to spend indoors tinkering with their latest creations.

Dave owns an automotive salvage yard and is a licensed auto body repair man, which explains why his choppers exhibit such expertly bent and painted sheet metal. His first bike was built from the frame of an Ironhead Sportster. Another of his first bikes, a 55-inch Little Twin, won third place in the Daytona

Beach Boardwalk Show. Now he builds Shovelheads, which is what we'll be talking about here.

Used Parts

From an economic standpoint, Dave's chopper-building efforts couldn't be more different than Michael Ballew's. Whereas the Blue Bike cost $100,000 to build, Dave built his Canadian Chopper for 14K. So, if you—like most of us—are on a budget, pay attention and you might pick up a few pointers from Dave.

According to *American Iron* magazine, Dave starts each of his builds by choosing a frame and wheels. Then he gets comfortable and stares at them until he has a vision of what the bike will look like when it is finished. Then he makes a shopping list and purchases the parts he needs.

Dave has a couple of aftermarket sources he relies on, but when he can he likes to get his parts through swap meets and from the backs of his friends' shops. A brand new shiny part holds no interest for Dave. Unless it needs to be polished, changed, or fixed, he's not interested in it.

Adapting to His Vision

It is an important factor, of course, that scrounged parts are cheaper than purchased parts every time, but that's not the only reason Dave does it this way. He believes that his bikes are more of an expression of himself when he adapts them, almost down to a molecular level, to his vision.

The gas tank on Dave's latest Shovelhead started out as a stock Sportster tank but Dave stretched it 6 *functional inches.* That tank is molded to fit the frame and is not welded to the frame. With consideration toward repairing a leak, the gas tank is removable.

def•i•ni•tion

Six **functional inches,** in this case, means that none of those 6 inches are for show only. All 6 inches hold fuel.

Rear Fender

The rear fender was purchased at a swap meet. It had originally been on a West Coast Choppers bike. Dave cut it, bent it, and welded it until he could call it his own.

Just as Dave doesn't like to weld his gas tanks to the frame, the same is true of his rear fenders. About that unwelded fender, Dave once told reporter Tom Johnson, "The fender follows the shape of the rim pretty closely. You can just wedge a finger between the fender and tire all the way around, and I want to keep it that way. If I have to move the wheel back to get the chain adjusted right, it won't change the looks. I can just shim the fender a little and keep it where it belongs."

Stock Motor

Dave tried to keep his Shovelhead (80-inch cone) motor as close to stock as he could. To build his own Shovelhead would have been prohibitively expensive, because parts would have been American, where the rate of exchange makes them more expensive for Canadians.

These Shovel-style pushrods are perfect and new, but Dave Green would rather use vintage pushrods found in the dark recesses of the back room of an ancient motorcycle shop.

(JIMS Performance Parts and Tools)

There were some custom parts to give the Shovelhead a little boost, however. To the stock components, Dave added an S&S carburetor, a Crane cam, and some freshly ported and polished heads. Dave's hard work paid off. The Canadian Shovelhead won first prize in the Custom Shovelhead Division at the London (Ontario) Motorcycle Show.

World Biker Build-Off

World Biker Build-Off is a weekly TV show on the Discovery Channel that cashes in on the chopper craze as well as the reality TV craze. This is another show in which real life is blended with game show sensibilities, and viewers at home, through the power of the call-in vote, are the judges.

In each episode, teams of bike builders, usually from different corners of the earth, each have a certain budget of money and time to build a bike. Camera crews, of course, follow their every move. When the time—usually two months—is up, they stop work and viewers at home are invited to vote for the bike they like best.

In This Corner ...

In the episode we watched, the winner was Joe Martin of Duncanville, Texas, who, with his brother Jason, operates Martin Brother Bikes. Joe was known for his long-forked choppers, and the bike he built for the television audience was no different. Joe did his own construction and painting, a silver and orange combo using Toxic Tom paint. Painting hot rods had turned Joe into an expert painter.

Joe was also in charge of the metal. He made the exhaust pipes, the fuel tank with its cobra-head swoop, the oil tank, the handlebars, the minimal rear fender. The stepped-down seat was also Joe's creation. The back wheel was single-sided, and the bike had a radiused springer front end. The engine on the Martin Brothers bike was a 2004 RPM Motors powerplant that displaced 96 cubic inches. It was based on Ultima cases and had billet cylinder heads.

Getting Real Comfortable

About the TV experience, Jason Martin later told a reporter, "Ron Kerr, the producer who came in to do this, was great. He took the time to get to know us first, before he ever turned a camera on. It became real comfortable, working with Rob, and we got to be real good friends. Next thing we knew, we were filming the show!"

Not everything went smoothly, of course. The Discovery Channel people like to put builders in situations where there is apt to be human drama, thus creating suspense for the audience. With difficulties comes conflict. For Joe Martin, difficulty emerged almost immediately. There were problems with the frame.

Flapping Lips

"They definitely like the tension for the TV screen," said Joe Martin. "I think they would have been happy if a few more things went wrong."

A Diamond frame provided the raw material for the frame Joe had in mind. He cut the original into several pieces. According to *American Iron* magazine, "The single-sided rear end was created by welding on a RC Components swingarm. Making a piece rigid when it's designed to be suspended is tough, because you've got to be sure the welds are strong enough to withstand all the road shocks, plus all the power the 96-inch motor can produce. Getting the perfectly aligned engine, transmission, and chain was tough, but it was something we knew we had to do right, because we knew we were up against some great competition." Joe's radiused springer fork also had some problems making it from paper to reality. "I wanted to use a curved springer," Joe later said. "A little like the old bicycle front forks, but it just didn't look right and we had to change our plans."

Hey, no pressure—just millions of people watching on TV. A 41 mm telescopic fork ended up on the bike, and all was well.

Computer Machining

Xtreme Machine used their computer expertise to program CNC machining. Because of this sophisticated technology the Martin Brothers logo was incorporated into the design for the front and rear wheels.

When the bike was done, they rode it to Daytona where the judging segments of the show would be taped. Joining them there were the crews from Scotty's Choppers of Australia and Russell Mitchell's Exile Cycles of Great Britain, with their entries in the contest.

When the votes were counted it was the Martin Brothers' bike that was the winner, which led businessman Jason to say, "Scotty's craftsmanship was phenomenal, and Russell is brutally hardcore. It was an interesting match-up between the three of us, but we all have different styles—styles that are difficult to compare."

Going with the "apple and oranges" analogy, Jason concluded: "It's like listening to three different bands play music. They may all be great at what they do, but one's country, one's rock and roll, one's heavy metal."

The Least You Need to Know

- Professional builders, unlike their amateur counterparts, often have to build choppers under seemingly impossible time constraints.

- Bobby Maione built a decidedly nonmainstream chopper when he decided to power it with a 100 ci Indian Powerplus motor.

◆ Michael Ballew builds expensive choppers, but they are as tough and durable as they are beautiful.

◆ On a TV show, chopper builders square off against one another, vying with their builds for the most votes from viewers.

Part 4

Maintenance with Style

Now let's spend some time talking about the needs of current chopper owners. I include in this category both routine maintenance—changing the oil of the air filter—and problems that come up that need to be fixed. Repairs come in two categories: those you'll do in your garage, and those you'll do at the side of the road while cursing a blue streak.

And finally, just because chopper fashion is different from that of the rest of the world, we look at what the most happening chopper riders are wearing these days—and why.

Take Good Care of Your Baby

In This Chapter

- ◆ Long live your chopper!
- ◆ Periodic checklist
- ◆ Picking a day
- ◆ Fork bearings

Okay, now you have learned how to find (or build) the right chopper for you. But, after you have a chopper, you have to learn how to keep a chopper—hopefully for a very, very long time.

The key to a long-lived chopper is twofold. It involves the following:

1. Safe riding. (Of course, your chopper will last longer if you don't lay it down every now and again, but that's the subject of another book, I think).

2. Proper maintenance—which is what we be discussing here.

Routine Maintenance Tools

It is important to be prepared before you start your first maintenance checkup. Here's a list of tools and materials you should have on hand when it's checkup time:

◆ One small and one large funnel to pour oil through

◆ Measuring cup

◆ Used-oil catch pan, oil-draining channel, and used-oil storage container

◆ *Spark-plug wrench*

◆ Wire brush

◆ Fork tuner

The Battery

One of the most important maintenance tasks you should perform regularly is checking your battery. You must check both the liquid level and charge condition of your battery.

If you're a longtime automobile owner, you're probably used to checking the fluid level on your battery by removing the battery cell caps and having a look-see. But you can't do that with a chopper battery, unless you have a sealed, maintenance-free battery. If you don't (and don't feel bad, most don't), the holes are too small to see the level of the liquid. The battery will need to be disconnected from the bike to properly check the liquid level.

When dismounting the battery, be sure to disconnect the ground terminal first. Anyone who forgets this will get a shocking surprise. Use a *hydrometer* to check the charge condition, but be sure not to use one designed for a car battery.

To complete your battery check, you need a hydrometer, a glass jar, distilled water, a drop light, and a 10 mm open-end wrench. After reconnecting the battery, make sure the lights work.

Other Routine Maintenance

Here's a routine that lends itself to good chopper health. In addition to the tasks already mentioned, here's a checklist of jobs to perform when you are giving your chopper its weekly maintenance once-over:

◆ Check the condition of the engine.

◆ Check oil. Make sure chopper is upright. If it is on a kickstand or otherwise tilting, you won't get an adequate reading. Put a block of wood under your kickstand to level the bike. After you're done checking the oil, leave the block of wood under the kickstand. Many maintenance checkup tasks will be easier if the chopper is kept perpendicular to the floor.

◆ Check both tires for signs of wear. The best part of this task is that it demands no tools. A good pair of eyeballs and you're all set.

◆ Check drive-train condition and tightness; lubricate and adjust the drive chain. This is a messy job. You have to reach down and grab the (hopefully well-lubricated) chain, either with your fingers or a wrench, and wiggle it to determine whether it is too loose or tight.

◆ Check fenders, sissy rails, and tanks for loose fasteners.

◆ Make sure the in-line fuel filter is not dirty.

◆ Make sure there are no leaks and no seepage in your fuel lines or engine.

◆ Make sure there is no seepage in your hydraulic brake lines.

◆ Check the rotors and brake pads on your disk brakes.

◆ Lube the kickstand. White lithium grease is best for this task.

◆ Check instrument lights, brakes lights, taillight, directional signals, and headlight to make sure they are operating properly.

◆ Check condition and lubrication of your control cables for the tachometer, speedometer, clutch, and brakes.

◆ Make sure your clutch and mechanical brakes are adjusted properly.

◆ Check fluid level and condition of master cylinders. You need a screwdriver or an Allen wrench.

Wheelie World _____

Some riders maintain their bikes on Saturday and ride on Sunday. Others ride both Saturday and Sunday. They do their maintenance checkup on a weekday (or night).

Different people pick different days of the week in which to do their chopper's regular maintenance checkup. It doesn't make any difference, obviously, as long as you stick to it—as long as it truly becomes regular and part of your routine.

My only recommendation would be to not pick the day of the week when you are most likely to ride your chopper. Maintenance Day and Riding Day should be separate days.

Replace Your Fork Bearings

Every bike has bearings. They keep the moving parts of your bike from grinding together like a knee without cartilage. The engine has three kinds of bearings—needle, ball, and roller—but there are other bearing, too. Your wheels have bearings, and so does the front end. These are the steering stem bearings in your forks.

Celebrity Bio

If you are into your engine, you should learn about Dave Mackie of Dave Mackie Engineering. Dave came out of a successful career building and racing drag bikes, and today he does custom headwork for high-performance Harley-Davidsons. According to the Mackie Engineering website, Dave says that H-D powerplants need some seriously specialized help these days, and this is the reason why: "Maximum airflow coupled with the highest possible intake velocity means horsepower for street or strip applications. With efficient airflow and sustained intake velocity, a 'ram' effect is created, significantly enhancing the breathing of Harley-Davidson cylinder heads, particularly Evolution models." Dave's greatest achievement was in speed testing. Dave built and then rode the world's fastest motorcycle, clocked at 322 miles per hour on the greatest drag strip of all, the Bonneville Salt Flats. Mackie also had a hand in the engine of Bob "Rat" Taft's motorcycle when it became the world's "First eight-second Evolution Harley-Davidson motorcycle" powered by gasoline.

Your front end can turn from side to side smoothly because there are two bearings, one under the top triple tree and another on the lower triple tree. The bearing races are pressed into the frame, and the bearings are fitted onto the fork stem. The front fork bearings are tapered rollers.

Russ installs the bearing races during his latest build.

(Precious Metal Customs)

Most Fork Bearings Standard

Most of the fork bearings used in American bikes are standardized, unless you're riding a bike built before 1949 (and if you are, you probably aren't reading this book). The tapered roller bearings and their bearing races are fairly standard. The steering stem has a 1-inch diameter.

Bearings keep the moving parts of your bike from grinding together like a knee without cartilage. Clockwise from top left, these are the four-speed bearing, Timken bearing; needle bearing, and inner-cam bearing.

(JIMS.)

Road Closed _____

It is important to get your fork stem bearings set up properly. If they are too tight, low-speed handling suffers. Too loose and the bike will shimmy at higher speeds.

The fork stem bearings should be replaced regularly. Always replace the bearings and the bearing races at the same time. To replace these parts, you need to remove the chopper's front end from the frame.

Fatty's Tips

Robert Edward's of Fatty's Aggressive Machinery in Burbank, California, offers a few tips on how to replace your fork bearings with a minimum of grief:

◆ Put the new bearing races in the freezer for about an hour or until cold. They will contract and be easier to install.

◆ To fit the lower fork stem bearing on the stem without damaging the bearing's rollers or cage, make a driver from pipe. Says Edwards, "Screw a 1-inch pipe nipple that is 3 inches long into a 1-inch by 1$\frac{1}{4}$-inch adapter. The pipe nipple fits over the fork stem, and the adapter gives it a larger footprint for use on the press.

◆ To make sure your new bearing is fully seated on the stem, try to rotate the lower dust shield. The new bearing is seated if the dust shield is tight.

Tools that are helpful when replacing your fork bearings are a bearing race punch with an oval end that allows for more contact area on the race; a front fork bearing race cup installer tool; and a race, bearing, seal driver.

Situational Shifting of Priorities

Some maintenance checkup items are situational. As your bike ages, your priorities in terms of maintenance change. For the first 5,000 miles or so, there's no reason to check the drive belt.

Then there are checkup items that change priority depending on any tune-ups or repairs your bike has recently experienced. For example, valves slowly reseat for about a month after having a valve job. Be sure to frequently check your valve clearances during that period of time.

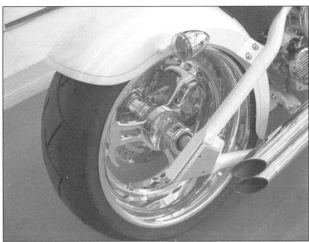

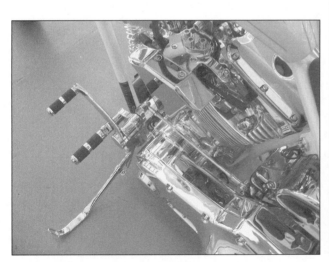

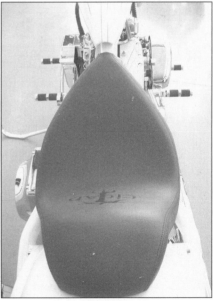

Anthony J. Matano keeps excellent care of his white-with-pinstripes chopper. It has a rigid frame, a 42-degree rake, a 250 rear wheel, 120 front tire, dual exhaust, inverted forks, and jewelry-finish chrome.

(Barry C. Altmark Photography)

Maintaining Your Paint Job

Paint for many riders is just a color. But for some it is so much more. It can be an expression of your alter ego or a dedication to someone special. Either way, you want to protect it.

Road Closed

I say don't put anything on chrome. To keep it clean, use Windex on a terry cloth rag, then—if you want—you can rub a bit of the same paint wax you use on it. There's no proof this helps prolong chrome, but it's something that has been passed down to me, and it has always seemed to work great.

After a freshly applied paint job, the worst thing you can do is wax it. Wax actually will trap solvents in. It is recommended that you allow the paint to cure for at least 90 days.

There is a major difference between wax and polish. Polish brings out the luster of the paint and wax protects it. For a stock paint job, both may be needed. Polish first, then wax.

For a high-end, "slicked-out" paint job, it has probably been polished better than you could ever hope for. So, just maintain it with wax after the 90-day period.

The Least You Need to Know

- Safe riding and proper maintenance are the keys to owning a chopper for a long time.

- Give your chopper a routine maintenance checkup once a week.

- Make sure your workspace is properly equipped before you begin your weekly maintenance routine.

- Your routine maintenance checkup should adjust to any recent repairs of tune-ups your chopper has had.

When You Break Down ...

In This Chapter

- ◆ Far from home
- ◆ Without shelter
- ◆ Tools to carry
- ◆ Progress

There was a time when breaking down on a chopper wasn't a matter of "if," but a matter of "when." Things have greatly improved since those good old, bad old days, but problems on the road still occur. Here's what you do.

Traveling in Packs

In days past, breaking down on the road was a problem that could delay a trip not just by hours, but by days. That's one of the reasons why, historically, bikers travel in packs. If someone had mechanical problems, there was always someone to go get help.

Riding alone was always a risk. Years ago, if you broke down in a remote place (21 miles out of Lovelock, Nevada, comes to mind), getting to help meant hailing down a friendly passing motorist. Now that everyone carries a cell phone, it's much harder to get stranded.

Flapping Lips

Ed Ryan of West London, England, described his first custom job to *The Horse* magazine: "I got hold of a 1938 Triumph T100 in 1970 for 30 pounds (then the equivalent of about $90) from a 'Teddy Boy' and started me on an unknown journey. At first it was a lash-up with 18-inch apehangers and high pipes. Soon, chopper shops started to appear selling extended fork tubes, 'Z' bars, forward controls, and fiberglass Sportster tanks. Here in London the nearest shop was Leon and Wallace in Putney.... They chopped everything. I even saw a Vincent Black Shadow in their front window once. Their specialty was chopping WLC 45s, raked and flaked."

As long as it's not raining, a parking lot, with a friendly bench nearby, makes a perfect place to do repairs.

(Barry C. Altmark Photography)

Of course, the cell phone can help you only to a point. If all of the cards are stacked against you, you still have a problem. For example, if you are immobile and you're in the middle of nowhere in the middle of the night, you might as well set up camp!

DIY: Give It a Try

Yes, despite cellular/satellite/GPS technology and all that, there will still be times when the problem that has halted your trip will be urgent enough, yet minor enough, for you to repair yourself. That's what this chapter is all about. I'll assume that if you break down across the street from a chopper repair shop, you don't need this book to tell you what to do.

Wheelie World

No matter which bike rally you attend—Daytona, Sturgis, New Orleans' Steel Pony Express, or the Fort Lauderdale Bike Rally—you will probably run into the Seminole Hard Rock Roadhouse, a multipart motorcycle tour. The show always includes four or more of the best custom bike builders in the world, and many examples of their work. They also bring along their own models, hold beauty pageants, and travel with their own mobile bar! Check out www.hrroadhouse.com.

So let's discuss more-difficult-to-solve problems. How can you be best prepared if you have a mechanical problem and there's no one in sight to help you?

If it is raining, you have a whole new set of problems. Some repairs cannot be done in the rain because they necessitate exposing internal parts that don't like getting wet. Do not do the repair until you either find shelter or it stops raining.

Minimum Needs

The first question to ask yourself is this: what is the minimum I need to fix the problem and get back on the road? In some cases, the object will not to be to restart your cross-country trip—but rather to get back on the road long enough to make it to a repair shop where more permanent repairs can be made.

You need two things: tools and a place to do the work. If at all possible, you want to do your repairs inside, where there is an adequate floor. Your tools will be in a pouch attached to your chopper. We discuss your emergency tool kit in greater detail later in the chapter.

Gimme Shelter

If you don't have shelter available to you, but you are near civilization, doing your repairs on a concrete surface is infinitely preferable to working where there is grass or even dirt. You don't want to do your repairs on a road because you might get run over. A driveway or parking lot might be available, however.

It's one thing if you break down a couple of blocks from your home, but what if it happens when you are halfway to Sturgis? Perhaps the nearest shelter is a day's walk away, and you're starting to suspect that it was true what they said on *The Simpsons:* There really is no North Dakota.

Rule number one: Get the bike away from the road.

(Barry C. Altmark Photography)

The first advice is, get the bike away from the road. You don't want to get hit by a car while performing your repairs. If no paved areas are available, find a hard-packed dirt surface as far from the road as possible.

Emergency Repair Kit

It is very difficult to find new parts when you are stranded on the side of the road. Here's a list of the items you need to perform emergency repairs on the road. Remember, space is extremely limited, so get the smallest available size for each tool:

- Phillips and slot-head screwdrivers
- Swiss army knife (by far the most valuable tool you will ever own)
- Key-ring flashlight *and* full-size flashlight (if possible, waterproof, such as those sold at outdoor-equipment shops)
- Repair manual—sealed inside a plastic bag
- Open-end wrenches (⅜ inch to ¾ inch; preferably with a clamp system that keeps all of the wrenches together when in storage)
- 10 mm combination wrench
- Assorted Allen wrenches (⁵⁄₆₄ inch to ⅜ inch)
- 6-inch and 8-inch crescent wrenches

> **Road Closed**
>
> Do not perform our roadside repairs in the grass. If you drop a small but essential part into the grass, you will never find it. Never!

- Spark plug wrench

- 5-inch long-nosed pliers

- 4-inch vise grips

- 5-inch channel-lock pliers

- Handheld digital multimeter (dMM); DMM test leads, DMM test probe tips (two alligator clips, two long probes, two needle probes, two spade-lug probes); keep in a separate waterproof pouch

- Tire-pressure gauge (sliding-scale version takes up less space than the kind with a dial)

- 6-foot test wire with alligator clip ends

- Spare breaker points

- Three #1157 brake light bulbs

- Two #53 instrument light bulbs

- Spare fuses as needed

- 5-inch tie wraps

- Thread-locking compound

- Scotch-Brite

- 8-inch by ⅝-inch extension handle

- Wire strippers

- Black electrical tape

- Feeler gauge set

- Teflon thread-seal tape

- 6-foot tape measure

Know Your Wires

As I stated earlier, the one system on your chopper that is most apt to break down in the electrical system. I've sometimes felt that the problem always seems to be electrical. Whether the ignition's gone bad or you just have a fouled spark plug, get to know your bike and its electrical system. That way you have a better chance of remedying the problem when it occurs.

If you built the bike, then you should understand it. You may want to keep a small wiring diagram of your bike's harness just to refresh your memory. I usually place one in a plastic bag under the seat. It came in handy for me in Daytona, year 2000. I had to rewire the ignition on the side of the road. Thank goodness I knew what was what.

Rethreading a Thrown Chain

Usually, a thrown chain is a broken chain. However, if it is not broken, you would loosen the rear axle and the axle adjusters. Slide the rear wheel forward, and hang the chain on the sprocket. Then reverse your procedure and slowly limp your bike to get repaired.

Not all jobs can be done on the spot with the help of your handy tool kit. For example, the correct way to seal a push rod is not easy, definitely not an on-the-side-of-the-road job (although it can be done). Some people have used super glue to seal the rubber grommet to get you to a permanent repair.

Replacing a Broken Ground Cable

Replacing a broken ground cable is difficult, even if you don't want the repair to be perfect, just good enough so that you can keep secure while riding.

If you are on the road and your ground cable breaks, there's really no choice except to sit and wait. (The alternative is to rig something up that you would never stake claim to while talking to your buddies.)

A ground is just a negative cable that attaches to the frame or drivetrain. I would probably strip back the wire and somehow temporarily attach it to the bike. Once again, you don't need the repair to be perfect, just good enough so that you can limp the chopper somewhere where you can permanently fix it.

Replacing a Brake Pad

Unless you are carrying around extra pads, which most don't on a chopper, you are screwed. However, if you have them, they're easy to change. Just unbolt the two screws that hold the caliper to the bracket. Find something like a screwdriver to compress the pistons back into their housings. Remove the necessary bolt pins holding the pads in. Drop the new pads in and reverse the procedure. Then pump the brakes until the pads are in contact with the rotor.

Modern Repair: It's a Beautiful Thing

Repairing your chopper is not nearly as difficult as it would have been a half a century ago. And I'm sure, repairs 50 years from now will make the repairs we are doing today look like caveman stuff.

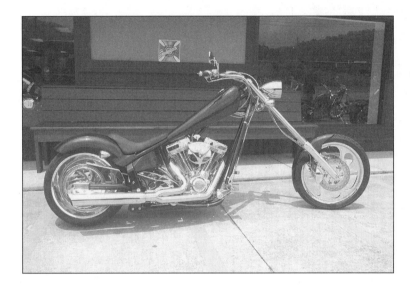

You might see this beauty cruising the roads in and around Birmingham, Alabama!

(Barry C. Altmark Photography)

Here are a couple of examples of difficult repairs that have been made greatly easier in recent days due to new-and-improved (not to mention easier-to-repair) parts.

Easy-to-Remove Rear Belt

As some of you may have had the misfortune of learning the hard way, it can take up to six hours to get repaired and be on your way if you break a rear cam belt while on a run astride a stock Harley.

However, Michael Ballew, the owner of Ballew South Central Customs in Poplar Bluff, Missouri, builds his choppers so that the rear cam belt can be popped out and a new one popped right back in again. As opposed to a six-hour delay, the rear cam belt can be replaced in a half hour.

Flapping Lips

According to maintenance and repair expert C. G. Masi, "If nothing can be done, then nothing is the best thing to do."

Anthony J. Matano's white-with-red-flames chopper has a 113-cubic-inch S+S polished aluminum motor, softail suspension, six-speed transmission, and PM brakes.

(Barry C. Altmark Photography)

Removable Gas Tank

It has usually been a rule of thumb that if your gas tank springs a leak when you are on the road, you need to push the bike to a shop to get it fixed. After all, the tank is welded directly to the frame and must be removed before the leak can be fixed.

That is, of course, unless you are riding a bike built by Dave Green of Ontario, Canada. He molds the gas tank to fit the frame but does not weld the tank to the frame. The tank is removable, allowing a rider many more options if that tank should spring a leak for whatever reason when you are far from home.

Road Closed

If you are alone and broken down on the side of the road, do not leave your bike!

The Worst-Case Scenario

I'd like to talk a little about imperfection, because nothing, not even the finest of choppers, is perfect. The idea is to get it as close to perfect as possible, of course, but you can't get frustrated and quit when something goes wrong. Because something always goes wrong. In this section we are going to look at problems that might (and probably will) occur—and what to do when they do.

So many things can go wrong during a build. It could be a manufacturer defect, electrical, paint, assembly, fabrication, hydraulics, the list is almost endless. I will tell a tale or two that will hopefully help you avoid these problems.

Electrical Malfunctions

I talk more about the electrical systems of choppers in Chapter 8. Here, as well as there, let me state that you have to know what you are doing to futz with the electrical system on your chopper.

I have an electrical story that illustrates Murphy's Law (everything that can go wrong will) and demonstrates how knowing what you're doing can help save the day even when it looks like the deck is stacked against you.

Road Closed

Guys who make mistakes while attempting to repair their chopper's electrical system develop instant Don King hairdos, and let me go out on a limb and guess that you don't want that.

Lance Blows a Fuse

My electrical story starts out with my friend Lance. Lance rides the tires off his bike. During the first year he rode it he must have put 10,000 miles on the odometer. Then, out of nowhere, Lance's chopper started blowing fuses left and right.

He found himself repeatedly stranded by the side of the road, muttering under his breath and calling the guy who built his chopper unmentionable names. (You'll never guess who the builder was. I'll give you a hint. His initials are R.A.)

The Case of the Missing Short Circuit

I rushed to his aid, like all good builders who are friends with their customers. I gave the chopper the once-over but, at first anyway, I couldn't find the problem. I assumed it had to be a short circuit somewhere, but I couldn't figure out where it was.

So we started examining why this problem was occurring now. What had we done to change the electrical? Or, what had we done to the bike that could affect the electrical? We made a list of all of the possible factors.

Detective Work

Included on that list was the fact that, not two weeks before, we had done a lot of powdercoating to the bike. You remember learning about that process in Chapter 10. The triple trees, rocker boxes, wheels—they'd all been recently powdercoated. After the painting was done, we reconstructed the bike, and Lance helped. As a matter of fact, I believe he put the rear tire on all by himself. He may say different.

Now there are only the bare essentials of wiring to get this bike going. Typical of bar hoppers. So we concentrated on these areas. Sure enough, we finally found the short circuit, and once I saw where it was I knew what must have happened.

The Answer

Regardless of how much of the reconstruction work Lance did and how much I did, the fact remained that his license plate bracket is mounted on the rear axle. It has a very clean little channel that has been cut out on the back side of the bracket to hide the wiring. Now of course we wanted everything as close and as clean as possible. The bracket was one-half-inch away from the spinning rotor and ¼-inch away from the spinning rotor bolts.

Plenty of clearance, right?

Well, not if someone forgets to put the wires back in the neat little channel and secure them down. In summary, every time Lance's wheel would turn around the button head bolts would skim the wiring, slowly removing the outer layers bit by bit until finally the positive grounded.

Check Your Clearances

Now, this didn't cause the bike to explode or electrocute Lance. It only popped the fuse. The wheel travels so fast when passing the wire that the contact only lasted a fraction of a nanosecond. Thank God for fuses or breakers. Without them a short could fry the whole electrical system.

Bottom line, always check your clearances before and after modifications. Never be in too much of a hurry to skip this step or you may end up on the side of the road like Lance.

Manufacturer's Defects or Errors

Sometimes a bike you purchased or a bike you built has problems because one of the parts from the manufacturer was faulty in the first place. In most cases, the problem is immediately apparent and it doesn't go on the chopper.

Other times, however, the problem with the part is not immediately obvious and doesn't *become* obvious until later, when the cause may be far more difficult to determine. Whichever way it happens, it is easy to figure out whose fault it is. It's the manufacturer's fault. However, even though the manufacturer screwed up, it is still the builder's responsibility to make sure everything is correct prior to final assembly.

My Sad Story

My story is short but typical of many builders. I was down to the wire before leaving for Daytona Bike Week. I had finished everyone else's bike but my own. We were leaving in exactly six hours and I was still in the shop trying not to panic.

My bike needed the starter put on, to be timed, filled with fluids, and cranked. So, part of putting the starter on is to assemble the starter gear and spring mechanism. Of course, I had done this before so I was taking my time. Then it hit me: half of the spring mechanism was missing!

Weekend Woes

First thing you do is blow a half hour cussing the manufacture, then another hour tearing the shop apart because you hope and pray that it is really your fault and you lost it. Then reality sets in. Where are you going to find these tiny parts on a weekend?

I can't call the manufacture or distributor and get the part in time. It's midnight on a Thursday and I am leaving around 5:00 A.M. to beat traffic. Since all hope is lost, I start doing other things that need to be done, just so progress is made.

I fill the fluids and then I time the bike. That took about 20 minutes. The only thing left is that damn starter mechanism! So, as any true fabricator would do, I say, "I'll make it myself!"

The Spring and the Top Hat

So that is what I did. The two pieces I was missing were a little metal cup thingy that sort of resembles a tiny top hat. It holds the spring in place as the starter depresses. The other piece I was missing was the spring.

Where am I gonna get a spring? Good thing I have built a bike or two and know the approximate size of the spring needed to make things work. It didn't hurt either that I had a mess of springs left over from who knows what.

So I have a spring now, but what about the metal top hat? Luckily, I own a metal lathe, which I use to turn-down material to the appropriate size. This made the job very easy for me. I just had to find some metal stock lying around and get to work.

Now after all this, my friend knocks on the door to see if I am ready to go *just* as I tighten the bolt ands fire the bike.

"Yeah, I'm ready," I say.

The moral is: don't assume anything is correct. I got out of it, but what about *you?* Do you have a mess of springs? A metal lathe and a piece of metal to shape? No? Well, then don't assume.

The Least You Need to Know

◆ If you travel in packs, there is always someone to go for help when someone breaks down.

◆ You need two things to do your own repairs on the road: tool and a workspace.

◆ You will be able to make most repairs if you carry the proper tools with you on your trip. There are so many people who don't realize that carrying a small set of Allen wrenches might mean the difference between sleeping in your bed that night or in a hotel.

◆ Modern technology—such as new easy-to-replace parts—has made many repairs much easier than they used to be.

Outlaw Fashion

In This Chapter

- Protection from the elements
- Helmet choices
- Second skin
- Jackets and boots

Okay, enough about your chopper. It's beautiful. It rides great. Now let's discuss the accoutrements, the clothes and other stuff you need to make sure your chopper doesn't look cooler than you do.

It is very tempting for the new rider with some disposable cash to go on a shopping spree and buy every biker dude (or gal) piece of apparel in the catalog. However, if you do this, you will be mistaken on the street for a member of The Village People.

Staying Comfortable, Staying Safe

The coolest thing about most biker attire is that being cool had nothing to do with it. For example, bikers don't wear leather jackets to make a fashion statement. Truth is, the leather jacket is the best material to protect the rider's skin from the elements—in particular, windburn.

Being out in the open air when riding your chopper is, of course, the point. But long trips can take a toll on the body. The wind and the sun on your skin, the heat—or worse, the cold—can wear a rider or a passenger out.

All fashionable chopper riders make sure their garb does not clash with their heavy metal. Just kidding.

(Barry C. Altmark Photography)

So biker clothes are geared toward keeping the body comfortable despite the wear and tear that can come with riding a chopper. They are also designed to keep bikers as safe as possible in case of a mishap.

> **Wheelie World**
>
> Just about any long trip necessitates at least one helmet, and because you are going to end up wearing one anyway, you might as well be both as safe as possible and look as cool as possible.

Helmets

Nobody likes to wear a helmet. Face it. Even those of who you are concerned about the state of your skull should you fail to negotiate Dead Man's Curve (and bikers tend not to dwell on things like that), still don't like wearing a helmet.

But the reality is that there are states where it is illegal to ride your chopper without a helmet on. There are some states in which the rider doesn't have to wear a helmet but a passenger does.

Aerodynamics

A well-shaped helmet can improve a rider's aerodynamics and make him or her slice through the air with greater ease. Over a long ride, an aerodynamic helmet can greatly reduce the stress on a rider's neck.

Helmets come in a wide variety of styles. There's open-face, closed-face, and novelty. Some helmets are just funny looking, like they could have been worn by Kaiser Wilhelm during World War I. Jack Nicholson wore a football helmet in *Easy Rider*, but he made it work for him.

Road Closed _____

Here's proof that bikers don't spend a lot of time worrying about fracturing their skulls. In states where it is not illegal to ride without a helmet, only between 28 and 40 percent of riders do wear one.

Advanced Carbon Composite

Today helmets are safer and more comfortable than ever before. That's because the plastics of yesteryear have been replaced by advanced carbon composites. The result is that the new helmets are both stronger and lighter.

Flapping Lips _____

David L. Hough says on www.soundrider.com/archive/safety-skills/crash_padding-pt1.htm, "Serious riders spend a lot of time on tactics for managing the risks of motorcycling. Riding a twisty road without taking a soil sample requires good cornering skills, not just dumb luck. Today's roads also have lots of booby traps that snag unwary riders, and we need to know what they look like and how to avoid them. And even if the road, the surface, or the traffic situation doesn't create problems, we also need to know how to maintain our bikes, ride with a group, carry passengers, negotiate muddy detours, and survive hazardous weather conditions. The point is, a serious rider gathers knowledge and skill to avoid accidents. What we can't avoid is the chance that sooner or later we all get our turn to crash. It just isn't possible to take all the risk out of riding. The statistics hint that a typical street rider will have one or two serious accidents in a lifetime of motorcycling. The point is, when you get your turn to crash, you'll be sliding down the road in whatever gear you decided to wear before you punched the starter button."

Face it, not everyone's head is the same size—or shape. These new helmets come with adjustable inside pads so they will fit whether your head is shaped like a football, an eggplant, or a basketball.

Helmet Safety

There's no doubt that your chances of surviving a serious accident on your bike increase if you are wearing a helmet. But that doesn't mean that everyone wants to wear one. Recent statistics show that biking in California is safer than it used to be. Deaths and injuries due to motorcycle accidents was down in 2004 from the previous year. And those stats do coincide with new state legislation requiring bikers to wear helmets.

> ### Road Closed
>
> While states across the U.S. debate whether helmets should be mandatory for riders of motorcycles, there's only one place in the world where helmets have been made illegal, and that's Pagadian City in the Philippines. They have a severe carjacking and shooting problem, and many of the criminals wear motorcycle helmets as a disguise. Now helmets are illegal. Carjackings and shooting are down, and Filipino bikers now get to ride with the wind in their hair.

But—and it's a big but—does that mean that the helmet legislation is responsible for the lower number of motorcycle deaths and injuries? The answer depends on who you ask. Some say that the helmets can take the credit. Others believe it has to do with safety classes that all bikers are now required to take.

The California Motorcyclist Safety Program has graduated 350,000 riders since 1985. Many feel that education and not legislation has resulted in the encouraging numbers, that it's not a matter of more bikers surviving accidents, but rather a matter of fewer accidents in the first place.

Jackets

It isn't like all motorcycle jackets are the same, or that one jacket fits all. Obviously, to look your best, you should choose a jacket that fits your coloring and build. In addition to normal leather, which is cowhide, jackets can also be gotten in deerskin, horsehide, and sheepskin.

Just like a sport jacket, motorcycle jackets can be bought either "off the rack" or tailored, depending on how much money you want to spend. Some mass-marketed jackets are stamped out like cookies and sewn together in a half hour.

Tailored jackets are made specifically for you, and because the material is cut to contour to your body, it will be more comfortable. Again, the other difference is price, which is to be expected.

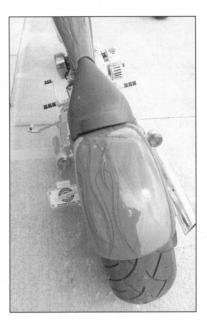

A rear view of Sonny Knighter's 2005 Legend Softail.

(Barry C. Altmark Photography)

And, like most men's fashions, they haven't changed much over the years. The jackets worn by Marlon Brando or James Dean 50 years ago would still look good today. Most prefer black, but the color is up to you—as are the number of zippers!

I realize that a lot of riders enjoy wearing denim jeans, and some prefer to wear denim jackets, but these are made of 100 percent cotton, which is cool (both in terms of temperature and style) but offer almost no protection to your skin in case there's a problem.

These Boots Are Made for Ridin'

Boots are another important part of a rider's garb. The rider has to use his feet in the balance and operation of the chopper, plus he must absorb the vibrations of the bike through his feet. Therefore, strong boots are important.

Leather boots provide better protection than fabric sports shoes. They help deflect debris, prevent burns, and will protect your feet from impact and abrasion. A stepped boot heel helps keep your feet on the pegs.

Wheelie World

And don't forget gloves. Especially in cold weather, gloves are essential, both as protection against the wind and to retain enough feeling to continue operating the controls.

Flapping Lips

An article about custom choppers from the Wild West Motor Company was called, "The Cycle Be Unbroken."

Writes boot expert David L. Hough, "Slip-on or zippered boots without laces are preferable, to avoid the hazards of a snagging your foot on a motorcycle part while reaching for the ground. Tall (11 inch or higher) boots help protect the ankles against flying stones, stinging insects, and hot exhaust pipes."

Many motorcycle boots have special features designed to keep the rider safe and comfortable. These include the following:

- Zipper flaps
- Close-fitting buckles
- Protection pads
- Oil-resistant soles
- Waterproofing to keep your feet dry

One of the best new boots is the Matrix Gore-Tex, made by Oxtar. (To order a pair check out www.fairchildsports,com.) Along with a lot of X's in their name, these boots have felt inner soles with DuPont Cambrelle to absorb perspiration and reduce odor. Just like old baseball gloves, old riding boots take time to break in and become comfortable, but that's no longer the case. These boots come prebroken in—yet they are strong enough to be dragged on the ground. They also have a hinge at the point where your ankle meets the top of your foot.

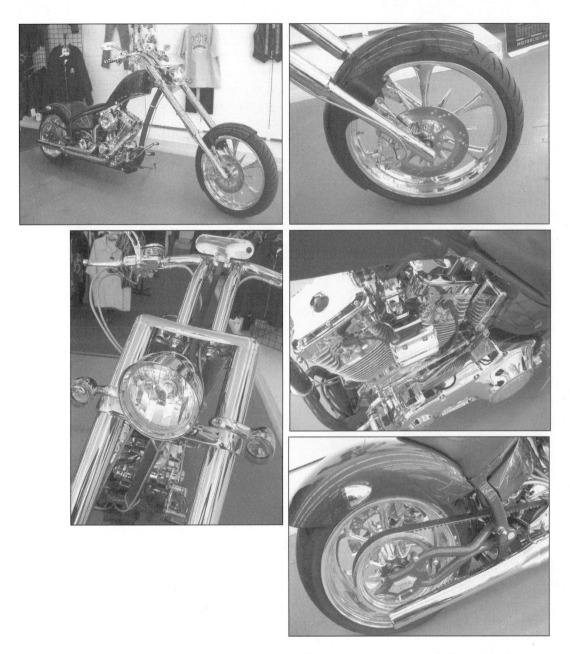

This red with flame Ultra Chopper softail belongs to Anthony J. Matano. It has a 113-cubic-inch S+S motor, a six-speed transmission, and right-side drive.

(Barry C. Altmark Photography)

An Overview of Underwear

If you go on long rides in very hot or very cold temperatures—or, if you race your chopper, you will quickly learn not to underestimate the importance of underwear. The best underwear will have the following qualities:

♦ will help keep the skin at a constant temperature;

♦ will fit snugly, not too tight or too loose;

♦ will be highly absorbent of perspiration.

The best long underwear out there is Alpinestars' Summer Tech-Race Underwear (www.alpinestars.com). This is probably too much technology for the bulk of riders, but if you are the sort who puts your body to the test and think of rides in terms of endurance, then these are the skivvies for you. The lightweight underwear consists of a lightweight, long-sleeve pullover and three-panel bottoms, which are woven from synthetic Lycra and feature flat seams for reduced friction (less chafing) and a compression to minimize fatigue.

Knights of the Open Road

For those who fear a wreck, or who have been in a wreck and don't want to go through the pain again, there is body armor that can be worn to protect the parts of your body most apt to be worn away if they unexpectedly are asked to function as a brake pad.

In the summertime, armor is prohibitively hot, but in the winter it has the advantage of providing another layer of protection against the relentless wind. Body armor is essential of you plan to race a bike, of course—and it is the reason that so many racers get up and walk away after horrendous wipe-outs sending them skidding over hundreds of yards of pavement.

def•i•ni•tion

Viscoelastic, the inner material in high-tech riding armor, is a flexible foam that stiffens upon impact to absorb energy.

Armor comes in a vest, which protects the upper torso, elbow and leg guards, and shoulder-pads not dissimilar to those worn by football players. State-of-the-art armor is made out of flexible *viscoelastic*. The outer shell of the armor is made of resin and is superhard.

Huh? Whadja Say?

You probably know that riding a chopper can be tough on your butt. And it must have occurred to you that bikers wear those boots for a reason. But, if you have never gone on a long ride on a motorcycle without wearing a helmet, then it may not have occurred to you that one of the body parts that takes the toughest pounding is your ears.

You know how you put your ear to a shell at the beach and you can hear the sound of the ocean? Well, ride a bike for more than a couple of miles and you can hear the sound of a Category 4 hurricane in your shell-like ears.

Some bikers say, "You get used to it." Others feel that ear protection is important—not just because all of that wind in your ears can get uncomfortable, but it will, temporarily, at least, make it harder to hear even after you've stopped.

The best earplugs out there today are Insta-molds, made by E.A.R., Inc (www.EarInc.com). They not only mold themselves to the shape of your inner ear, providing a tissue-to-tissue fit, but these silicone earplugs are also nonshrinkable and hypoallergenic.

In some cases a mold is made of your inner ear, and then earplugs are made specifically to fit you. The earplugs are soft, and have what are called *acoustical filters*.

In the past, custom-made earplugs were comfortable enough at first but they got on your nerves over time, because the fit was imperfect and they always seemed to expand and create pressure after being in your ear for a while. Now, thanks to modern technology, earplugs remain comfortable over the long haul. Plus, they come in a wide variety of colors.

def•i•ni•tion

Acoustical filters screen out high-pitched impulse noises, such as that of the wind in your ears during a long ride, yet somehow, magically, they allow for voice communication.

Head to Toe

So that's the deal. The idea is to ride, have fun, and feel free. And for some riders anyway, that means the freedom to not worry about personal safety while riding new roads when every turn and hill represents a mystery.

A wisely outfitted chopper rider will be looking good and be safe, covered in materials that represent a second, tougher skin, one that won't be so quick to wear away if unexpectedly confronted with the friction of 60 mph against blacktop.

The Least You Need to Know

◆ Nobody wants to wear a helmet, but it sure comes in handy when you land on your head!

◆ If you have to wear a denim vest because you are in a club, wear it over your leather jacket.

◆ Leather boots are preferable to any other kind of footwear when riding a chopper.

◆ Biker gear represents a second, tougher skin for the rider and passenger.

Part 5

Chopper Culture

The world of choppers is more than just a group of individuals who ride custom motorcycles. It's a whole culture, a whole way of life. In this part, I tell you about some of the coolest places to ride so that you can get together with others who share your obsession. Due to the rise in popularity of choppers and motorcycles in general, there are more festivals, rallies, and shows than ever before, so here's your guide if you're planning a chopper getaway.

If you're having trouble finding a chopper shop near you, there's a chapter that lists the location and attributes of a smattering of chopper shops from coast to coast. This section will be of interest to everyone, because the shops are so different.

Finally, we scan the world in search of clubs you can join and museums you can visit. Again, this information will be of interest to everyone who likes choppers, not just owners or builders.

Chapter 16

Choppers Are Different

In This Chapter

- ◆ Forget about blending in
- ◆ Social ramifications
- ◆ Crystal-ball time
- ◆ Disney World for bikers

Some people find comfort in blending in. They like to look and act just about the same as everyone around them. If no one notices them, that is okay with them. If you ride a chopper, you can forget about blending in.

If you are an experienced rider used to factory-built bikes, you need to remember that many aspects of your biking world will change when you switch to a chopper. You have decided to make a bold move. You have decided to stand out in the pack. You're the different guy. Maybe you're a really different gal.

Anyway, this chapter is about being someone who rides a chopper. It's about being a little different.

Effects of Customization

Chopper critics say that customization has a purely negative effect on a bike. Others say the effects of customization are equally positive and negative. Then there are folks like me. I think the effects of customization are 100% positive. As far as I'm concerned, every bike customization, as long as it is done by someone who knows what he or she is doing, is an upgrade.

> **Road Closed** _____
>
> When you ride a chopper, you will be noticed by those who love, admire, and respect your chopper. You will also be noticed by those who disapprove, and hate your chopper. And the latter group, I'll guarantee you, will come from both inside and outside the biker community.

I'm not the right guy to ask the pros and cons of owning a chopper, as opposed to, say, a stock factory bike—or an SUV, for that matter. That's because I can't think of any cons. Only pros. Anything you can do on a stock bike, you can do on a chopper.

Some may say that a chopper is not practical. I think practicality is different for each individual. What do people think is practical? Hauling bales of pine straw from your local home improvement store? Can't do that on any motorcycle. Cross-country riding? I would take one of my choppers for a coast-to-coaster and not think twice about it.

Your New Crowd

Some of the biggest changes created by your move to a chopper are social. You are apt to be hanging around with a new crowd made up of chopper enthusiasts. I think there are three types of bikers.

> **Wheelie World** _____
>
> Even in the biker community, custom bike builders tend to be the people who stray furthest from the norm, often in every possible way. Some dare to be different. Others don't have much choice. They just are different. They range from recently graduated high school kids to radiologists. The only thing they have in common is that they want to do it themselves.

The first group of people who venture to buy a motorcycle, whatever it is, tend to live life to the fullest. Stock Harley owners are those people who enjoy the camaraderie between riders and for the pleasure of riding.

Another type of person seems drawn to the store-bought custom market such as Big Dog or American IronHorse. These riders want instant gratification. They don't care how a motorcycle is built. They are only concerned with the quality of the ride. They have signed the dotted line and are ready to hit the road in style.

Then there is the third group, and this is the group I tend to see eye-to-eye with. They are custom bike builders. These guys and gals know every inch of their bikes. If their bike breaks down, they have no one to blame but themselves.

The third group likes to do everything with their own two hands, and they don't want anyone to tell them how to do it. (With the exception of the times, usually at around one o'clock in the morning, when they call me up because they can't figure out how to do something.)

These three groups may have different traits, but they all share a passion. The proof is in the surefire nods of approval you see as they pass each other on the road.

Rules Are Rules

Another thing you have to be aware of now that you are a chopper rider is that, yes, everyone will be looking at you, and that includes the brave members of law enforcement, many of whom consider a chopper a crime in general.

Celebrity Bio

Mike and Paula Stafford have owned and operated MGS Custom Bikes in Lancaster, California, since 2000. Known for quality work and slick designs, the Staffords work out of a 3,000-square-foot space where they produce, on the average, two choppers per month. Their workspace is divided up equally between assembly and showroom space, and includes the world's best fabrication equipment.

That said, there are a lot of laws that may affect the legality of your chopper. Also remember, you not only have to be in compliance with the laws of the state in which you live, but you also have to comply with the laws of all the states you ride through.

The laws regarding choppers can be funny. Not necessarily ha-ha funny. They are enforced according to their letter rather than their intent.

The Pimp and the Letter of the Law

Here's an example of a bike I built that was actually safer than its legal counterpart, but I kept getting tickets when riding it because the law had never taken my advancement into consideration.

The Pimp was built upon a custom drop-seat frame called the Spoon-Style Rigid.

(Precious Metal Customs)

def•i•ni•tion

The **Spoon and Scoop** drop-seat frame is called that because the neck is stretched up and out, leading the arching backbone to drop down into the seat pan. In other words, the seat scoops up under your butt and spoons it like Jell-O.

The bike, which was featured in *Street Chopper* magazine, was called the Pimp. I started out by building a custom drop-seat frame called the *Spoon and Scoop*.

The only real sheet metal on the bike was the gas tank, which needed to fit the size of the bike but still look good and flow with the frame's high backbone. I started to pound out the shape for the sides of the tank to have a concave look but a round, high back. The top had the same flow with just slightly rounded edges.

The Pimp's tank offered a challenge. It needed to fit the shape of the bike but still look good and flow with the frame's high backbone.

(Precious Metal Customs)

I then dropped the back of the tank down to the seat pan and trimmed the front panels in toward the top of the motor. I didn't like the design, but some of the guys in the shop did. I left it alone and hoped it would start to grow on me as I went to work on the motor and transmission.

On the Pimp, I used a 100-cubic-inch RevTech motor with a Mikuni carburetor and a set of Wicked Brothers pipes.

(Precious Metal Customs)

I used a 100-cubic-inch RevTech motor with a Mikuni carburetor and a set of Wicked Brothers pipes. I added a fully polished six-speed Baker transmission. At the same time, a BDL 3-inch primary drive was bolted to both.

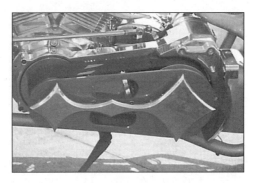

The Pimp's primary drive was a BDL 3-inch.

(Precious Metal Customs)

I then bolted up a 73 mm Mean Street front end with a set of 5-degree trees and 20-over tubes. By this time, I had decided I liked the gas tank. Now here comes the part where I got in trouble with the laws of the land.

The Perfect Rearview

I took a long look at my new bike and decided that I didn't want to clutter up its clean lines with anything that protruded, like, for example, rearview mirrors. So I had a better idea.

The LCD screen I mounted in the top of the gas tank offered a better rear view than if I had used mirrors.

(Precious Metal Customs)

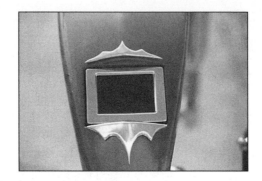

I installed a small camera on the back of the chopper and an LCD screen in the gas tank, so that a quick glance down offered a perfect rear view—in fact, a better rear view than would have been offered had I used mirrors. I figured that this was not only legal, it was better than legal.

Close-up of the Pimp's swingarm.

(Precious Metal Customs)

I put on wheels from Xtreme Machine. I let painters at Flashback do the paint job for me. They started with a champagne basecoat, then added tangelo graphics that looked like a cheetah fur coat, like a pimp might wear. Thus the name of the bike.

The seat had to flow with the paint so I made a snakeskin-covered seat to fit the drop pan.

(Precious Metal Customs)

I finished the bike off with a set of hand-carved billet blades added to the frame along the downtube and added spikes on anything I could. The seat had to flow with the paint, so I made a snakeskin-covered seat to fit the drop pan.

I finished the bike off with a set of hand-carved billet blades added to the frame along the downtube.

(Precious Metal Customs)

Three Tickets in One Week

I had it done just in time for Bike Week in Daytona. I hadn't been on the road with the Pimp for more than a few minutes when I was pulled over. I got a ticket. No mirrors. I explained the system I had put in. Didn't matter.

Hey, where's the rearview mirror, son?

(Precious Metal Customs)

The law says that you have to have a mirror. I picked up three tickets in the first week and eventually installed a small mirror on the handlebars, but I really think they should change the law. It's the rear view that is mandatory, not the mirrors!

Riding in Europe

We've learned that riding across this great land of ours means knowing state laws and how they apply to the chopper you are straddling. Well not everyone limits their riding experience to the United States—or to North America, for that matter. Some riders ship their choppers over to Europe and ride those wild, winding roads.

Wheelie World _____

Chopper builder Dave Finn, of Dave Finn Motorcycles in Tappan, New York got his first taste of fame when he was featured in *American Iron* magazine and then built that magazine's official custom for the 2005 Daytona Bike Week. But Finn didn't really feel famous until he got a call from the production manager of Saturday Night Live. Lindsay Lohan was hosting and, in one skit, they wanted her to straddle a chopper. Could he supply one? Finn not only said yes, he said he would be willing to ride the bike down to the City and deliver it in person! You can imagine Finn's disappointment when he got a call that Saturday saying that the show was running long and the chopper skit had been cut. Too bad. The sight of Herbie the Love Bug's pal in biker babe duds would have sent ratings through the roof. Don't feel too sorry for Dave, though. Soon thereafter he got another call, this time from Saks Fifth Avenue. They wanted one of their holiday windows to feature Santa on a chopper. This time the deal went off without a hitch and the chopper looked great with jingle bells tied on.

One of the toughest adjustments to make when riding in Europe is using the left-hand side of the road. It takes a while before your instincts stop screaming that everything is backward. After a while, though, you get used to it.

Roundabouts

Another adjustment is that there are far fewer stop signs and traffic signals in Europe. At major intersections, instead of a stop-and-go traffic pattern, there is a roundabout, what we call a traffic circle.

Everybody enters the circle and travels counterclockwise; when you get to the street you want, you pull off the circle and are on your way. If you are going straight you go around half of the circle. A right-hand turn means going around three quarters of the circle. A left hand turn is a quick one quarter trip around. A U-turn means traveling all the way around the circle and exiting at the same place you got on.

Road Closed

Since European countries are smaller than our nation, you can travel through nine, ten countries in a single trip. Be aware that almost all of the major highways (autoroutes, they are called) are toll roads. That's not a problem if you are not in a hurry to get where you are going and are willing to take the scenic route. But, the second you feel any deadline pressure at all, you'll want to hit the autoroute, and that means shelling out the change. The good thing about the autoroutes, though, is the lack of speed limit. They are finely kept roads and you have to go 80 mph just to keep from getting trampled in the stampede!

Oil Slicks

One major safety concern in Europe is oil slicks. They are far more common on roads over there than they are here, and they are particularly common at toll booths and border crossings, where there is a lot of stop-and-go driving. Be careful when starting and stopping, especially when you put your foot down.

Tollbooths in Europe are also more chaotic than the American version of the same. As many as 25 tollbooths can be working simultaneously, and all of those lanes have to merge. You'll feel like you need eyes in the back of your head. Proceed cautiously and make sure your neck is on a well-oiled swivel.

Flapping Lips

According to biker Donny Petersen, who had ridden many thousands of miles in Europe, "Once you learn some riding guidelines, traveling Europe becomes the ride of a lifetime. Europe has some of the best and safest riding in the world. History with varying cultures is everywhere in this fascinating continent."

Have Fun, Be Safe

I'm not much of a preacher, and I don't want to waste your time with a lot of things you've already heard (don't drink and drive, wear a helmet, and so on). But I will say, I don't want to lose any more friends to motorcycle accidents that could have been avoided.

I think that there is nothing more fun than riding around on a chopper, but the fun is over if someone gets hurt. So, to keep it simple, have fun but be safe. If you aren't being safe, well, you know who you are ….

A Look into the Crystal Ball

As I gaze into the crystal ball to predict the future of choppers, I see choppers becoming increasingly mainstream. They will be ridden not just by so-called "bikers," but by everyone from schoolteachers to scientists.

There are some concrete indications that my prediction is correct. Down in Daytona Beach, where annual biker festivals have already turned the town into a motorcycle Mecca, there are plans for a—get this—biker theme park!

Destination Daytona

The 150-acre complex will be known as Destination Daytona. It is still in the planning stages, but developers say that it will eventually include the following:

- Condominiums

- Hotel rooms

- A Harley-Davidson dealership

- A motorcycle maintenance school

- A parts shop

- Restaurants (The kids will say: "Can we go to Chucky Choppers? Can we? Can we? Can we?")

- Bars (The dads will say, "Can we go to the Thirsty Hog? Can we? Can we? Can we?)

- A civic center

The complex is going to cost $50 million and is the brainchild of Harley-Davidson dealership owner Bruce Rossmyer. According to an Associated Press report, "He plans to fly customers to Daytona Beach, put them up at a hotel at Destination Daytona, feed them, sell them bikes, take them to St. Augustine or Walt Disney World, and then fly them back. Several days later their Harleys would be delivered to their homes."

The Harley-Davidson dealership in Daytona Beach is already one of the largest in the world.

(Daytona Beach Area Convention and Visitors Bureau)

Changing Demographics

A generation ago, such a thing as a biker theme park would have been unheard of. A biker bar, yes—but a theme park? No way. But today the world of motorcycles is attracting a different crowd. They are richer, older, and increasingly coed.

Today, biking is more of a family affair, a tradition passed on from father to son.

(Daytona Beach Area Convention and Visitors Bureau)

Because of this, many motorcycle enthusiasts don't feel like they fit in at the bike fests as they exist now. (They want to stay in something slightly more solid than a tent, for example.) Destination Daytona would be the first complex to cater to the new generation of bikers.

Flapping Lips

One of the stores that will open at the new theme park is J&P Cycles, owned by John Parham. John says, "People have more discretionary income and want to enjoy their motorcycles and want to enjoy their nice hotel and aren't afraid to spend money to do that."

A chopper car?

(Andy Wyzga)

Motorcycle journalist Jim Betlach says, "This is like, if not a Fantasyland, a Disneyland for motorcycle enthusiasts."

Says Bruce Rossmyer: "Today, it's like doctors and attorneys. They come out. They don't shave for a week. They've got their pressed jeans and Gucci shoes and they think they're bikers. But they're out having fun."

An in-line bike?

(Andy Wyzga)

Swami Russ says, "That might not be the future, but it sure might be your future!"

The Least You Need to Know

♦ Beware that, when riding a chopper, your days of blending in are over—everyone will look at you, including those who do not approve of your chopper or your lifestyle.

♦ I built a chopper that obeyed the spirit but not the letter of the law. I got a fistful of tickets anyway.

♦ The 150-acre complex known as Destination Daytona will be Disney World for bikers.

♦ In the future, the world of choppers will become increasingly mainstream.

Chapter 17

Festivals, Rallies, and Shows

In This Chapter

♦ Granddaddy

♦ Rallies for all seasons

♦ Runnin' from coast to coast

♦ Checking out the greatest choppers

If you are like many bikers, you want to plan your vacations around biker rallies and shows. Here's a guide to help you set your schedule.

Sturgis

The Sturgis Motorcycle Rally, held in Sturgis, South Dakota, is known as the "Granddaddy of Them All." Folks have been riding their bikes to South Dakota almost as long as there have been bikes. There aren't too many people around who remember the first one.

The first Sturgis Rally was held in 1938. It was known as the Black Hills Classic back then. J. Clarence Hoel, known as Pappy, came up with the idea and the three-year-old Jackpine Gypsies Motorcycle Club made the run. The first race was held on August 14. Nine bikes raced, and spectators were few.

In 1940, the Black Hills Motor Classic incorporated, and the event was professionally organized and promoted for the first time. There was no rally in 1942 because of World War II and the gasoline rations. By 1949, the rally had grown so large that, for the first time, Main Street in Sturgis had to be blocked off from nonrally traffic.

Celebrity Bio

The founder of the Sturgis Motorcycle Rally was the legendary J. Clarence "Pappy" Hoel. Pappy got into the motorcycle business in 1936 when he purchased an Indian Motorcycle Company franchise.

Innovations

In 1961, the Jackpine Gypsies lent their own innovations to the proceedings by introducing the Hill Climb and the Motocross race. In 1963, the rally first became a three-day event. In 1964, it was decreed that a portion of Main Street would be blocked off for the entire length of the rally, and in 1965 that lengthened to five days.

In 1975, the event lengthened again, this time to a full seven days. Not that the rally wasn't always rambunctious, but, by 1983, the rally was beginning to get a rowdy reputation. That was the year that Sturgis' City Park was closed to camping because of repeated fire outbreaks.

Wheelie World

In 1974, the first temporary vendor was set up in the Sturgis Auditorium. People who made their living in motorcycles saw Sturgis as an excellent opportunity to show off their wares. By 1979, when the city of Sturgis began to license the vendors at the rally, there were nine licenses issued. That number has increased every year since. By 1988, the number was up to 117.

A Major City

In 1989, the proceedings were saddened by news of the death of Pappy Hoel, who was 85. The following year "Sturgis Rally and Races" was formed to organize and promote future events. In 1995, Sturgis Rally and Races was replaced as the sanctioning organization by Champion Rally Productions. By the year 2000, a record 600,000 were showing up for the rally. Sturgis was a town most of the year, but during the rally, it was a major city—certainly the largest city in the state of South Dakota.

In 2002, the city of Sturgis formed a department within its government to take the place of all prior contract labor hired to promote and organize the Sturgis Rally. In 2003, the name of the event was officially proclaimed to be the Sturgis Motorcycle Rally.

Old School Shovel Tour

One popular gathering spot in Sturgis is the Broken Spoke Saloon. Each year the saloon is the site of the S&S Cycle/American Iron Old School Shovel Tour. Five chopper builders are invited to build any style bike they like.

The only rules are they have to use the S&S 93 cubic inch shovel engine, have a functional kickstart, and use no more than $20,000 in retail parts. In 2005, the builders were Paul Cox and Keino of Indian Larry Legacy, Jesse Rooke of Rooke Customs, Chica of Chica Custom Cycles, Big Mike of BMC Choppers, and Kevin Alsop of Big Bear Choppers.

Wheelie World

The Sturgis Rally always starts on the first Monday after the first full weekend in August.

Endorsed by the King (No, Not Elvis)

Sturgis doesn't need celebrity endorsements, but gets them nonetheless, more often than not in actions rather than words. In 2005, for example, "King of the Choppers" Arlen Ness celebrated his 34th consecutive year at Sturgis by bringing 15 of his best choppers for his fans to gawk at.

Of course, Sturgis isn't just for choppers, but many of its shows and contests are for choppers and other customs. Annual awards are given out for the best, Radical Rigid Chopper, Rigid Chopper, Radical Softail Chopper, Custom Softail Chopper, Softail Chopper, and Sportster Chopper.

Today

Sturgis remains the most beautiful place in the world to just ride around and look at the view. At Sturgis, there are 21 desirable destinations to ride to and back. They range from the Full Throttle Saloon, which is only 3 miles from downtown Sturgis, to a run to Hot Springs, which is 84 miles away.

Sturgis is a rally well attuned to the twenty-first century. Today, they are using a digital approach to lure motorcycle enthusiasts to South Dakota from around the world. TDG Communications, Inc. is in charge of spreading the message.

For more info, visit www.sturgismotorcyclerally.com. Phone 605-720-0800, or write The City of Sturgis Rally Department/2030 Main Street/Sturgis, SD 57785. The 2005 rally was the sixty-fifth annual.

V-Twin Expo, Cincinnati

This is a big bike show, held annually three days in late January or early February. The show is sponsored by Easyriders and held in the Cinergy Convention Center in Cincinnati, Ohio. For more info, visit www.vtwin-expo.com.

To be a bona-fide dealer/retailer at this event, you need two forms of proper ID (proper meaning retail business license, vendor's permit, resale license, paycheck stub, W2 form, or business card). Those interested in reserving exhibit space for upcoming V-Twin Expos should log on to www.vtwin-expo@reactionmanagementinc.com.

def•i•ni•tion

The V-Twin was a popular powerplant in the early days of motorcycles. The motor's two cylinders were built in a *V* shape to fit in the bicycle-style frames of the day. The prototype of the V-Twin was built in conjunction by Harley and the Davidson brothers in 1907. Not all V-Twins are perfect. According to the editors of *Motorcyclist* magazine, "Some designs, like Harley-Davidson's 45-degree V-twin, vibrate excessively. Some Harley touring models … compensate for that vibration with elaborate rubber mounting systems … The reason [for the vibration] involves the crankshaft design used in all Harley V-twins, but the vibration is also caused by the narrow angle of the V."

Bike Week

Ahhhh, 10 days in March in Daytona! Bike Week is a celebration of the joy of motorcycling. One of the highlights of Bike Week is the Rats Hole Chopper Show, where the best chopper builders in the United States show off their hottest new bikes.

There's a contest for chopper builders, and the winner gets sent to Germany to compete against the best chopper builders in the world.

Contact the Daytona Beach Area Convention & Visitors Bureau or e-mail info@daytonabeach.com for more info.

Bike Week in Daytona. So many bikes in need of a good chopping!

(Daytona Beach Area Convention and Visitors Bureau)

Fans mull around a show chopper in Daytona.

(Andy Wyzga)

Bikers' Ball

The 2006 Bike Week in Daytona will be held from March 8 through 11. On the final day of that party, a "V-Twin Biker's Ball" will be held to raise money for charity. The cost of a ticket is $225 per person.

According to the ball's publicity material, the price of admission enables you to "rub elbows with master bike builders and industry icons, and raise money for the Boys and Girls Club of Broward County. Join us for police-escorted rides to one-of-a-kind places, four-star meals, and ride your bike around the world-famous Daytona International Speedway." There also a charity auction and an awards banquet at the Plaza Resort and Spa.

Laughlin River Run

The Laughlin River Run in Laughlin, Nevada, is five days in April. The event has been held annually since 1983. Because Laughlin is a hop, skip, and a jump from Las Vegas, there's an endless variety of places to stay and things to do between events. And the run itself features stunt shows, freak shows, and beautiful creature shows.

Wheelie World

For more info on the Laughlin River Run, visit www. laughlinriverrun.com.

There are retro but hot concerts. Recent performing acts include Steppen "Born To Be Wild" Wolf, Styx, and Eddie Money. And finally, for all you guys who can whistle the loudest, there's a Ms. River Run Contest.

The Heritage

The Heritage Motorcycle Rally is held annually at the Exchange Park Fairgrounds in Charleston, South Carolina. It lasts 10 days in the spring. A newcomer on the list, it has been held since 2003.

Flapping Lips

On why he prefers to sleep in his bike hauler/ camper in a campgrounds when he goes to bike shows rather than get a room in a motel, Dave Green of Ontario, Canada, says, "Campground dwellers tend to be more social. There's always someone dropping by to say hello at the campgrounds. At a motel, once you close the door, you're done."

The Heritage Rally has been called "the wildest bike show in the South." Features include stunt shows and a $125,000 Bike Build-Off contest. As this was written, this rally could get away with calling itself the "newest national rally in the United States," a claim one can only make until a newer one comes along, which usually comes sooner than later.

Featured events are the bike build-off, a drag race, and a special old-school show. There is easy access from camp sites, and exhibits by lots of local bike shops. Contact www.heritagemotorcyclerally.com for more info.

Myrtle Beach Bike Week

Held annually, 10 days in May, the Myrtle Beach Bike Week in Myrtle Beach, South Carolina, has been called "the Carolinas and Mid-Atlantic greatest motorcycle event." Put on by Chopper Road Shows and Sonny Productions, the Myrtle Beach get-together even boasts that it's the "third largest motorcycle rally in the United States." Many of the top shops go all-out to get their hottest new custom bikes ready for the Myrtle Beach show.

There are concerts. This rally doesn't always get the biggest names, but you can count on a biker theme, such as last year's entertainment, Joey J and the Shovelheads. (Autographed copies of Joey J's single "Open Road" were available.) For more info about the Myrtle Beach Bike Week, visit www. myrtlebeachbikeweek.com.

Laconia

The Laconia Motorcycle Rally and Race Week, in Laconia, New Hampshire, is nine days each June. The 2006 event will be the eighty-third annual. This event is the home of the "Biker's Ball and Vintage Reunion Riders Dinner," which is such a feast that it fills the Winnipesauke Expo Center. Proceeds go to a local children's charity.

Each year you can purchase a DVD of highlights from the previous year's Rally and Race Week. A lot of people buy it to see if they're on it. For more info, visit www.laconiamcweek.com. Phone 603-366-2000, or write Laconia Motorcycle Rally and Race Week/P.O. Box 5399/Laconia, NH 03247, or, if you're surfing, go to www. laconiamcweek.com.

Wheelie World

Laconia gets great concerts. Lynyrd Skynyrd and the Marshall Tucker Band have played.

Every June the biker world gathers in Laconia, New Hampshire.

(Andy Wyzga)

The strip at Laconia.

(Andy Wyzga)

Bikers from the Northeast love the fact that, for nine days in June, the world comes to them.

(Andy Wyzga)

Las Vegas Bikefest

The advantages of going to a bike rally in Las Vegas need not be explained. An article about this rally in the February 2005 issue of *Hod Rod Bikes* magazine was called "Sin City Overload," which gives you bit of an idea what it is like there.

That magazine has its own display at this Bikefest, which they call "Artistry in Iron." In addition to professional displays, there are the thousands of bikes you can check out just because they're parked next to yours—right down the middle of the walk on Freemont Street.

Flapping Lips

In 2004, the top bike award was given by the magazine to Roger Goldammer's BTR3. According to motorcycle journalist Brian Moore, "The winner was a flashy retro board tracker that mixed vintage looks with cutting-edge technology."

Biketoberfest®

Biketoberfest® lasts four days in October. Bike Week is the big spring break get-together, and this is the autumn shindig, the second major highlight of Daytona's year-long celebration of the joy of motorcycling.

Biketoberfest® in Daytona is where it's happening.

(Daytona Beach Area Convention and Visitors Bureau)

The event started in 1992, and has been held every year since. It's been known by its current name since 1993. That year 15,000 bikers attended and pumped more than $4.5 million into the Daytona Beach economy. By 1995, the number of visitors had risen to 43,000. By 1996, there were more than 300 activities on the schedule, and the event had spread out so that it now involved two Florida counties, Volusia and St. Johns.

A custom bagger draws stares in Daytona.

(Andy Wyzga)

By 1997, the event had been named one of the top 25 annual events in Southeastern Tourism. In 1998, the fest received a tremendous boost because it was scheduled to coincide with the Pepsi 400 NASCAR event at the Daytona International Speedway. That was the same year that Biketoberfest® received a visit from Evel Kneivel.

In 1999, attendance was up to 75,000. Discovery Channel stars the Teutuls and Jesse James were guests in 2003, and in 2004, for the first time, the number of bikers heading into Daytona for the fest surpassed 100,000. Every year, there are rides, shows, concerts, and more. There's a huge party hosted by the American Legion called the "Legion Riders Blast."

All the saloons in the area host big parties with music. The major motorcycle apparel companies have giveaways. Contact the Daytona Beach Area Convention & Visitors Bureau or e-mail info@daytonabeach.com for more info.

> **Flapping Lips**
>
> "There's a little biker in all of us!"—Official motto of Biketoberfest®

> **Celebrity Bio**
>
> The "Mother of Biketoberfest®" is Daytona Beach native, Janey Kersey, who was hired years ago as director of tourism events and promotions by the Daytona Beach Area Convention and Visitors Bureau. Her first job was to find a way to get tourists to come to Daytona Beach during off-season periods. Her solution, in October 1992, was what was then called the "Daytona Fall Tour."

Steel Pony

The Steel Pony Express Rally in New Orleans, Louisiana, is held annually at the University of New Orleans Arena Grounds during the last weekend of October. Attendance is usually around 70,000, with more than 300 vendors. The rally is also known for its music. Lynyrd Skynyrd and Blood, Sweat, and Tears played at the 2004 rally.

The 2006 Steel Pony Express Rally figures to be the biggest and best one yet. It is scheduled for October 26–29, 2006.

Other talent that regularly perform at this rally are stunt riders Team X-Treem, and Walton & Johnson, who perform annually as the "Steel

> **Road Closed**
>
> Don't make the mistake of thinking of New Orleans as a fall destination only. The Steel Pony Express people also sanction a spring show, held in late April or early May. The show is known as the Louisiana Bike Expo and is held in the Louisiana Superdome.

Stallions." For more information, contact Scooter Promotions, P.O. Box 8407/ Metairie, LA 70011, or call 504-362-7434.

Easyriders **Rodeo**

Easyriders magazine sponsors this touring bike show. The show features rodeo action, motorcycle exhibits, weekend camping, a ride-in bike show, trophy girl contest, and barstool races (and all that implies).

Road Closed _____

Absotively, posilutely, no kids at the *Easyriders* Rodeo Tour. No teenagers either. Adult visitors are invited to be themselves. Therefore, no one under 18 will be allowed in.

At the moment, the tour hits North Carolina, Pennsylvania, Kentucky, Ohio, and Michigan—but it is getting bigger every year. Check out www.easyridersevents.com to see if the rodeo is coming to a town near you.

The Ultra Chopper So-Cal pro-street bike has an S+S motor that displaces 113 cubic inches, a silver-with-blue-flames paint job, a softail suspension, a 42-degree rake, and a six-speed transmission.

(Barry C. Altmark Photography)

Friday the Thirteenth Parties

If you are from Canada or from the Great Lakes region of the United States, you might want to check out the Friday the Thirteenth parties, held in a small fishing town called Port Dover, Ontario, on the northeastern shore of Lake Erie.

To find out when the next one is, just check your calendar. They are held every Friday the thirteenth. They close down Port Dover's Main Street to all traffic except motorcycles, and it is said that the party rivals any biker get-together found in the United States.

Word to the wise: if you do have to cross the border to get to the Port Dover party, be polite and serious with the guys at the border. As is true when going through security procedures at an airport, there are no senses of humor. If you are a joker, the border patrol will find a way to inconvenience you.

Tornado Rally, Wichita

In June 2005 the very first Tornado Rally was held in Wichita, Kansas, and it was a tremendous success. The rally was held at one of the state's largest bike stores, Big Dog Motorcycles. Big Dog's marketing director Paul Hansen said, "When developing this new rally our ultimate goals were to promote the city, to show the motorcycle community our home, and to thank Wichita for its continued support through the excellent exposure this annual rally could bring. And the event was phenomenal! The support from the city government was also excellent. With all of this support, next year's Tornado Rally (scheduled for June 10–11, 2006) should be even better!"

About 15,000 people attended the event, most from Kansas, but many from other parts of the country as well. The furthest trip was made by a biker from Alaska. It was estimated that there were 4,000 bikes there, and they represented every style and make imaginable. Naturally, there were plenty of choppers.

Rolling Thunder

Rolling Thunder isn't a wild party but a solemn remembrance. Each year during the Memorial Day weekend motorcyclists gather in Washington D.C. and ride to The Wall, the Vietnam War memorial, to honor the almost 100,000 Americans who are still unaccounted for from World War I, World War II, Korea, the Vietnam War, the Gulf War, Afghanistan, and Iraq.

The procession, which in 2005 attracted an estimated 175,000 riders, begins in The Pentagon's parking lot and is led by the motorcycle club known as the Nam Knights. Along with the Wall, the ride also stops at Arlington National Cemetery, where there are 220,000 veterans buried.

Up on Cripple Creek

Another patriotic biker get-together is the Salute to American Veterans Rally, held each August in the small Colorado town of Cripple Creek. It began in 1987 and currently boasts of being the seventh largest biker event in the United States.

The Cripple Creek rally is always held the weekend after Sturgis, so it's a place to go for those who don't want to go home after that long, and sometimes lost, weekend. Colorado doesn't have a helmet law, and riding through the Rocky Mountains is beautiful.

There's a VIP banquet, and each year a notable veteran is a guest speaker. Military bigwigs often attend. Two kinds of choppers are plentiful at the Cripple Creek Rally. In addition to the motorcycles, military helicopters can frequently be seen, shuttling VIP guests in and out.

There is 14-mile parade with 5,000 motorcycles going from Denver to Cripple Creek, with cheering supporters lining the road the whole way. Both the Marines and the Army provide flyovers during the parade and the ceremonies that follow it. For more information about Cripple Creek visit www.pro-promotions.com.

Dealer Shows

Not all chopper builders and dealers are mom and pop shops like mine. Your bigger chopper manufacturers will behave like the makers of stock bikes in that they will hold annual shows to debut their new models.

It's called a dealer show because it is hoped that motorcycle dealers from across North America will attend the show, be impressed, and order zillions of the new models to sell in their showrooms.

At dealer shows the press is invited, and the hopes are that photos of the debutante bikes making their public debut will appear on TV, in

Road Closed

These being attractions for bikers, a huge party inevitably develops and, here and there, young women have trouble keeping their shirts all the way on.

daily newspapers, and in the many bike magazines that you get at the newsstand. For both dealers and members of the press, test rides are available.

Because the new bikes may, by themselves, not be the kind of draw the party-givers need to draw maximum attention, motorcycle celebrities are invited to chat with visitors, sign autographs, and say a nice word or two about the new bikes on display.

One of the best annual dealer shows is the Big Dog Motorcycles Dealer Show, which in 2005 was held in Sedona, Arizona. The brand new model on display at this dealer show was the K-9. (Get it? From Big Dog Motorcycles.)

Another reason for the name of the new bike is that the K-9 has been stretched out until it's a full nine feet long. It has a 117-inch motor, a "Balanced Drive System," a six-speed transmission, and hidden shocks.

The Least You Need to Know

- The rally in Sturgis, South Dakota, is the "Granddaddy of Them All."

- The Heritage Motorcycle Rally at the Exchange Park Fairgrounds in Charleston, South Carolina, is called "the wildest bike show in the South."

- At Daytona's Bike Week, there's a contest for chopper builders, and the winner gets sent to Germany to compete against the best chopper builders in the world.

- Biketoberfest® in Daytona is a young rally but already one of the largest.

Chapter 18

Two-Wheeler Dealers: A Shop Near You

In This Chapter

◆ Teutul time

◆ My shop

◆ Both coasts, both schools

◆ Best of the aftermarket

In this chapter, we take a quick coast-to-coast review of the major shops out there that either sell completed choppers, kits for constructing choppers, or chopper parts. Hopefully, after finishing this chapter, you will have a better idea of where you want to do your future shopping.

Orange County Choppers

I begrudgingly start with the most famous chopper shop: Orange County Choppers. I have nothing against the show *American Chopper*. I like the Teutuls, and the fact that the show is so popular is good for everyone's chopper business, not just theirs. But I don't watch the show religiously.

When you spend as much time in a chopper shop as I do (I practically live in one), watching someone else build choppers isn't my idea of relaxation.

Wheelie World _____

Orange County Choppers

Founder: Paul Teutul Sr.
Chief designer/fabricator: Paul Teutul Jr.
Established: 1999
Location: Rock Tavern, New York
Employees: 20
Bikes produced annually: 150

Because of the success of the show *American Chopper* on the Discovery Channel, the Orange County Choppers shop, which is featured on the show, may be the most famous chopper shop in the country. Maybe in the world.

Orange County Choppers (OCC) isn't located in the more famous O.C. in California, but rather in the county nestled along the Hudson Valley, about 80 miles north of New York City. If you're looking for it on a map, it's in the town of Rock Tavern, New York.

Celebrity Bio

Paul Teutul Sr. is best known as the dad on the Discovery Channel's *American Chopper* program. He first got into building choppers back in the 1970s when he opened up Orange County Ironworks. It was a steel-fabrication enterprise in a small space that steadily grew until in 1999 it became Orange County Choppers, or OCC, which operated out of a large warehouse in Rock Tavern, New York, about 80 miles north of New York. By this time, Paul had his sons and many others working for him. Paul's big break came in 1999 when his chopper "True Blue" caused a fuss in Daytona. After that, the family signed on to be filmed by a crew as they built their bikes and lived their lives, like *The Osbournes* for the chopper set. Paul and his sons became instant celebrities, and have made guest appearances on many TV shows, including Jay Leno and David Letterman.

Wheelie World _____

Another signature bike to be built during the early days of the shop was called the Spider Bike, which was eventually purchased by musician Wyclef Jean of the Fugees.

Orange County Choppers, as it exists today, has only been around since 1999, but it is an offspring of a steel-fabrication shop called Orange County Ironworks, the brainchild of Paul Teutul, Sr., which had been around since the mid-1970s.

Of the early custom choppers built by OCC, the one that put the shop on the map was called True Blue. It was a classic chopper built in the basement of Paul Sr.'s house and was shown off at the 1999 Daytona Biketoberfest®.

The first OCC chopper seen by most people was the Jet Bike, which was built to honor U.S. military forces in Afghanistan. The reason that bike is so well known is that it was featured on the very first episode of *American Chopper*, which was broadcast in September 2002.

In addition to being TV darlings who have made appearances on *The Tonight Show* with Jay Leno and *The Late Show* with David Letterman, the Teutels have also received critical acclaim from less-mainstream sources, sources with unimpeachable motor-cycle savvy. In 2002, OCC was recognized by American Iron as one of the world's top 12 builders.

 **Road Closed**

If you are on a tight budget, don't even consider buying a chopper from OCC. Their choppers are among the most expensive in the world.

Celebrity Bio

Paul Teutul Jr.(a.k.a. Junior or Paulie) started helping his father in the sheet-metal business when he was 12. After graduation, he went to work for his dad full time. By the time he was an adult, he was an expert, a skill that helped him tremendously when he began to design and build choppers. Soon he was promoted to head of its railing shop. Paul Sr. became increasingly obsessed with building motorcycles for pleasure, and he "asked" his son to assist. Senior soon recognized Junior's gifts. Together they decided Junior should quit his job in the railing shop, and together they started Orange County Choppers in 1999, with Junior as the chief designer and fabricator, and with Senior lending his considerable business acumen.

For those of you—there might be a few—who have not seen the show, it centers around the tough old man, Paul Sr., who runs the shop. Among his staff are his two sons, Paul Jr., who is a major designer and builder of choppers, and lovable goofball Mikey, who answers the phones and takes out the trash.

In each episode, the father and sons quarrel and spar as fathers and sons do, while building an often patriotically themed chopper against incredible deadline pressure. The bikes are high and wide by industry standards.

Celebrity Bio

Michael Teutul, a.k.a. Mikey, the youngest son of Paul Teutul Sr., worked for his father's ironwork company during summers and part time from the age of 12 until he was 20. For a time, he moved to Arizona, where he had five jobs—bouncer, busboy, telemarketer, valet parking attendant, and "movie theater guy"—before returning home to New York State. He was working for his brother Daniel when he met Russell Muth, the man who would produce the *American Chopper* TV show. Russell could tell star appeal when he saw it. He wanted Mikey on the show and arranged for him to be hired on at OCC as the guy who answers phones and takes out the trash, not to mention the occasional popping of bubble wrap. Now that the show is so popular, Mikey's duties have expanded, and he has a staff (of two) of his own.

A Classic from OCC

If you are an avid viewer of *American Chopper*, you are familiar with the types of choppers they make. The Teutuls are into themes—that's an understatement. Here's a quick look at one of their most famous choppers.

The Spider Bike

This was designed by Paul Jr. using the patterns and colors popularized by Spiderman of comic book and motion picture fame. The gas tank is red with black web detail, all under a chromed lattice, also web shaped. Spiderman's eyes in white are painted on the side of the gas tank. The spider motif even appears on the license plate.

Even the front fender is just the skeleton of a fender, designed as chromed web. The porous nature of that fender exemplifies the design over practicality that makes the Spider Bike so innovative.

Flapping Lips

About the Spider Bike, OCC's Paul Teutul Jr. said, "I built this bike to make man, motorcycle, and spider all one."

Paulie admitted that he was not eager to sell this one. He had poured his heart and soul into it, and he didn't mind keeping it around the shop for a while so that he could glance over at it now and again. "The bike will have an owner, but we're holding on to it right now," he said.

"It started as a project between projects," Paulie said. "I started doing some spider web round bar work and soon those projects turned into a complete bike. I thought of the bike as alive, with superhero eyes staring out of the tank, ready to transform into another guise."

Love and Grief

Many fans of the American Chopper show enjoy the gruffness of Paul Sr. and the way that the Orange County Chopper workspace seems to be steadily on the verge of becoming a battleground. They remind us of ourselves and of our own families—that is, full of love and grief all at the same time.

So one of the most fascinating episodes of the show was first shown in November 2005. It was called "American Chopper: The History of O.C.C." Many had listened to Paul Sr. and Paul Jr. argue about arriving to work late or losing a tool, or something equally trivial, and figured there must be more to it than that. The arguments must have a basis in something deeper. This episode confirmed those suspicions.

Past Problems

Paul Sr., it was revealed, had had a drinking problem as a younger man when his children were young. And though the ol' man had been sober for more than 20 years, his sons remembered the times when he frequently forgot his promises.

They also recalled the time when Paul Sr. divorced their mother, and how they sided with their mother during that difficult time. Paul Sr. wasn't alone in his struggles with substance abuse. Paul Jr. revealed that he did a stint in rehab as a teenager and Mikey admitted that he, too, had spent a period of his life "getting wasted every night."

> **Flapping Lips**
>
> Referring to the father/ son squabbles that have provided so much entertainment for their fans, Paul Jr. comments, "Usually the arguments aren't what they start out to be. They end up being something more, something having nothing to do with motorcycles." For most of us, that sounds familiar, too.

The Price of Celebrity

In a recent interview in the January 2006 edition of *V-Twin Motorcycles* magazine, Paul Sr. admitted that he sometimes got tired. The success of the TV show has made him a bigger businessman with more money than he had really anticipated.

Being a celebrity has taken its toll. Seeing fans is great, but it gets harder and harder to go out in public. In 2005, when Paul and his crew went to Daytona, they caused such a fuss that they needed a police escort to get from one place or another.

OCC Mania

And, because of their celebrity, their schedule is nuts. They are like a famous band on tour, playing a seemingly never-ending series of one-night stands. They are in Daytona one day, off to Vegas for a show the next, and then down to Georgia the day after that.

Being in the shop and working on a bike is the downtime, the quiet time, even if there is some father-son bickering going on and a film crew taking in all the action. At least once a day some well-minded tourist knocks on the door to see the American Chopper crew in person.

Most of the time the people who visit are nice and it's not too much of a hassle, but Paul Sr. would prefer they didn't drop by in person unless they had serious interest in buying an Orange County Chopper.

Still, Paul Sr. acknowledged that, if he was given the choice to do whatever he wanted for his remaining days he would choose to build motorcycles. Even if he had to go back to building bikes in his basement, which was how he did it when he first began, it would be okay.

On the day of the interview he was showing off an orange bobber he had built, an ultimate old-school bike, with "hardly nothing on it." He used a repro Harley frame, with a 2004 88-inch pan/shovel motor and a RevTech five-speed transmission.

Building bikes was what made him happy. There was nothing else he wanted to do. It was a sentiment I could certainly understand.

Shopping List

The first thing Paulie did after coming up with the concept for the Spider Bike was put his head together with his dad, Paul Sr., and determine what they would have to order. Item one was a 113-cubic-inch S&S motor.

They also decided the bike needed a six-speed Baker-built transmission and a 3-inch primary belt drive. The frame is stretched. The gas tank has been stretched 5 inches to match the stretch of the frame, and there are 20-inch over-wide glide forks.

The web motif spreads over the shift lever, belt guard, handlebars, and sissy bar. The frame is a RC Components rigid. It is stretched 5 inches on the backbone, and 8 inches upward. The rake angle is 40 degrees. To create strength, the triple trees are offset from the vertical by 5 degrees.

Maybe it's me, but I can't think about how good a chopper looks unless I can imagine myself looking good while riding it. The only way to look good when riding the Spider Bike is to wear a colorful costume, mask and tights, and I don't think that's going to happen.

Big Dog Motorcycles

In January 2005, Big Dog—which employs 340 people—decided that their inner-city Wichita space wasn't big enough. President Sheldon Coleman Jr. purchased 106 acres east of the city as a location for a new plant.

Here's how your new 2005 Big Dog chopper would look just as you were straddling it for the first time.

(Barry C. Altmark Photography)

Big Dog has quickly grown since 1994 when Coleman first began to use his garage to add power and style to factory Harley-Davidsons. Estimates were that Big Dog made 5,700 motorcycles in 2005. That is 27 percent more than in 2004. That growth was expected to continue.

S+S Cycle, Inc.

S&S Cycles is headquartered in Viola, Wisconsin. This is the shop that sanctions the "Old School Tour" at the Laughlin River Run each spring. The shop was founded in 1958 by George J. Smith. The first shop, which George opened with his wife Marjorie, was in Blue Island, Illinois. They started out highly specialized, selling high-performance push-rods for Harley-Davidsons.

> **Flapping Lips**
>
> George J. Smith, the founder of S&S Cycles, had a simple motto: "I want to make all bikes go faster!"

Today that mom-and-pop shop in Illinois is one of the world's most respected shops in Wisconsin. They specialize in making the best high-performance engines and components for American V-Twins.

Biker's Dream

It's known as Biker's Dream of Colorado, and there are two shops, one in Denver and the other in Colorado Springs. The idea here is that they make your dream come true. No matter what kind of bike you need, they oversee its creation and sell it to you. The products they create range from stock performance machines to custom orders. It's a good place to go for biker garb, too.

In addition to selling great bikes, Biker's Dream serves the biker community in other ways, too. They sponsor the Tejon Street Bike Fest each year in June. In 2005, the Marshall Tucker Band played. There were 10,000 bikes and 20,000 people.

Careful when approaching a hardtail from the rear. This one has a 300 rear tire.

(Barry C. Altmark Photography)

East Coast Ironhorse

Out of Charleston, South Carolina—with an affiliate in Savannah, Georgia—East Coast Ironhorse has only been around since 1999, but today it is only one of three platinum American ironhorse dealers in America. Every Thursday night the shop presents "Bike Night" at Big Deck Daddys, a Charleston bar. There's live music, a "burn-out contest," and great food.

The shop was founded by father and son Ron and Tony Sprovero. They call themselves the "leading purveyor of high-end V-twin custom motorcycles. They make wild choppers. Perfect for bar hopping," is their motto.

West Coast Choppers

West Coast Choppers is the shop owned and operated by Jesse James, who you learned about earlier (Chapter 2) in a celebrity biography. The shop opened in the 1990s. The shop started as the ultimate small operation, but today James has an 18,000-square-foot facility, 50 employees, and sells his choppers for up to $150,000 apiece.

West Coast Choppers has built choppers for basketball star Shaquille O'Neal, singer Kid Rock, model Tyson Beckford, and Atlanta Falcons wide receiver Shawn Jefferson. With Jesse's regular appearances on the Discovery Channel, business back at the shop is booming.

Big Bear Choppers

Another California shop. Here's their pep talk to those considering designing and building their own chopper. "You are able to swap out different swingarms, different fuel and oil tanks, different fenders, and so on in your order. Design your own motorcycle!

Here's a f'rinstance when it comes to designing your own motorcycle: You just called Big Bear on your cell:

"Yes, sir, may I help you?"

"Yeah, I'd like to purchase a bike," you say. "Nothing ordinary, you understand. Start with a Venom Chopper frame with a Merc swingarm, a Merc fuel tank, a Reaper oil tank and a Merc springer front end."

"No problem."

"No, I changed my mind. I want the Sled 300 frame with a Devil's Advocate swingarm, a stretched tank, a Sled oil tank, and an inverted front end. Can you do that?"

"Yes, sir!"

It's as easy as that. We're sure you can come up with some good ideas with all the options we are throwing out at you. With 11 different frame models, three swingarm designs, five fuel tanks, five oil tanks, three front ends, custom-cut fenders, or whatever, build a custom chopper the way you see it!

American IronHorse

A chopper manufacturer, American IronHorse sells completed bikes. Their most popular model is the Texas Chopper with polished six-speed transmission, 280 mm rear tire, and a stretched front fender. Texas Chopper also has a stretched one-piece fuel tank, a skirted oil tank, custom-style grips and pegs, and proprietary controls.

The standard engine is a 111-cubic-inch S&S, but that can be upgraded to either a 117-cubic-inch or 124-cubic-inch S&S. You also have your choice of a 240 or a 280 rear tire. You choose from a number of possible graphic/paint combinations.

Choppers, Inc.

Choppers, Inc. is the shop of Billy Lane (see his bio in Chapter 2). The address is 1243 North Harbor City Boulevard, #C/, Melbourne, Florida 32935. Hours: Mon–Fri 10 A.M. to 6 P.M., Sat 12 P.M. to 5 P.M., Phone: 321-757-7262, Fax: 321-757-3117. Store/order e-mail: orders@choppersinc.com.

If you're in the area, here are the directions from I-95: exit 183/Eau Gallie Blvd. Go east 5 miles. At US-1/N., Harbor City Blvd, turn right (south). Choppers, Inc. is 2 blocks south on the left.

Custom Chrome

If you're looking for the best of the West Coast aftermarket, seek out Custom Chrome. This innovative shop started out more than 40 years ago run by four friends out of a space behind a two-car garage on West San Carlos Street in San Jose, California. The shop was opened in response to the trend toward customizing stock bikes.

The shop, originally called Coast Cycles, became one of the first aftermarkets. They simply sold custom parts and accessories at first, but after a time they began to design their own. In 1970, the name changed to Custom Chrome.

Today Custom Chrome is the world's largest independent supplier of aftermarket parts and accessories for Harley-Davidson motorcycles. How did it get so big? They say it was because they knew how to "satisfy the marketplace with unique and innovative product designs that rely upon an intensive research and development effort by our in-house staff of engineers and product specialists."

Flyrite Choppers

Do not, I repeat, *do not*, call Flyrite Choppers "old school." They prefer the term "traditional." "We are the most traditional chopper shop around," says Flyrite spokesman Marty Stillwell. "We're very much into hot rods and early-style bikes. By hot rods I don't mean street rods—flatheads and hemis. No fiberglass."

The guys at Flyrite in Austin, Texas, say, "We love motorcycles. We love building motorcycles. We ride what we build. We realize that not everyone can afford $30K+ for a custom bike, or, $20K+ for a stock one. We build bikes the way they used to be: basic, bare bones, wrench-on-it-yourself real for the real motorcycle rider. We have basic principles that we adhere to when building a bike. We use 1-inch tubing. We use springer front ends. The largest tire we offer is a 180 mm × 1 inch. No long bikes here. No twin cam engines. Six models are currently available with options to make one of them the bike you're dreaming of.

"Custom? You want a bike that nobody else has? All of our bikes are a little bit different, but if you want a true 'one-off' frame, we can do that, too. Check some of the one-off projects on the Project Bikes page. Pricing is not the same as our production models, but we believe we can give you the most for your money in the custom motorcycle world. Give us a call for a custom quote." (See the Chopper Shop Directory in Appendix C for contact info.)

Most of the bikes they build are built to order. They offer quite a few options. You can change out engines, transmissions, exhaust, etc. They don't accept "swap outs" because they are a manufacturer. They offer a discount on bikes for active duty military. Build time: between 8 and 12 weeks.

Road Closed

Most shops will not deliver a bike you have ordered until they receive the final payment.

Love bobbers! Anthony J. Matano's Von Zepper bobber has a 93-cubic-inch shoverlead S&S motor with five-speed transmission. It has a Springer front end, baby apes bars, a sissy bar with its two-seater setup, a rigid frame, and a black-with-orange-flames paint job.

(Barry C. Altmark Photography)

Wild West Motor Company

The Wild West Motor Company, out of San Diego, California, has a new custom that comes in three variations: the Gunfire, the Vigilante, and the Dragoon.

The gorgeous front end of a 2005 Texas Chopper Softail.

(Barry C. Altmark Photography)

The Vigilante is known for its low seat, which is only 21 inches off the pavement. So the rider can sit right inside the bike, oil is stored in the frame. The Dragoon features a stretched gas tank and high-tech four-piston brake calipers, billet aluminum wheels, and a state-of-the-art instrument cluster. Gunfire has carbon-fiber Integrated Strut Technology (IST) and a custom paint job.

The chopper has a 117-cubic-inch engine, V-twin with more than 115-plus-horsepower, and aircraft-grade billet aluminum wheels, 300 rear tire, sleek single-riser handlebars, and six-speed transmission. It has a two-in-one chrome exhaust system. Base price is $39,000.

Wheelie World _____

To find contact info for more chopper shops, see the Chopper Shop Directory in Appendix C at the back of the book.

According to their website, "Over the past decade, Wild West Motor Company has been designing, testing, tooling, and building some of the most exotic motorcycles in the world. Wild West was founded by a mechanical engineer with a creed to revolutionize motorcycle design." For more info check out wildwestmc.com.

Proper Chopper

Proper Chopper out of Santa Cruz, California, manufactures bobbers. This is an ultimate old school shop. Their bobbers have nothing on them that isn't absolutely essential. They have whitewall ties and shotgun pipes that make it impossible for this bike to sneak up on anyone—anyone who isn't deaf, that is.

> **Road Closed**
> Beware. The engine is a 107 cubic inch S&S with a compression ratio of 9:6:1, which is beyond the limits of the law in some states.

The seat is only 24 inches off the ground. It has a 66-inch wheel base, a 4 ½-inch ground clearance, a two-inch stretch in the frame, a 34 degree rake and it only weighs 540 pounds, even when it had a tank full of gas.

Word is that the Proper Chopper bobber is going to be updated in 2006 to include optional hidden shocks. For more info: www.proper-choppers.com.

Dipping a Toe

Sometimes a guy or gal will just dip their toe into the murky waters of motorcycle customization, and—with only the slightest push or prod—they will dive right in, and the next thing you know they're riding around on a jaw-dropper.

That was the case with Tommy Deluca down in Florida. He bought himself a stock Harley-Davidson Road King, and for a time all was right with the world. Then he began to feel the urge for just a little bit more. He yearned to sew a little dream onto his stock bike.

Taking the Plunge

Deluca went to see a motorcycle customization expert, namely Pete Giaruso of Pete G's Chopper Design in Longwood, Florida (407-834-5007; www.chopperdesign.com). He hemmed and hawed and said he wanted Pete to transform his stock Harley into something special.

Giaruso sensed that before him was a man dipping his toe, yet teetering on the edge of the pool, ready to take the plunge. By the time Deluca left Pete's shop he had agreed to finance a from-the-ground-up chopper project. The bike would be called *Ghostrider*, based on the favorite comic book of Tommy's son.

def•i•ni•tion

Ghostrider is a hero who derives his power from touching a magic motorcycle.

The bike was originally covered in a flame design. Then, in 2004, Deluca and Giaruso rode together to a Daytona rally. While there they couldn't help but notice how many choppers were covered with flame designs.

So, they decided to change. The flames were stripped off and replaced by a new design. Ghostrider's face appears on the back fender and the comic's logo is painted on the sides of the gas tank, a fiery red emerging from a black background.

So if you are currently the rider of a stock bike and you're looking to experiment with customization, be aware that these things are addictive. And you might wind up riding a totally radical bike, like Tommy Deluca did. His Ghostrider masterpiece was so cool that it won its class in 2004 at the *Easyriders* Bike Show in Atlanta.

The Least You Need to Know

♦ The chopper that put Orange County Choppers on the map was called True Blue, a classic chopper built in the basement of Paul Sr.'s house and shown off at the 1999 Daytona Biketoberfest®.

♦ Looking at it as objectively as possible, there are still plenty of reasons to shop at Precious Metal Customs for all of your chopper needs.

♦ If you're looking for the best of the West Coast aftermarket, seek out Custom Chrome, which started out more that 40 years ago in a space behind a two-car garage in San Jose, California.

♦ The Wild West Motor Company, out of San Diego, California, has a new custom that comes in three variations: the Gunfire, the Vigilante, and the Dragoon.

Clubs and Museums

In This Chapter

◆ Harley heaven

◆ Choppers conquer Europe

◆ Women only

◆ People come just to see 'em

Now that you have your new chopper, you want to meet other chopper riders. You need places to visit on your chopper—reasons to go on a road trip!

In this chapter, we take a look at clubs you can join and places you can visit to make friends and learn more about choppers and chopper culture. Here are a few clubs you can join, and museums you can visit.

So throw on your colors and get ready to ride.

H.O.G.

The initials stand for Harley Owners' Group, and they have chapters all across North America and Europe. Many chapters also have a female wing of the club known as *L.O.H.* Folks to customize Harleys are welcome, so there are plenty of chopper people around.

def•i•ni•tion

L.O.H. stands for Ladies of Harley. In some chapters, a full third of the members are women.

The group has, if you count all of the chapters, almost a million members. They're looking for people, they say, who are "making the Harley-Davidson dream a way of life." For more info, check out the official Harley-Davidson website.

The Chopper Club

For chopper fanatics in Europe, there's the Chopper Club, a motorcycle club that has dedicated the past 30 years to promoting, protecting, and enjoying custom biking across Europe.

The club was created in England in 1973. At first it was called the National Chopper Club. Since then it has expanded into Chopper Club Nederland (or The Netherlands), Chopper Club Belgie (for Belgium), Chopper Club Luxembourg, Chopper Club Ireland, Chopper Club Germany, Chopper Club Wales, Chopper Club Scotland, and Chopper Club Norway.

Wheelie World

The Gold Wing Road Riders Association is the world's largest "social organization" for owners and riders of Honda Gold Wing and Valkyrie motorcycles. More info at www.gwrra.org.

Wheelie World

The club was founded by Bill Gill, Pete Gaertner, and Syd Wellings.

According to their website, the United Kingdom discovered choppers following the release of *Easy Rider*, and the chopper craze that followed resulted in the formation of the club—a club "devoted purely to riders of custom machinery."

The club's stated goals are to

- Generate better understanding between chopper enthusiasts, other road users, and the general public.

- Improve standards in safety and construction of choppers.

- Bring all chopper riders closer together.

You can write them at Chopper Club/P.O. Box 1433/Luton, Bedfordshire, England; or e-mail: info@chopper-club.com.

The Antique Motorcycle Club of America

It's all about turning the old into new. Folks in this club, which is made up of regional chapters all meeting regularly for four-day "national tours," are into detailed restoration. The topics of the day are often technical questions, both practical and philosophical. Style is discussed, too, but not as much. According to their website, "It all boils down to is this ... having fun with *Old Iron!*"

The club members get to ride to nine national meets spread throughout the country. Best Restoration gets a prize. Four times a year, they also run four national road tours.

Here's the pitch: "Here you and the family can enjoy some beautiful scenery and put a few miles on your bike over a four-day period. All club activities are designed so the entire family can participate." So leave your "Show Us Your [Blank]" signs at home.

def•i•ni•tion

Old Iron is a loving term for an antique motorcycle.

Road Closed

If you are only into the state of the art, the here and the now, then the Antique Motorcycle Club of America is not for you.

American Motorcyclists Association

As it turns out, anyone who has ever had a good time at a run, rally, or festival has a debt of gratitude to pay to the founders of the next club, the AMA. Designed to address issues that are important to bikers, the American Motorcyclists Association is the oldest and largest biker club.

It's formerly known as the FAM (Federation of American Motorcyclists, and M&ATA (the Motorcycle and Allied Trades Association), but it can nonetheless trace its roots back to the infancy of motorcycles, the beginning of the twentieth century.

Wheelie World

The name of Marlon Brando's motorcycle club in *The Wild One* was the Black Rebels Motorcycle Club. They were outlaws. Most current biker clubs, however, are not composed of chronic rulebreakers.

Celebrity Bio

Jeff Huggins and his wife, Pam, own a store called Biker Rags, a leather and accessories store, in Knoxville, Tennessee. In addition to helping run the store, Jeff also likes to tinker out in the garage. Inside the store a number of antique bikes are always on display. His most recent project didn't involve an antique, but it was interesting nonetheless. That's because he, with the possible exception of a quick trip to the paint store, accomplished his customization without shopping. Jeff customized a 2001 Softail standard into a bike he calls the "Beater Bike." It was a stock Harley Softail that Jeff chopped. He also painted it "rattle-can black." He added Samson pipes but otherwise, everything was either a stock part, or something Jeff had lying around. Very few purchases were made.

On September 7, 1903, the FAM was officially formed during a meeting of 93 enthusiasts at a clubhouse in Brooklyn. The meeting was chaired by George H. Perry, and one notable attendee was George M. Hendee of the Indian Motorcycle Company, who brought 109 membership pledges from the New England area.

First Run

Maybe the first road run of all times was organized by the FAM in 1913 in Milwaukee, Wisconsin. It was called a "Good Fellowship Tour." This developed into the "Gypsy Tours," which really caught on. In 1925, the FAM (now known as the AMA) organized 212 individual Gypsy Tours. The tours were held simultaneously on June 20 and 21.

Flapping Lips

The *Motorcycle & Bicycle Illustrated* issue of March 19, 1925, stated: "The Gypsy Tour idea originated eight or nine years ago, the object being to set a certain date for an outing, where riders, dealers and everyone interested in motorcycles would tour to some convenient spot for a day's sport and a real old-fashioned good time."

Women on Wheels

One of the best clubs for biking women is Women on Wheels (WOW). Their recruiting pitch goes like this: "If you are a lady who loves to drive or ride as passenger on motorcycles, motorbikes, scooters, or trikes, then this is the group for you! This organization welcomes your family members and you to indulge your passion for riding with other discriminating hobbyists, at rallies, chapter meetings, tours, and other events."

Their stated mission is to "unite all women motorcycle enthusiasts for recreation, education, mutual support, recognition, and to promote a positive image of motorcycling." More info at www.womenonwheels.org.

Now let's take a look at some top museums of interest to chopper lovers.

The Shop

The Shop—on Highway 101, a.k.a. the Pacific Coast Highway—is a store that also houses a hot museum. Generically named, The Shop is an entrepreneurial idea of some note (although it is fairly common—some would say mandatory—to build a gift shop as a moneymaking adjunct to a museum).

But David Hansen at The Shop, took the moneymaking angle one step further. It's a shop that services and sells parts for exclusively American motorcycles and built a museum to help attract customers. For chopper aficionados, The Shop is a piece of old-school heaven!

Road Closed

There is absolutely, positively no foreign iron allowed at The Shop.

Amazing Collection

The Shop is the home to one of the most amazing collections of antique American motorcycles. Exhibits include '02 Indian, '13 H-D "Silent Gray Fellow," '16 Indian "PowerPlus," '19 Excelsior, '20 Indian Scout, and many more.

It's a very cool place to go. If you're taking the PCH on a run, you will see it. And if you're chopper needs a checkup, there's one reason to stop. Love antique bikes, ancient American heavy metal? Then this is the place to go, too. It's two, two, two Shops in one.

Biker Oz

Inside, it's like biker Oz. Commenting on the décor, which has been described by a Shop publicist as "a blend of industrial carpet, art deco black & white tile floors, old gas pumps, redwood latticework and shelves filled with motorcycle esoterica," David Hansen says: "No one planned the decor at the outset—it just emerged. We wanted something comfortable and unique; something warm so people would feel at home when they walked in.

"We had plenty of wall space to hang all the junk and memorabilia we had. I figured if there was an overflow of customers, which there is quite often, and limited counter help, which there is all the time, people can look around and be entertained.

"I have several friends that collect motorcycles, so we're always changing the bike displays. It encourages people to come in—there is always something new—and old—to see."

Next to the Truck Stop

Why is The Shop so popular? It doesn't hurt that it's next to one of the biggest truck stops between San Francisco and Los Angeles, but David has another explanation: "The thrust of a contemporary Harley-Davidson dealership is the 'Evolution' engine. Because of the very large and growing customer base, many Harley dealers don't have the time or resources to supply the needs of the clientele that are into the obsolete models such as the Panheads, Knuckleheads, Flatheads, Shovelheads, or even iron-head Sportsters."

He continues, "The parts inventory for these motorcycles would be substantial, as would the workforce, especially coupled with all the accessories carried for the Evos. More and more places are dealing with the older Harleys, and more shops dedicated to Indians have opened up. There are very few shops that deal with both brands to the extent that we can. Our service department can be putting a set of four-valve heads on an Evo while restoring an Indian chassis and rebuilding a Henderson four-cylinder motor."

The Motorcycle Hall of Fame Museum

Located just east of Columbus, Ohio, on the 23-acre campus of the American Motorcyclist Association in Pickerington, the Motorcycle Hall of Fame Museum is home to an impressive collection of motorcycles and memorabilia. The museum tells the exciting stories of motorcycling by creating rotating exhibitions covering a wide range of topics featuring many motorcycles borrowed from the foremost collectors in North America. The Hall of Fame recognizes the great racers, inventors, promoters, designers, enthusiasts, and journalists who have made our sport so exciting by placing the people and their machines in the context of their time and place in the history of motorcycling.

A guiding principle of the Motorcycle Hall of Fame Museum is that motorcycling is more than the machines.

(Motorcycle Hall of Fame Museum)

The Motorcycle Hall of Fame Museum offers excitement and education for everyone, with unique exhibits showcasing some of the most elegant and remarkable designs and technologies from motorcycling's past and present. The two-story, 26,000-square-foot facility houses three main galleries, showcasing machines of every description and age—from the board-trackers and streamliners of the sport's early days, to competition Superbikes and motocrossers of the modern era. Come see why motorcycles have long been on the cutting edge of transportation and motor sports.

Motorcycle Hall of Fame Museum
13515 Yarmouth Drive
Pickerington, Ohio 43147
Phone 614-856-2222
Fax 614-856-2221
Website: www.motorcyclemuseum.org
e-mail: info@motorcyclemuseum.org

Just east of Columbus, Exit 112A on I-70

Spindly motorized bicycles from the turn of the century keep company with today's championship-winning racers.

(Motorcycle Hall of Fame Museum)

I hope you've learned something from this book, and I wish every one of you happy riding.

The Least You Need to Know

- The Harley Owners Group (H.O.G.) has almost one million members.

- The Chopper Club of Great Britain now has chapters across Europe.

- Clubs come in all gender combos: men only, women only, and—my personal favorite—coeducational!

- When cruising the Pacific Coast Highway, stop at The Shop, Pop!

Appendix A

Glossary

aftermarket Place to buy parts and accessories other than those that come on an original factory-built motorcycle. Market for custom parts rather than replacement parts.

apehangers Extremely high handlebars. They got their name because riders using them resembled apes.

bagger Motorcycle equipped to carry bags. If you do not pack lightly and you want to go on vacation, a bagger is the right bike for you.

balancing Adding or removing weight from the flywheels to equalize weight distribution.

big twins The powerplant on a big ol' Harley.

billet Very strong yet light aircraft-grade aluminum.

blueprinting Procedures used by engine builders to make sure that various engine parts have dimensions and operating clearances within a certain range.

bobber Predating the term *chopper*, a bobber was a post-WWII bike owned by a rider who, seeking more speed, had cut off (bobbed) most of the body work.

combination wrench Wrench that has a box-end wrench on one end and, in the same size, an open-end wrench on the other. The most valuable American sets range in size from $^3/_8$ inch to 1 inch. Best metric sets span 8 mm to 19 mm.

computer-aided design (CAD) Method of designing choppers made possible by computer software. The program helps the designer do the complicated math involved with determining the chopper's rake and tail, and allows the designer to view the chopper under design in three dimensions. Designers who previously sketched out the choppers they were designing, now "sculpt" them.

digger A bike characterized by gooseneck frames that combined the stretch chopper's radical 38- to 40-degree rake dimensions with telescopic front forks that were often shortened, rather than lengthened, for dramatic effect.

digital fuel optimizer Modifies the outgoing signal from the ECU to your injectors, increasing the duration of the spray of fuel, thereby richening the mixture.

donor bike Bike you customize to make your chopper. It is the raw material, the blank canvas upon which you paint your masterpiece.

electronic control unit (ECU) Machine that helps optimize air intake to engine speed.

Evolution The Evolution engine, sometimes shortened to "Evo," is the first build by Harley-Davidson to feature aluminum cylinder jugs.

fork length The distance between the top of the fork tubes to the centerline of the axle.

forks Metal tubes that connect a chopper's front wheel to the rest of the bike. Long, angled forks are one of the trademarks of a chopper.

gaiter Rubber protective sleeve that slides over a chopper's front forks and protects them from the elements. The term comes from England, where the weather greatly resembles that in the American East.

gearhead Man or woman who is a born mechanic, the sort of person who could take a bike apart and put it together again, the first time he or she tried, without an instruction manual.

hardtail Bike with a rigid frame, essentially suspension-free.

knucklehead The first (1936) overhead-valve Big Twin engine made by Harley-Davidson. Sometimes referred to simply as a "knuckle."

L-twin engine   This is basically a V-twin engine that has had its cylinders pushed outward so that they form a right angle (an L).

massive stroker   Truly big engine.

old iron   Loving term for an antique motorcycle.

panhead   Name of the second-generation Harley-Davidson overhead-valve engine, which first appeared in 1948. Sometimes referred to just as a "pan."

rake   The angle in degrees of the steering neck from the vertical cord.

roll your own   Build your own chopper.

roller   Short for rolling chassis, the frame and wheels combo that is the starting piece for most first-time chopper builders.

rolling chassis kit   Kit that comes with the chassis and the wheels already assembled. You can see what your finished product will look like after the engine and other parts are added. This is perfect for the kit builder who doesn't look forward to welding his or her own mounts. That has been done for you.

R-U-B   Rich urban rider (beware!).

shovelhead   Harley-Davidson model first produced in 1966, known for its overhead-valve Big Twin engine. Sometimes referred to just as a "shovel."

softail   Bike with suspension in the rear end only. The travel is around two to three inches. It has two struts or shocks that are mounted beneath the transmission. These bikes can appear to look rigid due to the lack of exposed shocks.

spoon and scoop   A drop-seat frame that earns its name because because the neck is stretched up and out, leading the arching backbone to drop down into the seat pan. In other words, the seat scoops up under your butt and spoons it like Jell-O.

stroke   In a motor, the distance the pistons travel up and down.

supercharger   Device that increases the power produced by an internal-combustion engine by increasing the air charge beyond that drawn in by the pumping pistons.

trail   The distance defined by the vertical line from axle to ground and the intersection of centerline of the steering neck and ground.

Appendix B

Sources and Resources

Books

Holstrom, Darwin. *The Complete Idiot's Guide to Motorcycles, Third Edition.* Indianapolis, IN: Alpha Books, 2005.

Hough, David L. *Proficient Motorcycling: The Ultimate Guide to Riding Well.* Irvine, CA: BowTie Press, 2000.

Lane, Billy. *Chop Fiction.* Osceola, WI: Classic Motorbooks, 2005. Photos by Michael Lichter.

Masi, C. G. *How to Set Up Your Motorcycle Workshop, Second Edition.* North Conway, NH: Whitehorse Press, 2003.

Remus, Timothy. *How to Build a Cheap Chopper.* Stillwater, MN: Wolfgang Publications, 2004.

———. *How to Build a Kit Bike.* Stillwater, MN: Wolfgang Publications, 2002.

Seate, Mike. *Outlaw Choppers.* St. Paul, MN: Motorbooks, 2004.

Zimmermann, Mark. *The Essential Guide to Motorcycle Maintenance.* North Conway, NH: Whitehorse Press, 2003.

Newspapers and Magazines

Anderson, Steve. "Modern Armor: Motorcycle Protective Clothing, Body Armor, and CE Standards." *Cycle World*, January 2006, p. 67.

Ball, Keith. "What Skool Do You Ride From—the New School or the Old School?" *Street Chopper*, February 2005, p. 12.

Blake, Adrian. "Flying Low: Ron's Brazilian Blaster." *American Iron Magazine*, February 2005, p. 63.

———. "Tomahawk." *American Iron Choppers*, 2005, p. 20.

Buckman, Adam. "Family Fueled: What's Eating 'Chopper' Teutuls?" *New York Post*, November 14, 2005.

Friend, Greg. "Variety Is the Spice of Life." *Street Chopper*, March 2005, p. 12.

Johnson, Tom. "Canadian Chopper: And some good news about Friday the 13th, eh?" *American Iron Choppers*, 2005, p. 60.

Kanter, Buzz. "We've Come a Long Way, Baby!" *American Iron Choppers*, 2005, p. 10.

Kress, Joe. "David Covington's Pagan Gold Hot Rod: Lucifer 1." *Easyriders*, January 2006, p. 8.

Lopez, Ernie. "The Pimp: One Long-Azz Chopper." *Street Chopper*, March 2005, p. 80.

Lumenick, Lou. "Motorcycle Tale Hits on All Cylinders." *New York Post*, December 7, 2005, p.56.

Moore, Brian. "Sin City Overload: Las Vegas Bikefest 2004." *Hot Rod Bikes*, February 2005, p. 27.

Moore, Jeff. "Ghostrider: A Dream Come True For Tommy Deluca." *V-Twin Motorcycles*, January 2006, p. 139.

Padgett, Nina. "Rebel Ride: Rolling Tribute to a Hollywood Legend." *Cycle World*, January 2006, p. 56.

Petersen, Donny. "How It Works." *American Iron Magazine*, December 2005, p. 34.

Puddin', Cheese. "Oddi Enough: Drop It on Down." *Easyriders*, June 2005, p.18.

Queso, El. "Hitman: Hit the Button and Hang On." *Easyriders*, January 2006, p. 56.

Scott, Alex. "Building BERT's Bike: Bert Baker's Green Dream, with Six on the Side." *American Iron Choppers*, 2005, p. 12.

Scraba, Wayne. "Hurricane Force: The Less-Is-More Approach." *American Iron Magazine*, December 2005, p. 70.

Sullivan, John. "'Cool Bikes': Primary Cover/Oil Cooler From Tauer Machine." *Easyriders*, June 2005, p. 153.

"Their Theme Park: Bike Enthusiasts and aficionados to Get Their Own 150-Acre, Self-Contained Haven in Daytona Beach." *Newsday*, March 13, 2005, p. A30.

Voorhis, Dan. "Big Dog Prepares for Possible Growth Out East." *Wichita Eagle*, February 1, 2005, p. A3.

Williams, Greg. "Skin-Deep Beauty: Tom Reiter's Shoestringed Panhead Chopper." *American Iron Magazine*, December 2005, p. 132.

Wordman [sic, no first name]. "Tattooed Chrome: On Chrome or Polished Metal, Chemical Etching Offers a World of Opportunities." *Easyriders*, June 2005, p. 154.

Great Biker Movies

Angels from Hell: A 1968 movie directed by Bruce Kessler. Tom Stern plays a guy who gets back from Vietnam and starts a biker gang, only to run into trouble with rival gangs and the fuzz.

Easy Rider: Directed by Dennis Hopper and starring Hopper, Peter Fonda, and Jack Nicholson, this is the classic freedom-on-the-open-road flick that turned choppers into a national fad. Fonda played Captain America, whose stars-and-stripes-themed chopper remains the most famous of all time.

Glory Stompers: Released in 1967, Dennis Hopper and Kasey ("American Top 40") Kasem play gang members who plot to steal the good guy's girlfriend, take her south of the border, and sell her as a prostitute.

Hells Angels Forever: Documentary 10 years in the making, started in 1973 and released in 1983, made by the same filmmaking team that produced *The Grateful Dead Movie*. Directed and produced by Richard Chase and Leon Gast, and written by Richard Chase and Sandy Alexander. Film defends Angels leader Sonny Barger, who at the time faced drug-distribution charges. Music by Bo Diddley, Jerry Garcia, Willie Nelson, and Johnny Paycheck.

Hells Angels on Wheels: Directed by Richard Rush and released in 1967, this one stars Jack Nicholson as a gas station attendant turned biker named "Poet." Sonny Barger is credited as "technical advisor."

Rebel Rousers: Released the year after *Easy Rider*, and starring Jack Nicholson and Bruce Dern. Directed by Martin B. Cohen, this film also stars Cameron Mitchell and Harry Dean Stanton. Check out Nicholson's striped pants!

The Wild Angels: Made in 1966, and produced by low-budget master Roger Corman, Peter Fonda plays a member of the Hells Angels known as Heavenly Blues. The script, by Charles Griffith, follows the outlaws as they destroy stuff and themselves. Also stars Bruce Dern and Nancy Sinatra. Great guitar soundtrack by The Ventures and Davie Allan and the Arrows.

The World's Fastest Indian: Made in 2005, Anthony Hopkins plays Burt Munro, a real-life 72-year-old eccentric motorcycle racer in this Rocky-style movie made in New Zealand. The movie, directed by Roger Donaldson, begins in 1962 as Munro is souping up his 1920 Indian Twin Scout so that it can hit 200 miles per hour. His big dream: to go to America and win the Big Race on the Salt Flats of Utah.

Videography (Includes DVDs)

American Chopper: The Series—First Season. Columbia Tristar Home Video, 2005. DVD version of the Discovery Channel series starring the Teutuls of Orange County Choppers. Three-disc set.

American Chopper: The Series—Second Season. Columbia Tristar Home Video, 2005. Three-disc set. Includes outtakes and an interview with Paul Sr.

How to Build a Radical Chopper or a Bike in a Box with Inside Knowledge from Professional Mechanics. Chopper Assembly Videos (Chopper Assembly Videos, 233 Illinois Avenue/Westerville, OH 43081; 614-882-5975; chuck@chopperassemblyvideos.com), 2005.

Monster Garage—Season Two. Columbia Tristar Home Video, 2005. Three-disc set. Starring Jesse James.

Motorcycle Mania 3—Jesse James Rides Again. Columbia Tristar Home Video, 2005. Jesse James builds a chopper for Kid Rock!

Websites

www.bikerbeach.com—The place to go for all information about Daytona Beach events and other happenings for bikers all year long. You can also use the site to book your stay while in the Daytona Beach area any time.

www.chopper-club.com—Website for Europe's number one chopper organization.

www.chopperdaves.com—The website says, "Chopper Dave's is dedicated to real kustom motorcycles and all the riders of the pre-war era (1930–1941), the guys that bought new bikes, bobbed them and rode the hell out of them! This is the place to see choppers, bobbers and kustom bikes that are built to ride! I am going to be posting pictures of bikes that reflect the heritage of pre-war riders all over the U.S. I do not advocate bolt-on crap, trailer-queens or chrome abominations."

www.choppersinc.com—Online ordering from the "Motorcycle Shop Your Mother Warned You About." This is Billy lane's shop in Melbourne, Florida.

www.choppersrule.com—Wild site. Their motto states: "These pages are devoted to those tireless men and women who, with blow torch in hand and wrench in teeth—turn the commonplace into rolling works of art. This is the land of the chopper. Form doesn't follow function here, bucko, it just is. It's been like this for almost thirty years, the billet barges and crotch rockets will be dead and buried—moldering in junk yards or unridden forgotten toys, but you can bet one thing: CHOPPERS RULE!"

www.hondachopper.com—Website says, "From their launch in 1969, the Honda CB 750 was chopped, rode, wrecked, and rebuilt! Choppers *are* the people who ride them—they're inventive, fast and free, and of course they're resisting repression." Website offers a chat room for folks looking for device, parts, swaps, or just chitchat regarding their Honda choppers. There's some info on the CB 750, tips for those who are building or repairing a Honda chopper, and a link to join the club and become an official member of the Honda chopper community. They say, "Choppers are a uniquely American form of motorcycle, just as jazz is a uniquely American form of music. This site is a dedicated tribute to the solitary souls who split the night with their ungodly roar searching for whatever is left of the frontier."

www.paragoncustoms.com—Great parts shop up in Wisconsin. They do in-house custom painting and fabrication, and build bikes, too. If your favorite color is skull, this is the place for you. They can work a skull motif into any design. Check out their skull headlights, made of A356 billet. You can also get skull tanks, skull fenders, skull mirrors, skull wheels and pulleys, and … you get the idea.

www.preciousmetalcustoms.com—My website. Visit often. Buy some stuff.

www.streetchopperweb.com—Online edition of *Street Chopper* magazine. It contains a schedule of upcoming chopper events, profiles of notable choppers and chopper-builders, a technical department, a forum for readers to discuss their favorite subject, motorcycle manuals, and links to both *Hot Bike* and *Hot Rod's BikeWorks* magazines.

www.unitedbikers.com—"United Bikers: United We Ride, United We Stand." Website includes a chatroom forum, plus links to ride info, weather, road conditions, repair tips, and the best deals on accessories and gear.

www.xtrememachineusa.com—A great source for custom motorcycle wheels and accessories.

www.wickedbros.com—Website of a great source for custom exhausts. Wicked Brothers have pipes to fit all Evos and Twin cam models. You can get pipes in chrome, stainless steel, and some double wall.

Chopper Shop Directory

Aeromach Manufacturing
11423-B Woodside Ave.
Santee, California 92071
Phone: 619-258-5443
Order toll free: 1-800-990-9392
Fax: 619-258-8515
techsupport@aeromach.net

American IronHorse
Motorcycle Company
4600 Blue Mound Road
Fort Worth, Texas 76106
Phone: 817-665-2000
www.americanironhorse.com

Arlen Ness Enterprises, Inc.
6050 Dublin Blvd.
Dublin, CA 94568
Contact: Arlen Ness
Phone: 925-479-6350
Fax: 925-479-6351

Big Bear Choppers
477 Eureka Drive
Big Bear Lake, CA 92315
Phone: 909-878-4340
Fax: 909-878-4341
www.bigbearchoppers.com

Big Dog Motorcycles
1520 East Douglas Avenue
Wichita, KS 67214
Phone: 316-267-9121
www.bigdogmotorcycles.com

Big Mike's Choppers
63018 Plateau Drive #2
Bend, OR 97701
Phone: 541-312-2760
www.bmcchoppers.com

Bourget's Bike Works, Inc.
21407 North Central Avenue
Phoenix, AZ 85024
Contact: Roger Bourget
Phone: 623-879-9642
Fax: 623-879-9629
www.bourgets.com

Broadway Choppers
1518 Bradley St.
Schenectady, NY 12305
Phone: 518-374-0008

Burr Built Custom Manufacturing
1028 Lake Ariel Highway
Lake Ariel, PA 18436
Phone: 570-698-5428
www.burrbuiltcustoms.com

California Customs
2609 Charleston Road
Mountain View, CA 94043
Phone: 1-888-707-CUSTOM
www.calcustom.com

Carefree Custom Cycles
7020 North 55th Avenue
Glendale, AZ 85301
Phone: 623-209-0060
www.carefreecustomcycles.com

Cenzi Motorcycle Company
42 Nichols Street
Spencerport, NY 14559
Phone: 585-349-0120
www.cenzimotorcycles.com

Choppers Inc.
1243 N. Harbor City Blvd. #C
Melbourne, FL 32935
Contact: Billy Lane
Phone: 321-757-7262
Fax: 321-757-3117

Echelon Motorcycles
2320 West Airport Boulevard
Sanford, FL 32771
Phone: 407-322-0095
www.echelonmotorcycles.com

Exile Cycles
9249 Glenoaks Blvd.
Sun Valley, CA 91352
Contact: Russell Mitchell
Phone: 818-768-7667

Flyrite Choppers
13200 Pond Springs Rd. #B-12
Austin, TX 78729
Phone: 512-918-CHOP

HotMatch Custom Cycles
201 W. Truslow Avenue
Fullerton, CA 92832
Contact: Matt Hotch
Phone: 714-680-3462
Fax: 714-680-3874

Indian Larry's
151 N. 14th Street
Brooklyn, NY 11211
Phone: 718-609-9184

Jim Nasi Customs, Inc.
21622 N. 7th Ave
Suites #1 & 2
Phoenix, AZ 85027
Contact: Jim Nasi
Phone: 623-879-8600

KC Creations
7524 Frontage Road
Overland Park, KS 66204
Phone: 913-642-3279
www.kc-creations.com

Logic Motor Company
10359 West South Range Road
Salem, OH 44460
Phone: 330-332-2323

Orange County Choppers
27 Stone Castle Road
Rock Tavern, NY 12575
Contact: Paul Teutul Sr.,
Paul Teutul Jr.
Phone: 845-567-0595
Fax: 845-567-0630

Paul Yaffe Originals
2211 East Indian School Road
Phoenix, Arizona 85016
Contact: Paul Yaffe
Phone: 602-840-4205

Precision Cycle Works
109 East Sanilac Road
Caro, MI 48723
Phone: 989-673-8555
www.precisionconceptsinc.com

Swift Motorcycle Company
3846 West Clarendon Avenue
Phoenix, AZ 85019
Phone: 602-248-2836
www.swiftmotorcycle.com

Thunder Cycle Design
629 E. Sunrise Blvd.
Fort Lauderdale, FL
Contact: Eddie Trotta
Phone: 954-763-2100

Titan Motorcycle Company
2222 West Peoria Avenue
Phoenix, AZ 85029
www.titanmotorcycle.com

**Vengeance Performance
Products, LLC**
4501 Etiwanda Avenue
Mira Loma, CA 91752
Phone: 866-483-6432
www.vengeancemotorcycles.com

Von Dutch Kustom Cycles
10743 Edison Court
Rancho Cucamonga, CA 91730
Phone: 909-481-0600
www.vondutchmotorcycles.com

West Coast Choppers
718 West Anaheim St.
Long Beach, CA 90813
Contact: Jesse James
Phone: 562-983-6666
Fax: 562-983-6556

Wild West Motor Company
8230 Miralani Drive
San Diego, California 92126
Phone: 858-547-9780
Fax: 858-547-9760
www.wildwestmc.com

Index

D

X-Y-Z

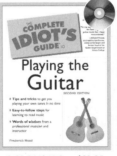